—PRAISE FOR—

# PLUNDER!

Greenhut has performed a great service for ordinary citizens and taxpayers with PLUNDER: *How Public Employee Unions are Raiding Treasuries, Controlling Our Lives and Bankrupting the Nation.* But be forewarned: If you take high blood pressure medicine, better take a double dose before reading this book. It will surely amplify the current distrust and disgust with government today as reflected in the resurgent taxpayer revolt and the Tea Party movement. With clarity and a compelling writing style, he reveals how public employees have, indeed, become "America's Protected Class." The good news is that Greenhut gives valuable advice at the end of the book on what we can do to turn the tide on this seemingly unstoppable socialistic encroachment. Frederick Douglas, when asked how to affect change, famously responded "agitate, agitate, agitate." With PLUNDER, Greenhut does more than his share of agitating. Except for government labor bosses and bureaucrats, we will all be better for it.

—**Jon Coupal,** President, Howard Jarvis Taxpayers Association

Government employees are supposed to work for the public—not the other way around. Unfortunately, because of the overwhelming political influence of government unions, public employees have gained an unsustainable level of pay and benefits. Taxpayers will be saddled with higher taxes, depleted services and unconscionable levels of debt. As Greenhut's timely book explains, the public servants have indeed become the public's masters.

—**Robert W. Loewen,** President, Lincoln Club of Orange County

All too often, critics of government concentrate upon the real abuses committed by the federal government but ignore what happens at the state and local levels. Steven Greenhut has not forgotten the federal spending scams, but he turns here against the abuses being committed in our backyards by public employee unions and state and local politicians, who band together to pick the pockets of taxpayers while exempting themselves from huge swaths of the law. He correctly challenges the "public servant" fiction, pointing out time and again that those who supposedly "protect and serve" people are the ones who are protected, who receive salaries out-of-proportion to the work they do, and who ultimately control the local councils and state legislatures. Many conservatives will react negatively to this book because he challenges the so-called heroes of the police and fire departments, but Steven Greenhut has done his homework. Governments at all levels have fostered a culture of abuse against regular citizens, who not only bear the brunt of official abuse, but are forced to pay for it, and no one better exposes this sad state of affairs better than Steven Greenhut.

—**William L. Anderson, Ph.D.**, Associate Professor, Department of Economics
Frostburg State University, Maryland

With the help of the Tea Party movement, much has recently been made about the unrestrained spending of Obama's Washington. But state and local governments are also wasting enormous amounts of their constituents' dollars. Fortunately, with his new book PLUNDER, Steven Greenhut is on the case. While it's natural to want to return to the Founding Fathers' small government ideals in DC, don't ignore the waste and rapaciousness that goes on every day at the local level – Greenhut certainly hasn't.

—**Ed Driscoll,** Multimedia Journalist working with Pajamas Media
www.eddriscoll.com

Steve Greenhut deserves credit for shedding light on an issue that deserves far more attention than it has gotten so far: the sweeping powers and reckless actions of government employee unions. As Greenhut shows, the people of states like California and Michigan where public-sector unions are at their strongest tend to wind up with dysfunctional governments and have suffered the worst in the current economic slump. This is an especially timely book and one can only hope Greenhut's warning is heeded through the country.

—**Paul Kersey,** Director of Labor Policy, The Mackinac Center for Public Policy

# PLUNDER!

HOW PUBLIC EMPLOYEE UNIONS
ARE RAIDING TREASURIES
CONTROLLING OUR LIVES
AND BANKRUPTING THE NATION

## STEVEN GREENHUT

THE FORUM PRESS

PUBLISHED BY THE FORUM PRESS, INC.
COPYRIGHT © 2009 STEVEN GREENHUT. ALL RIGHTS RESERVED.

THE FORUM PRESS
3100 W. WARNER AVE., SUITE 7
SANTA ANA, CA 92704

REPRINTED BY PERMISSION OF THE FREEMAN: "GOVERNMENT WORKERS ARE AMERICA'S NEW ELITE," BY STEVEN GREENHUT, JULY 2008.
REPRINTED BY PERMISSION OF THE ORANGE COUNTY REGISTER: "BREAKING THE CODE OF SILENCE," BY STEVEN GREENHUT, MAY 15, 2009 AND "COP LOBBY FLEXES ITS MUSCLE," BY STEVEN GREENHUT, JULY 1, 2007.

COVER AND INTERIOR DESIGN BY KIRA FULKS COPYRIGHT © 2009 | WWW.KIRAPRODUCTIONS.COM

CATALOGING-IN-PUBLICATION DATA IS ON FILE WITH THE LIBRARY OF CONGRESS.
ISBN-13: 978-0-9842752-0-5
ISBN-10: 0-9842752-0-7

PRINTED IN THE UNITED STATES OF AMERICA

10 9 8 7 6 5 4 3 2 1

To Donna, Laura, Diana and Teresa

Officeholders are the agents of the people, not their masters.
– GROVER CLEVELAND


The art of government is to make two-thirds of the nation pay all it possibly can pay for the benefit of the other third.
—VOLTAIRE


When the people fear their government, there is tyranny; when the government fears the people, there is liberty.
– THOMAS JEFFERSON

## ACKNOWLEDGEMENTS

I owe a great deal of thanks to my family for allowing me to spend the bulk of our summer working rather than vacationing and for their constant love and support.

This book would not have become a reality without the support of the Lincoln Club of Orange County, whose hundreds of members voluntarily give of their time and treasure to many worthy causes such as this. Special thanks go to Mark Bucher and Robert Loewen, in particular, who championed this project and who are dedicated to leading the charge for reform on the political front. Individual Lincoln Club members Steve Borowski, Jean Michel, Kristopher Diulio and Paul Louchis provided time-saving research assistance.

Jack Dean's pensiontsunami.com Web site was an invaluable resource. I'd also like to thank Marcia Fritz of the California Foundation for Fiscal Responsibility for her timely suggestions. My former colleague John Seiler did a fine job editing this book. Thanks also to the *Orange County Register* for its support on this project and for its willingness to focus attention on pension- and union-related issues. Had it not been for the encouragement and zeal for this project by Jim Riordan and Publisher Kira Fulks, this book would never have gotten off the ground.

This battle is just beginning, and this book is meant to be a call to action. I still have faith in the willingness of Americans to stand up and do the right thing even in the face of powerful interests. This book is dedicated to them and to the eternal struggle for freedom.

# CONTENTS

# FOREWORD

## Tom McClintock
U.S. Congressman (R-CA)

A generation ago, California was truly America's Golden State. Paying far lower taxes and shouldering far less debt, Californians enjoyed the finest highway system in the world and the finest public school system in the country—including a free university education for every Californian who wanted one. Water and electricity produced by California's rapidly expanding public works became so cheap and abundant that many communities didn't bother with metering. Jobs were plentiful and California's diversified economy was nearly recession-proof.

How different things are today. California has now reached the paradox of the bureaucratic state. Despite record levels of expenditures, it can no longer afford to build a decent road system, educate its children or protect its citizens from criminals. In recent years, a population exodus has begun, with many ex-Californians finding a better place to raise their families in the middle of the Nevada and Arizona deserts than they had found in bountiful and beautiful California.

No conceivable act of God could wreak such devastation as to turn California into a less desirable place to live than the middle of the Nevada Nuclear Test Range. Only acts of government could do that. And they have. The political Left gradually gained dominance over California's government and imposed a disastrous agenda of radical and retrograde policies that have wrecked California's economy and bankrupted its government.

Americans have developed a morbid fascination with California, in much the same way as they can't resist the story of the celebrity who has fallen on hard times or the macabre wreck on the highway.

Steve Greenhut indulges our fascination by taking us on a slow drive past that wreck, but there's a respectable purpose for doing so. Just as a wreck on the road offers the opportunity to lecture the kids, "See what happens when you don't pay attention while you're driving," Greenhut offers a more important lecture: "See what happens when you don't pay attention while you're voting."

Greenhut spent years at one of California's flagship newspapers, the Orange County Register, warning about the policies and laws that have laid the state low, and now catalogs them into a single morality play for the rest of the nation. It's the tale of how the rise of a pampered mandarin class of government officials, aided by powerful public employee unions, could systematically and methodically gain political power and use it to destroy the quality of life in what was once a legendary land of opportunity.

It's a tragedy the nation can't afford to ignore. The very same policies debated in the halls of the California legislature and enacted into law during those decades are now being debated in Congress. Californians at least had the consolation that if the Left succeeded in wrecking California, there were still 49 other states that offered offer safe haven.

But where will Americans escape if the Left ultimately succeeds in wrecking America?

So enjoy Steve Greenhut's lively and entertaining chronicle of California's folly, but heed the medieval epitaph: "Remember man as you walk by, as you are now so once was I; as I am now so you will be." And then, maybe, perhaps, Americans can learn from California's mistakes without having to repeat them.

# FOREWORD

## MARK BUCHER

CO-AUTHOR OF PROPOSITION 226, THE CALIFORNIA PAYCHECK PROTECTION INITIATIVE

PLUNDER is a field manual of information and examples for the millions of Americans who are wondering what has gone wrong in America, and what can be done to fix it. From the title of this book to the very last sentence, Steven Greenhut lays the truth out for everyone to see—public employees are raiding our treasuries, controlling our lives and destroying our country.

Growing up and living in California, I have had the misfortune of watching this great state go from golden to bankrupt during my generation. I remember in grade school asking my teacher why the grass in our ball field was turning brown. Her answer was that there is not enough money to water the lawn. It was not until years later that I realized the school district was using our playground as a propaganda tool in a campaign to get more money for schools.

Public employee unions did not have the power then that they have today. In fact, it was not until a decade later that they were given the right to unionize by Governor Jerry Brown in 1978, and now hold such complete political control in this state that it makes me long for the days when the destruction they could do was limited to killing the lawn at my elementary school.

I was first introduced to the power of the public employee unions in 1993 during my involvement as a volunteer for a California school choice initiative that would have provided more educational opportunities for children and parents, at half the cost of what the state was spending on our schools. I had no idea at the outset of that campaign how completely the California Teachers Association controlled our education system, but watched in amazement as they used their power and money to defeat that initiative.

In the 16 years since, I have seen firsthand many examples of unbridled public employee union power that you will read about in PLUNDER. As the only special interest group with the right to withhold money from the pay of public employees, these unions have a steady flow of ready cash to elect politicians who support them, and punish those who oppose them. As a result, most legislators are elected with their support, and the rest, save a rare few, will not dare oppose them. Since these union-controlled politicians are effectively the employers of the unions, it is not surprising that salary and benefit packages for public employees now substantially exceed those in the private sector, to the point of bankrupting cities and our state.

In 1998 I authored a paycheck protection initiative which would have required the unions to at least ask their members before using their money for politics. Despite polls showing initial support of this common sense idea by 85 percent of the public, the initiative was defeated by outright lies—that if this proposition were adopted, police officers would die because their addresses could be on the form granting permission to deduct political contributions. Nothing in the initiative even suggested this, and numerous laws prohibited disclosure of police addresses. But we learned in that election that a lie backed up by tens of millions of dollars of campaign spending, and phone calls to voter's homes from "concerned police officers," can fool most of the people—at least for a while.

Today, unemployment in California exceeds 12 percent. Businesses are leaving, jobs are being lost, and people are suffering. Yet, in the county where I live, the politically conservative city council for Costa Mesa just increased pension benefits for firefighters, police in Irvine are picketing to get salary increases, and the water district serving most of Southern California is considering boosting pensions 25 percent. Why? Politicians who are beholden to, or fearful of, the warchests of the public employee unions. PLUNDER is the story of what public employees have done to California, and what they are doing to our country. Read it, become informed, get angry, and then help take our country back!

—Mark Bucher is a businessman who resides in Orange County, California and is one of the authors of an initiative, targeted for the November, 2010 California ballot, which would stop unions from using dues withheld from public employees for political donations.

## Chapter One

# HOW PUBLIC SERVANTS
# BECAME THE PUBLIC'S MASTERS

*We are becoming the servants in thought, as in action,*
*of the machine we have created to serve us.*
**– John Kenneth Galbraith**

As a child, I would ask my mother on Mother's Day or Father's Day: "Why isn't there a Children's Day?" After she stopped laughing, Mom explained: "Every day is Children's Day." I didn't understand the joke then, but now that I'm the father of three children, her answer makes perfect sense.

I recalled that exchange recently after reading that government employees get an entire week dedicated to their "service." In 2008, "Public Service Recognition Week" ran from May 5 to 11, and state government workers got their own recognition day on May 7. The U.S. Senate and House of Representatives honored the occasion by passing proclamations commending the nation's noble public servants.

Special weeks or not, many of us have no special appreciation for government workers. Many, if not most of them, perform jobs that should either be eliminated or handled by the private sector (the real private sector, not "private" firms using taxpayer dollars). Besides, even workers who perform arguably legitimate tasks are well paid for their efforts. Roofers, car mechanics, taxi drivers and journalists perform important services also, but one doesn't find entire weeks devoted to their heroics. Furthermore, government officials do not behave like noble doers of the public good. Instead, they are regular human beings who use their power and position to advance their own interests. That's to be expected, so why treat them like heroes?

But the best argument against honoring public "servants" is the one made by my mother in her concise rebuttal: Isn't every day Public Employees' Day?

## PUBLIC EMPLOYEE SMORGASBORD

Thanks to craven politicians seeking government-union support, shameless exploitation by those unions of national tragedy (such as the death of firefighters in the World Trade Center collapse), and other factors, including the public's increasing embrace of big government, government workers have turned themselves into a coddled class that lives better than its private-sector counterparts and is exempt from many of the standards and laws that apply to the rest of us. Instead of offering accolades and honors, the public should be mad at the current situation and ought to question what the situation says about the nature of our society. We should be outraged that the public's servants have turned into our masters.

The *Orange County Register* published a front-page investigation in April 2008 about a special license-plate program for California government workers.[1] The drivers of nearly 1 million cars and light trucks—out of a total statewide registration of 22 million—have their addresses shielded under a confidential records program.

"Vehicles with protected license plates can run through dozens of intersections controlled by red light cameras with impunity," according to the *Register*'s Jennifer Muir. "Parking citations issued to vehicles with protected plates are often dismissed because the process necessary to pierce the shield is too cumbersome. Some patrol officers let drivers with protected plates off with a warning because the plates signal that drivers are 'one of their own' or related to someone who is."

As I wrote in the *Register*, "Readers have been shocked to learn that California has about 1 million citizens who are literally above the law. Members of this group . . . can drive their cars as fast as they choose. They can drink a six-pack of beer at a bar and then get behind the wheel and weave their way home. They can zoom in and out of traffic, run traffic lights, roll through stop signs and ignore school crossing zones. They can ride on toll roads for free, park in illegal spots and drive on High Occupancy Vehicle lanes even if they have no passengers in the car with them. Chances are they will never have to pay a fine or get a traffic citation."[2]

Yes, rank has its privileges, and it's clear that government workers have a rank above the rest of us.

If officials who claim to be protecting the public's safety were told that one out of every 22 California drivers had a license to drive any way they chose, these officials would be demanding action and more power to protect Californians from the potential carnage. But until the newspaper series, we'd heard nothing about the situation from police officials and legislators. The reason, of course, is that the scofflaws are the police, their family members and other government agents.

The special-license program started in 1978 with the seemingly unobjectionable purpose of protecting the personal addresses of officials who deal directly with criminals. Police argued that the bad guys could call the DMV and get home addresses. The bad guys could then go harm the officers and their family members. There was no rash of such actions, only the possibility that this danger could take place.

So police and their families got their confidentiality, but then the program expanded from one set of government workers to another. So now parole officers, retired parking-enforcement employees, DMV workers, county supervisors, social workers and many other categories of workers get the special protections. By the way, the protections are pointless now, given that the DMV long ago abandoned the practice of giving out personal information to the public. Yet the list of categories keeps growing and growing.

A few days after the newspaper investigation caused a buzz in Sacramento, legislators voted to *expand* the protections to even more classes of government workers. An Assembly committee, on a bipartisan 13-0 vote, agreed to extend the protections to veterinarians, firefighters and code officers. One legislator justified the vote with a horrific story about code officials who were murdered after breaking up a dog-fighting ring. After the vote, the story was revealed as largely bogus. But just as government officials constantly parade their heroes in front of the public to secure more funding, so too do they tell tales of the grave dangers they face.

## RATIONALIZATIONS FOR SPECIAL PRIVILEGES

One Democratic Assembly member justified her support for the bill this way: "[T]his is a public safety issue. And there are lives of public workers, public safety officers, that are put on the line every day on our behalf that need to be protected." Said a Republican member of the committee: "I don't want to say no to the firefighters and veterinarians that are doing these things that need to be protected."[3] Never mind that there is no longer any need for the protection and that the main result of the special plates is to protect government employees and their families from tickets and tolls while they drive in their personal vehicles on their personal time.

With the government employees' addresses kept confidential, toll-road operators, parking enforcement and red-light-camera operators either cannot access them or don't go through the extra steps necessary to find the addresses. So the government employees often rack up thousands of dollars individually in unpaid fines or in tolls. This costs the quasi-private toll operators millions of dollars. Furthermore, when police spot these special plates or pull people over and look up the plates, they realize that the driver is special. They then extend what the police call "professional courtesy" — that is, they don't ticket other members of the brotherhood of government enforcers.

"It's a courtesy, law enforcement to law enforcement," said one police spokesman to the *Register*.

I have gotten calls from police whistleblowers alerting me to, for example, a local cop's spouse who allegedly was pulled over stone drunk, then given a courtesy ride home. Any average citizen pulled over for a DUI would end up in the county's notoriously abusive jail system for a day or more.[4] Don't ever expect such "courtesy" for a mere citizen or taxpayer! This obviously is the type of thing more appropriate to an authoritarian society, where the rulers get to behave according to a different set of laws than the ruled.

In California, law enforcement gets its own "Peace Officers Bill of Rights,"[5] which offers a comprehensive list of special protections in case officers are accused of wrongdoing. Even the name of that law is offensive — the Bill of Rights is meant to protect the public from the government, but this one offers an added layer of protection from public accountability for the agents of government.

## 'MORE'

Being largely exempt from traffic laws is bad, but government workers are always pushing the envelope. It's like the union leader who was once asked, ultimately, what it was he wanted for his members. His answer: "More." That applies not only to salary and benefits but to special protections.

In April 2008, the California Assembly Public Safety Committee was set to consider—and most likely pass, with little apparent opposition—Assembly Bill 2819 by Democratic Assemblyman Mark DeSaulnier. The bill states, "No firefighters, EMT-1, EMT-II or EMT-P employed by the state or a local agency shall be subject to criminal prosecution for any legal act performed in the course and scope of his or her employment to carry out his or her professional responsibilities."[6] The only way a firefighter could be prosecuted was if he or she committed an act "with demonstrable general criminal intent"—an extremely high standard for a prosecutor to meet. An earlier version of the legislation would have prevented firefighters from "civil or criminal liability unless the act was performed in bad faith or in a grossly negligent manner with demonstrable, willful criminal intent."

Despite the words "legal act," the clear result of the legislation would have been to protect firefighters from prosecution for gross negligence. If, say, a firefighter committed an intentionally illegal act such as murder or theft, he would still be subject to prosecution. But if he was involved in otherwise legal behavior, such as driving, but acted in a grossly negligent way when doing so, he would be exempt from prosecution. This went far beyond the current civil protections for "good faith" mistakes a firefighter or paramedic might make in the line of duty.

The impetus for the legislation was a controversial prosecution by a district attorney against a firefighter who killed someone because the firefighter was driving a fire truck allegedly in violation of department standards. Even though prosecutors are loath to file charges against firefighters, the firefighter unions grabbed onto this one incident as a means to gain blanket immunity for their members, even for outright misbehavior. One Assembly member told me that if the legislation became law, a firefighter or paramedic would be protected from any civil or criminal claim even if he showed up at an accident, saw someone in severe distress, but decided to get a hamburger instead of doing his job.

As the *Register* opined at the time: "The Assembly Public Safety Committee today is considering one of the most noxious, special-interest pieces of legislation we've seen in a while—one that will endanger public safety, tread on the California Constitution and reinforce the perception that some government workers are part of a special, coddled group that's exempt from the normal legal and ethical standards that are applied to other Californians."[7]

The constitutional problem: the Legislature cannot dictate to the executive branch whom it can and cannot prosecute. This legislation was first introduced for firefighters, but before long police, animal-control officers and others would be demanding the same protection. The bill was pulled from the calendar at the last minute due mostly to the bad publicity the editorial generated, but it will surely be back again. Government workers and their unions are quite shameless about pushing their self-interest.

There was a time when government work offered lower salaries than comparable jobs in the private sector, but more security and somewhat better benefits. These days, government workers fare better than private-sector workers in almost every area—pay, benefits, time off and security.

"Today, government employees in the vast majority of job classifications earn considerably more than those in the private sector doing similar work," wrote Jon Coupal of the Howard Jarvis Taxpayers Association and Richard Rider of the San Diego Tax Fighters in a column on the CaliforniaRepublic.org Web site. "They have even better job security than before and they enjoy many far superior benefits—including a pension which can exceed the salary they earned while working."

The *Asbury Park Press* in New Jersey reported recently that "Federal workers, on average, are paid almost 50 percent more than employees in the private sector." The reason, according to a Heritage Foundation legal analyst quoted in the article: "The government doesn't have to worry about going bankrupt, and there isn't much competition."[8]

One result is the huge public liability created by government pension and retiree health-care plans. Elected officials are generous in granting expanded benefits to government employees. They buy labor peace and political support, letting future legislatures, councils and taxpayers deal with the growing debt. This is no minor problem. "The funds that pay pension and health benefits to police officers, teachers and millions of other public employees across the country are facing a shortfall that could soon run into trillions of dollars," the *Washington Post* reported.[9] "But the accounting techniques used by state and local governments to balance their pension books disguise the extent of the crisis facing these retirees and the taxpayers who may ultimately be called on to pay the freight."

The second part of that quotation is harrowing. The unions and government agencies have cleverly hidden the extent of the deficit. But courts have ruled that the promises made by elected officials to government unions are ironclad contracts that must be kept. That leaves the nation's taxpayers stuck footing the bill. Even as private-sector workers must toil longer to shore up their eroding retirement funds, so too must they work extra to make good on the unsustainable promises elected officials have made to government workers. Only the best for our rulers!

## PERVERSE INCENTIVES

It's easy to understand why the pension deficits continue to grow. In California, for instance, public-safety employees—police, fire, prison guards, and an expanding number of law-enforcement categories—receive "3 percent at 50" retirements. That means at age 50 they are eligible for 3 percent of their final year's pay times the number of years worked. So if a police officer starts working at age 20, he can retire at 50 with 90 percent of his final salary until he dies, and then his spouse receives that for the rest of her life. The taxpayer typically makes the complete retirement contribution throughout the officer's years of work. Many police—more than half in some agencies—claim an injury (such as back pain or bad knees) a year before their retirement age, which not only gives them a year off for disability, but protects half their retirement from taxes.

Police and firefighters are legally presumed to have a work-related illness when they get common ailments such as heart attacks or cancer. The bottom line: Public-safety officials have many ways to gin up their already generous retirement benefits to astronomical levels. Most garden-variety government employees get lucrative pensions also. It is common for them to retire at age 55 with more than 80 percent of their final year's pay. Most public employees receive defined-benefit retirement plans, in which the taxpayer promises a set rate of return, as opposed to private-sector workers who have 401(k)'s and other defined-contribution plans in which the market sets the return.

## TROUBLE WITH VALLEJO

This situation is bringing trouble. Vallejo, a city of 120,000 in the San Francisco Bay area, declared bankruptcy because tax revenues remained relatively static while public-employee salaries continued to grow out of control. Police and fire budgets consume three-quarters of the city's budget, leading to the reduction of other government programs (libraries, museums, senior-citizen centers). Despite the enormous spending on public safety, city officials have warned citizens to be judicious in their use of 911 calls. When government overspends, the public has to suffer.

The *San Francisco Chronicle* reported that the base salary of firefighters in Vallejo is $80,000 a year, that 21 firefighters earn more than $200,000 (out of approximately 190), and that 77 of them earn more than $170,000. The *Chronicle* also reported that these excessively paid folks have been spending their time "going abalone diving, grilling tri-tip and drinking cocktails on the public's dime."[10] The city manager, by the way, earns a total compensation package of $400,000 a year. The downtown is decrepit, in large part because the city has no money to spend on infrastructure.

Even with bankruptcy, it's uncertain whether Vallejo can get out from under the outrageous union contracts that are turning it into a Third World city—one that comes complete with an arrogant and corrupt aristocracy that doesn't care about the public.

Even worse than the fiscal mess is the kind of society we're creating. It's one where the government elite get special pay, special benefits, special privileges and special exemptions from the law, and where the rest of us have to play by the rules and work extra hard to pay for these excesses.[11]

## THE $100,000 PENSION CLUB

While the average household income in the United States hovers around $50,000 a year, the nation's government-worker elite often earns more than double that amount in their retirement years—perhaps the most striking symbol of an out-of-control system that is bankrupting cities and leading to the creation of a two-tier society where the government elite live far better than the public. In summer 2009, the California Foundation for Fiscal Responsibility used the Freedom of Information Act to create a $100,000 Pension Club database: www.californiapensionreform.com/calpers. The database allows members of the public to search for the names of the 5,115 California government workers who earn more than $100,000 a year in pension benefits from the California Public Employees Retirement System (CalPERS).[12] Twenty-four employees have retirements above $200,000. This reveals only part of the problem, given that many other government workers are part of county and other retirement systems, but it alerted the public to the degree to which government employees had gamed the system. When *all* California retirement systems are considered, the number of $100,000 Pension Club members is 8,205, according to Reason Public Policy Institute. Reason notes that 100 percent of California's retired state employees receive taxpayer-funded health benefits.

Many workers earn well above $100,000 a year in taxpayer-funded retirements. The top 10 pension earners range in pay from $224,000 a year to nearly $500,000 a year. They worked for a variety of agencies, ranging from a small city government, to a water district, to the state's university system. The list is filled with police and firefighters, who not only often retire in California with large pensions, but get to do so at extremely young ages (in their 50s) and generally go on to earn hefty salaries at other police and fire agencies. The current retirement system, with its combination of exorbitant payouts and low retirement ages, really is a scam designed to double the income of public employees in the last decade of their working lives. As a *Sacramento Bee* editorial explained, "That firefighters and police officers dominate the list of $100,000 retirees should come as no surprise. At the state level and almost all local jurisdictions, public safety personnel have the richest retirement formulas. If they work for 30 years, police and firefighters can retire in their early 50s with 90 percent of their last year's salary, which is usually their highest."[13]

The *Bee* made another important point, which explains why the pillaging of the public treasury goes on to this day: "Managers also dominate the $100,000 club list. These are the people who are supposed to represent the public when employee benefits are negotiated. But when government managers sit down with union leaders to dicker over compensation, they are negotiating for themselves as well. If rank-

and-file workers get a wage or benefit boost, non-union managers get a commensurate hike and a matching pension benefit."[14]

CFFR had to fight to gain access to the data. Even though these pensions are paid for by taxpayer dollars, government unions insist that the information actually is private and an invasion of workers' privacy rights. Fortunately, the courts sided with full public disclosure.

This is from a July 4, 2009 *Legal Newsline* report: "California's leading taxpayers' rights group says the public scored a major legal victory this week when a judge ruled that a county's pension records are not entirely confidential. The judge ruled that the Howard Jarvis Taxpayers Association and California Foundation for Fiscal Responsibility, a public pension watchdog group, are entitled to a list of names and total retirement benefits for all Contra Costa County employees receiving an annual pension of at least $100,000. Retired Contra Costa County Deputy Sheriff Donna Irwin sued the county retirement board, claiming that releasing her pension amount was an invasion of privacy. Attorneys for the taxpayers' group intervened in the case, arguing that unlike the IRA and 401k plans of private citizens, public employee defined benefit plans pay a guaranteed amount that are funded by taxpayers. ... In his ruling Wednesday, Contra Costa Superior Court Judge Barry Baskin ordered the records released, saying a 'transparent government is the cornerstone of our democracy.'"[15]

Thank goodness for that ruling. Increasingly, government employees are shielded from public disclosure requirements, which is part of Chapter 4's discussion of special privileges enjoyed by the government elite.

The top pension earner in the state, Bruce Malkenhorst of the tiny industrial city of Vernon, earns a half-million bucks after serving as the sort of Boss Hogg of his little Los Angeles County burg. He was the $600,000-a-year city manager, clerk, finance director, treasurer, redevelopment agency boss and head of the city's "independent" light and power company. It's amazing that anyone could perform all these tasks at once, but, even though Vernon is a legal oddity (a glorified industrial park incorporated as a city), this reveals a great deal about the lack of accountability throughout the public sector in California and elsewhere.[16]

"We are becoming a nation of government aristocracy, much like Russia was in the days before it collapsed from the weight of it," wrote *Grass*

*Valley Union* columnist Jeff Ackerman.[17] "Take the former San Francisco police chief, for example. Heather Fong just retired at 53 years old and will receive a pension of $229,500 per year FOR LIFE. Assuming Ms. Fong lives an average lifetime (say...75), her pension is potentially worth more than $5 million. ... So how is your 401(k) performing these days? How close to $5 million is it? ... It's tough to say exactly when government desk jockeys replaced coal miners as the nation's strongest labor union force, holding taxpayers hostage and politicians in their pockets. Those unions are crippling our ability to manage taxpayer money prudently, which is one of the big reasons most municipalities are broke today. And ... no ... it's not because we aren't paying enough taxes. Sorry. That one doesn't fly anymore, not so long as we are handing out $5 million retirement packages."

The level of enrichment is obscene. The ElkGroveNews.net, a blog covering this suburban Sacramento community, focused on a *Public CEO Newsletter* cover story about Elk Grove City Manager John Danielson, which featured his photograph and this headline: "Elk Grove Robber Baron?" Writes the blog: "The story illustrates how Danielson, who was the city manager of Incline Village, NV before being hired by Elk Grove in 2001, was able to amass over $4.8 million in compensation, leave buybacks, lifetime health insurance and pension before being fired in late 2006."[18]

The size of the pension payouts is raising concern even in the most liberal locales. In the city of Los Angeles, the $100,000 pension club has 841 members, including the retiring head of the Department of Water and Power, Ronald Deaton, who will retire with more than $327,000 a year. The *Los Angeles Times* headline captures it all: "Amid the cutbacks, pensions soaring."[19] And amid the tax increases, also. Taxpayers in Los Angeles are frequently asked to pay more to protect public services, but in reality they are paying more to protect these millionaire public "servants."

People often say in response that private companies offer absurd levels of compensation to their top-level executives, which often is true. Of course, those executives are paid with private dollars. If a company wants to squander its money on absurd compensation packages, ultimately it must answer to stockholders and to consumers. Poorly run businesses can go out of business. And rank-and-file employees rarely receive multi-million-dollar guaranteed pensions. By contrast, the public sector uses taxpayer dollars, cannot go out of business and the enrichment schemes are spread across every category of worker, from the top to the bottom.

The $100,000 club is not exclusive to California. The *Albany Times-Union* reported in June 2008 that "Almost 700 retired public educators in New York are receiving at least $100,000 annually in pensions, and many more than double their income by returning to work for school districts. The 690 school retirees join 899 state and local government workers in the six-figure state pension club."[20] Some of the top pensions in New York state are doled out to retired public librarians, according to a February 23, 2009 *New York Post* article. In one case spotlighted in the article, a retiree from the New York Public Library received more than $188,000 a year. As the *Post* put it in classic *Post* fashion: "Being expert in the Dewey Decimal System really pays off."[21]

When government employees retire early, they often go on to take other jobs. They get to pursue their passions while collecting large paychecks or, often enough, they continue working at the old job as part of Deferred Retirement Option Plans (DROP) that allow them to collect two paychecks (the retirement check, which goes into a deferred account for a later payout, and their salary). Others go on to take other government jobs and earn additional retirement benefits. They can't receive more than one check from the same retirement system, but there are many retirement systems. So they go on to work for an agency that has, say, a county system rather than the state system. They typically don't collect Social Security, but they don't pay into it either. Ironically, many public employees aren't satisfied with these cushy deals—they complain and demand that their retirements be brought up to even higher levels enjoyed by other civil servants.

This taxpayer-funded enrichment really is outrageous. Something needs to be done about it. The first step, of course, is to alert the public to the problem, which is what this book is about. By the way, this is a non-partisan issue. In my newspaper coverage of the matter, I've found both parties to be eager to expand government pensions for government workers. Democrats are more closely allied with public-sector labor unions and have been on the forefront of these pension-hiking deals, of course, but Republicans have been particularly aggressive in pushing expanded benefits for public-safety workers. Both parties created the problem and people from across the political spectrum will be needed to fix things. During one pension battle, one of the most eloquent speakers against a proposed retroactive pension increase was a liberal Democrat who argued correctly that as pensions begin eating up more and more of her city's budget, there will be far less money available for libraries, social services, road improvements and other programs that were important to her. Many conservatives realize that the coming pension tsunami will lead to higher taxes and increased debt loads. Here's an area where there's much room for a bipartisan solution. Everyone should be appalled at the excesses and abuses inherent in the current retirement system. Public employees should receive a fair level of pay and decent retirements, but they should not be able to use their political muscle to secure absurd compensation levels, or be allowed to engage in dubious pension-spiking schemes or get such rich deals that future generations of Americans are going to be stuck with the debt.

## THE PUBLIC'S CHOICE

This is not a book about political theory, but about rubber-meets-the-road reality. Nevertheless, it's important to spend a short time discussing one of my favorite political theories, called Public Choice Theory. Understanding its basic point is crucial for any discussion of government workers and its relevance will become clear in later chapters as the book reviews the political reasons that all this enrichment has taken place. Public Choice debunks some of the childish defenses used by unions to protect their outsized pay and benefits.

When critics point out the high pay, special protections and enormous pensions that government employees, especially police and firefighters, receive, the main argument in response is an emotional one: "We are doing the public good. You need us to provide these essential services!" Public safety officials always use this catch phrase: "We put our lives on the line to protect you."

Sorting through these notions could be the subject of an entire book in and of itself. Before we address this directly, it's important to raise three points relating to the nature of government and "government service":

First, while we need a certain level of government to enforce the rule of law and provide certain services, it's not true that everything government now does needs to be done in the public sector. This is a deeper philosophical argument, but the public assumes that if, say, the schools weren't run by the government, then there would be no schools and little education. That's not true. In a true free market, every sort of educational opportunity would arise, courtesy of entrepreneurs operating in the marketplace. I'm not trying to engage an argument on the existence of public schools. I'm only raising the obvious point that much of what the government does—even in areas that most people view as fundamental— could and certainly would be done in other ways. One city in Georgia, Sandy Springs, has privatized its entire city government outside of public safety. Most fire departments in the United States remain volunteer fire departments. Many large private entities use private security forces rather than public police. In Southern California, a quasi-private toll road agency built some of the most impressive freeways in the state using private funds when it became obvious that the state government wasn't going to build the roads.

Readers need to recognize that, for starters, there are plenty of alternatives to the government provision of services. So, yes, most of these essential services—education, firefighting, police, roads, etc.—can at least partially be provided by other means. And in an alternative world the public workers would simply be workers for private or quasi-private enterprises whose pay and benefits would better reflect the marketplace.

Second, many things government does should not be done at all. Government should not provide corporate welfare to businesses, so those involved in such a provision shouldn't be doing this at all. Government should not be, say, arresting medical marijuana users (or any marijuana users, for that matter), so those engaged in that form of work should be doing other things. There's no need for government workers to do things that are not properly the sphere of government —but government unionization and the political support these unions receive create constant pressure for more public workers.

Third, everyone who provides productive and useful labor in society is doing the public good. The idea that government workers are doing this more so than others is a fallacy, especially when one puts government work into the proper perspective. In fact, most Americans have typically had a skeptical view toward government work, at least in past decades, given that those who work in the public sector are involved in activities that require little risk, have power over others (and often abuse that power, given human nature) and have widely known civil-service and union protections that most Americans don't have. It's commonly understood that it's nearly impossible to fire even the most incompetent government workers, and that the best and brightest head to the private sector.

Here's my point: Government work should not be honored above other forms of work. That's not to say that government workers are not necessarily honorable or don't often provide valuable and necessary services, but many of us are tired of the constant union drumbeat seeking to elevate public-sector workers above the rest of society. That elevation has provided the intellectual rationale for the excessive benefit increases that politicians have endorsed. The politicians might fear union backlash if they don't vote for the increases, but they can tell themselves and their constituents that they are helping protect the public's protectors. Note the Public Service Recognition week referred to above.

"Why should we in the private sector take all the risks, and labor under the burden of ever-higher taxes, so we can pay for the lavish salaries, pensions and benefits of public service employees?" asks Wayne Allyn Root, the vice presidential candidate for the Libertarian Party in 2008, in his recent book. "Why do we work 12 to 14 hour days, while government employees work 9 to 5? … Why should we slave away at work until the day we die, so we can pay for the early retirements at age 50 (or younger) of public employees who get to play golf for the rest of their lives … ?"[22]

Perhaps it's a little overstated. But those are good and fair questions, and ones that get to the heart of increasing populist anger at the unfair and unaffordable system we've created.

When "public safety" officials point to the dangers they face, it's useful to turn to the Bureau of Labor Statistics.[23] Recent data show the most dangerous professions as follows:

1. Fishing-related workers
2. Logging workers
3. Pilots and flight-related workers
4. Iron and steel workers

5.  Taxi cab drivers

6.  Construction workers

7.  Farmers and ranchers

8.  Roofers

9.  Electrical power workers

10. Truck drivers and sales-related drivers

11. Garbage collectors

12. Law enforcement

You can see that most of these categories are private-sector categories. According to the BLS, 90 percent of those killed on the job are in private industry. Consider that about 20 percent of America's workers are government workers; it's far safer to work in the public sector, all things considered. About half of police and sheriff's deputies killed each year die in automobile and motorcycle accidents. Firefighters are far down on the list. This is not meant to minimize any death, but to put the public safety argument in perspective. Even the most dangerous public sector jobs— civilian ones, with military combat service exempted—are not particularly dangerous in comparison to the overall U.S. workforce. No one forces anyone to take any job, so it's fair to assume that anyone who chooses to be a roofer or a police officer has intelligently weighed the risks vs. the payoff for pursuing that career. Yet police and firefighters constantly use this argument to guilt the public into accepting ever-larger amounts of compensation. Many police and firefighters have a sense of entitlement and complain constantly about how difficult and dangerous their jobs are. The evidence doesn't support this, even though these can indeed be tough jobs. Bottom line: If a person doesn't like a job or a profession, that person should do something else!

As the outrageous pension benefits and high pay levels of public-safety workers get more attention, police organizations are fighting back by using misleading campaigns that emphasize the dangers of their work. The *Sacramento Bee* blogger Andrew McIntosh writes about a late summer 2009 police lobbying campaign as the governor proposed a new pension benefit level for new hires only: "In the PORAC [Peace Officer Research Association of California] videos, a male and female officer take turns saying they work dangerous streets and complain that their pensions are 'under fire.' A gun appears on screen as they discuss their concerns. The problem is, that's not true for current officers. Changes to pensions under consideration by the administration would only affect future recruits, not officers already working the streets. Why deliver that message now? This fall, police pensions are certain to come under intense scrutiny if the state's financial condition worsens."[24]

The reason for the ads: Whenever any public policy issue arises regarding police and firefighters, their unions reach for the cheapest emotional ploy. And they don't mind resorting to outright deception.

Again, these jobs have their dangers, but are not particularly dangerous in the scheme of all U.S. jobs. And people who take these jobs are very well compensated for them, especially considering their educational levels. The vacancy problem referred to in the PORAC ads stems directly from the "3 percent at 50" benefit itself and from the tendency of elected officials to always call for hiring more police officers. So-called shortages are the result of police unions getting their way, not because benefit levels aren't high enough.

Granted, people appreciate firefighting in particular. But it was appalling when a newspaper showed some California residents pitching in money to firefighters after they had saved their neighborhood from flames. The gratitude is understandable, but the firefighters are well paid for their work and it's just part of the job. There's no need to offer more than a simple thank you for a job well done. One reader called to yell at me after I criticized firefighter pay packages: "Pay them anything at all. They are worth any amount," he said. It's hard to know where to begin to debunk such emotionally driven fiscal insanity, but suffice it to say that this appears to be the policy undertaken by public agencies. We are finding out, however, that the enrichment of certain classes of government workers is coming at the high price of higher taxes, unsustainable debt loads and reduced public services.

Now, let's get back to the theoretical discussion at hand.

Underlying the "we protect you" argument, and the support it often receives, is the traditional civics-book concept about public work—that the public votes for representatives who promote the public's interest and that the bureaucracy is filled with public-spirited folks who serve the people.

As William Shughart II writes in the *Library of Economics and Liberty*: "As [renowned Public Choice economist] James Buchanan artfully defined it, public choice is 'politics without romance.' The wishful thinking it displaced presumes that participants in the political sphere aspire to promote the common good. In the conventional 'public interest' view, public officials are portrayed as benevolent 'public servants' who faithfully carry out the 'will of the people.' In tending to the public's business, voters, politicians and policymakers are supposed somehow to rise above their own parochial concerns.

"In modeling the behavior of individuals as driven by the goal of utility maximization—economics jargon for a personal sense of well-being—economists do not deny that people care about their families, friends, and community. But public choice, like the economic model of rational behavior on which it rests, assumes that people are guided chiefly by their own self-interests and, more important, that the motivations of people in the political process are no different from those of people in the steak, housing or car market. They are the same human beings, after all. As such, voters 'vote their pocketbooks,' supporting candidates and ballot propositions they think will make them personally better off; bureaucrats strive to advance their own careers; and politicians seek election or reelection to office. Public choice, in other words, simply transfers the rational actor model of economic theory to the realm of politics."[25]

Public choice is used to explain not only how politicians behave, but also how bureaucrats behave. It recognizes that most decisions within government are made by the permanent bureaucracy. As such, it gets at the real motivations of government decision-making. The theory doesn't suggest any conspiracy, but helps us understand the obvious: that people in government, although they may be diligent and professional, are trying to improve their pay, benefits, salaries, power and so forth. All people do such things. My underlying argument throughout this book is not that government officials are necessarily bad people, but that they constantly have pushed their prerogatives and have been particularly successful at it because of political forces at play. It's crucial that Americans realize that government work is not about some ill-defined public good even though some of what government does arguably advances the public good. The sooner we disregard the myopic view of government, the sooner we can bring government's fiscal problems into line. We need some government and those who work for it should be fairly compensated. My view, however, is we have far too much government and those who work for it have manipulated the system to enrich themselves far beyond what most of us would have imagined. It's coming at a big cost to the rest of us.

The key word is *manipulate*. "Anglo-American jurisprudence emphasizes the rule of reason; it grossly neglects the reason of rules," write Public Choice theorists Geoffrey Brennan and James M. Buchanan. "We play socioeconomic-legal-political games that can be described empirically only by their rules. But most of us play without *an understanding or appreciation of* the rules, how they came into being, how they can be changed, and, most important, how they can be normatively evaluated. … We note with a mixture of admiration and envy those clever strategists who manipulate existing rules to their own advantage. It is these persons in the role of spivs rather than the sages that all too many emulate."[26]

Indeed, the public employee unions and the politicians who support them have learned how to write and then manipulate the rules for their own advantage. Then those who try to fight against this process are stuck playing by rules that give the other side huge advantages. It's a no-win game for the taxpayer. For instance, a fiscally responsible politician might oppose a plan to enhance the pension formula and might even win, but the rules of the game are so rigged that it's nearly impossible to move the ball in the other direction and all such victories are only fleeting. It's only a matter of time before the unions re-introduce the proposal or come back with another plan to achieve the same sort of enhancement. Having worked 14 years for newspapers, I've watched this process many times. We would fight a plan, but even when the public won, the plan came back again thanks to the constant efforts of the bureaucratic forces in favor of it. Like rust, government never sleeps.

One story during California's 2009 budget crisis came from a conservative Republican who explained that even some prominent Democrats are upset at the power that public-sector employee unions wield. But the Democrats are completely beholden to those unions and cannot stand up to them publicly, which is yet another example of how unions have understood and manipulated the political rules to their advantage. The Republican told me of Democrats who were urging the

GOP to please tackle pension reform, even though they admitted that there was no way they could possibly help out. Even some Democrats know that the current situation is unsustainable. The Brennan/Buchanan quotation is a reminder of how deep the problem has become. It's not just a matter of electing politicians with the courage to fight union proposals. Reform is a hard road. It requires an intense rewriting of the political rules that push in one direction. That's another area where a little understanding of political theory can help those interested in change.

It also is crucial for readers to understand a thing or two about the nature of government itself. After appearing on the Air Talk radio program on Southern California public radio in July 2009, I received an angry e-mail from a listener who didn't like our panel's comments regarding public employees. We were discussing the Orange County Planning Department. As the *Los Angeles Times* explained it, "Orange County's planning department is in 'critical condition'—employees have not been performing required safety and environmental inspections, morale is down and customer service is nearly nonexistent, according to a county performance audit released Wednesday."[27]

All of the panelists took a "this is what you expect from government" approach. My point: government employees often treat the public like subjects rather than customers. I said that these employees have excellent pay and benefits and much power—especially in planning departments, where the officials can make or break a person's building or remodeling project. The listener was a public employee who explained how hard she works and how nice she is to members of the public. Her salary was less than $50,000 a year, she explained. She was polite, but angry at me.

All of that is no doubt true. There are plenty of dedicated and decent public employees, many of whom earn relatively low salaries. Many of them perform necessary tasks. Many of them will no doubt write to the publisher after this book is published, just as many of them write to the newspaper in response to my columns. But these folks always misunderstand the nature of government. As George Washington said, "Government is not reason, it is not eloquence, it is force; like fire, a troublesome servant and a fearful master."

Government takes its money by force. That's reality. Despite the IRS fiction that our system is voluntary, if an American doesn't pay his taxes he will end up in jail. Because government is funded in such a way, it need not compete for business. It takes what it wants, or at least what it can get away with in a democratic system. Government agencies and agents have power over people. They can force us to bend to their will. Sometimes that's necessary, as when a police officer arrests a suspect. But let's not forget the nature of things here. If a customer goes to a Best Buy store and the salesman demands that he buy a computer, the customer can laugh and walk out. If the Department of Motor Vehicles, the IRS, the local deputy sheriff, Child Protective Services or the Franchise Tax Board tells you to do something, you better obey immediately and fully ... or else. That's what is meant by being a subject rather than a customer. Even the so-called government "helping" professions are backed by policies and procedures that give officials certain coercive powers. So, yes, many government employees are decent and honorable, but let's not overlook the very nature of the government system and the relationship between the official and the public.

Regarding dollars and cents, economist Murray Rothbard correctly captured the nature of government, "By its nature, government is not subject to the profit-and-loss test, to the domination by the consumers, of the free market. Even voluntary non-profit organizations, while not seeking maximum profit, at least have to be efficient enough to avoid severe losses or bankruptcy. Furthermore, such voluntary organizations at least must satisfy the values and demands of their donors, if not the users of the good or service as in the profit-making market. But government is unique among organizations in attaining its revenue via the coercion of taxpayers. Hence, government suffers no worries about losses or bankruptcy; it need serve no one except itself. The only limit on government is the enormously wide one of people rising up to refuse to obey its orders (including taxes); short of such revolution, however, there is little to limit government or to check the entrenchment or burgeoning of its elite."[28]

Keep these concepts in mind as we look at the massive transfer of wealth and power that has flowed in recent years from the private to the public sector.

## NOT QUITE FRANCE

Fortunately, the United States has avoided the militancy of organized labor that has dominated Europe. In France, workers have been known to stage nationwide work shutdowns. In April 2009, the *Times* of London reported on union gas and electricity workers in France sabotaging electricity substations in order to deprive hundreds of houses and businesses of electricity.[29] They were angry about the outsourcing of jobs and a rejection of their demands for 10 percent pay increases. Workers bemoaned competition from market forces. In Europe, the labor movement often is tied to communist and socialist political organizations. In many cases, workers actually take their bosses hostage as they make their demands.

In the United States, the labor movement has been rather bourgeois in its values. Many pundits attribute this to the nation's lack of a strict class system. Americans value their upward mobility, and blue-collar workers believe that they can indeed move up the economic ladder through hard work rather than labor demonstrations. American politics has rarely tolerated radical extremes. This is a good thing. Certainly, the American labor movement has had its share of violence, but nothing like what routinely goes on in Europe. Of course, it's even worse in South America, where new leaders buy off the bureaucracy by spiking pensions and where union protests routinely turn violent.

As the Manhattan Institute's Steve Malanga explains in a May 14, 2009 *Wall Street Journal* column, private sector employees "are accepting cost-saving measures with equanimity—especially compared to workers in France, where riots and plant takeovers have become regular news. But then there is the U.S. public sector, where the mood seems very European these days."[30] He points to angry protests and overheated ad campaigns by unions refusing to share in any of the nation's economic pain. More recently in California, public unions have voted to authorize strikes, even though such strikes are illegal. An authorization vote doesn't mean a strike will happen, but it shows the mindset of government workers. But Malanga explains the difference in approach: "Call it a tale of two economies. Private-sector workers—unionized and nonunion alike—can largely see that without compromises they may be forced to join unemployment lines. Not so in the public sector."[31] Never mind that satiating the unions is causing higher taxes and reducing dollars for genuine public services.

So far, the government-worker protests have been more bluster than anything else and they have not been violent. Still, the increasing testiness of their protests—in the face of only modest cutbacks, and cutbacks that are far less severe than those faced by private-sector workers—shows the public-sector-union mindset. Government workers get high pay and outrageously generous benefits, but their sense of entitlement knows no bounds. Ironically, a few furloughs and occasional cutbacks aside, America's government workers have largely escaped the impact of a bad recession. They may be acting a bit like the French workers/mobs, but, as this book will show, there has been absolutely no need for unionized government workers to get the least bit agitated, let alone violent, about their working conditions and salaries. They have been enriched beyond belief, and the real question is whether the rest of Americans—the folks who will pay higher taxes and work later into their lives to pay for these promises—will decide to protest. Clearly, the world has been turned upside down when it comes to government unions in America.

CHAPTER TWO

# UNBELIEVABLE PAY AND BENEFITS

To greed, all nature is insufficient.
— SENECA

Every time I write something about public employee pay and pension packages, or talk about them on TV or radio news programs, people find the statistics cited hard to believe. Most recently, I referred to the average total pay and benefit packages for firefighters in my newspaper coverage area of Orange County, Calif., during a short segment on the "Glenn Beck Show" on Fox News. "It can't be so," said one Midwestern caller, who contacted me the day after the segment aired. But it is true. The number, double-checked in the county's fire authority budget, is an astounding $175,000 a year,[32] which includes overtime and all the various benefit goodies (total cost). The amount —a compensation package worthy of a CEO—literally is unbelievable, especially to people who live outside the aptly named Golden State. But while California is on the cutting edge of this absurdity, just as it is on the cutting edge of various other trends for good or ill, this is a nationwide problem. It is being felt in every state, although it is most pronounced in union-dominated blue states. States such as Massachusetts, New Jersey and Illinois have similar problems.

It's crucial that people grasp the extent of the raiding of the public treasury. Back to the original example—thanks to the overtime system, rigged to boost employee pay rather than protect the public till, many California firefighters earn more than $200,000 a year in pay alone. One local firefighter amassed so much overtime his annual pay was nearly $300,000 a year. These are not aberrations. Firefighters aren't the only government employees who have discovered a gold mine, but their situation best illustrates how terribly the public is getting plundered and how out of balance the entire government pay situation has become, especially with regard to the most demanding class of "public safety" workers who can retire as early as 50 with nearly full pay—and at times at pay levels beyond their final year's pay—guaranteed for the remainder of their lives, and the lives of their spouses.

Whenever discussions turn to their compensation packages, safety union officials (police, fire, probation, prison guards, etc.) proclaim, "We put our lives on the line," and that generally ends the discussion. Few politicians want to be portrayed as "soft on crime," or enemies of other "public protectors" such as firefighters, when before elections those political hit mailers get sent out—especially in California, with its regular wildfires. In fact, one local Orange County tax initiative was languishing in the polls, but then wildfire season struck, the firefighters produced ads portraying their successful firefighting efforts, and that was that—the public voted "yes."

Politicians desperately seek public safety union endorsements and to be photographed in campaign literature next to police cars and fire trucks. When the fire department in Laguna Beach, Calif., got into a contract dispute with the city, the fire union drove a (rented) fire truck around the city plastered with images of 9/11. It's hard for politicians to stand up to this type of shameless negotiating tactic. Americans appreciate the heroism displayed by New York City firefighters, but does that mean they have no right to question the demands of every fire union in the country during every contract dispute? From a political standpoint, however, it's far better to just go with the flow and let future generations of taxpayers figure out how to make good on all the promises than to take on some of the most powerful political forces in local or state politics. This isn't a place where nuanced discussions or cost-benefit analyses matter. It's about emotions and political power, which explains in part how the country has gotten into its current fiscal mess.

The local firefighters' union gets annoyed when anyone refers to that $175K number. Officials there confirm its accuracy, but complain that it unfairly angers taxpayers because the number includes the cost to the county for every benefit that firefighters receive. In other words, the union is uncomfortable when average people learn about the *total* compensation package for its members. The union prefers that reporters either not write about the salaries and benefits at all or that they use the low-sounding base-salary figures the union always uses, and simply neglect the common gaming of the overtime system and Cadillac-style benefits its members receive. Actually, the $175,000 number is too low, because it does not include the unfunded liability—the debt incurred on future taxpayers to make good on the retirement promises for current workers. Politicians have promised these workers a benefit that is not sustainable and not even budgeted to reflect the true future costs. Courts have ruled that such benefits are vested, so the benefits are the equivalent of binding legal contracts no matter what happens to state and local budgets. No wonder union officials will tell elected boards virtually anything when benefit increases are being debated, because once the benefits are passed, it's a done deal. It doesn't matter if the investment-return numbers justifying the expansion are unrealistic or even downright deceitful. Taxpayers will have to pay for these deals, just as eventually someone will have to pay for the Social Security and Medicare Ponzi-like schemes. Just because our grandkids and great-grandkids will have to make good on those promises instead of us doesn't mean these promises don't come with real costs.

With the economic downturn in 2008 and 2009, this future problem—addressed in more detail in Chapter 3—is already here as some localities are facing bankruptcy to deal with unfunded liability problems related to government employee pensions. As a 1970s rock group used to sing, "The future is now!" So, too, in the here and now, we turn back to public firefighters who have, in the words of one politician friend of mine, "skinned the hog." They receive an inordinately high salary, guaranteed millionaires' pension, some of the finest health benefits known to mankind, limited working hours and so much free time on the job that they can work on side businesses or exercise and play games. They can retire at age 50 and try something else with their lives after that without having to worry about saving for retirement. The local fire union leader wanted a correction after my column explained that firefighters are paid *for* sleeping. "They are paid *while* sleeping," he retorted. Nice work if you can get it.

The legal privileges and special benefits public employees receive are generally unknown and at times quite astounding. If public safety union members get common ailments such as heart attacks or cancer, these are considered by law to be work-related ailments, and that unleashes disability retirements and a tide of other benefits. The real kicker is that in addition to all these absurdly generous benefits, firefighters also get to bask in the glow of admiration, as the public—generally unaware of the way they and their elected officials have been played as fools by the firefighter unions over the years—believes these folks are underpaid doers of the public good. This is not an effort to demean the work they perform. But they reflect the public-employee problem at its extreme.

My family certainly was glad when firefighters showed up to put out the wildfire raging around my Southern California neighborhood in 2008. (Although it's fair to share the story of how difficult and infuriating it was to get the department to cut down the dry tinder on public land surrounding our homes given the level of bureaucratic indifference within the department, which is a common story.)[33] Yes, firefighters perform an important service. And we all understand that they will, to an extent, have an easy job most of the time—we pay them a premium so they are trained, rested and ready in the rare occasions when we need them. Although these jobs aren't high on the Bureau of Labor Statistics list of dangerous professions, they do entail serious dangers at times. Firefighters die battling blazes nearly every fire season. But many private-sector jobs are far more dangerous (roofers, contractors, fishermen, etc.). Good pay and benefits are in order, but we've gone into the world of the unreasonable.

It's worth putting this in context of supply and demand, which determines the pay and benefits of private workers. The high pay and benefits go far beyond what the market requires to keep local fire departments fully staffed, even considering that staff levels are artificially inflated from union featherbedding rules. These rules require as many as four firefighters per fire truck and require fire trucks to show up for paramedic calls. Firefighters' pay and benefit levels are especially amazing given the low number of fires in most urban areas. Typically, about 90 percent of emergency calls to fire departments are for paramedic services[34]—services that could be privately provided, by the way, but which have been co-opted by the firefighters as unions have used their legal muscle to drive out most private competitors. Keep in mind, also,

America's tradition of volunteer fire departments. This is a job that many people will do for free, out of the enjoyment and sense of purpose they get from the work. But again the unions have done what they can to squelch this lower-cost alternative. *Parade* magazine reports that "72 percent of America's firefighters are volunteers. … Of the 118 U.S. firefighters who died in the line of duty in 2007, 68 were volunteers."[35] This should debunk the notion that volunteer firefighting is not a reasonable alternative to massive budgets and CEO-like salaries and benefits for firefighters. Actually, the firefighting situation highlights the huge disparity in America today, with a large percentage of people who make actual sacrifices of time and money to perform an important task and a smaller group that has taken the road to self-enrichment. In my view, the market, left to its own devices, would provide various high-quality firefighting and paramedic services that would apply downward pressure on costs. Yet powerful firefighter unions have been able to tap deeply into public treasuries across the country—and mainly to the benefit of employees, not the public. These costs, in other words, are not entirely necessary. One can have an honest debate about the best way to provide firefighting services, but my point is that these decisions are made based on what's best for the union and its members. How taxpayers are best served is not even part of the equation.

I've often heard firefighter unions complain that they don't have enough money for necessary equipment or to replace aging fire trucks, as they lobby for tax increases or higher diversions of property tax revenues to their budgets. Often, it's true that such equipment is badly in need of replacement, but no one likes to explain the reason why: Fire authorities already have blown the bulk of their budgets on salary and benefit payments. In a debate with one fire official, he cried poormouth about the aging truck situation. When we brought up the huge increases his department made in pension benefits in the past few years, he said that such an argument was beside the point because pay and benefit dollars came from a different budget item. In the private sector, managers must deal with a real budget. If a manager spends too much on salaries, he will have to cut back on the quality of products or services offered to consumers, consumers might become dissatisfied and might start shopping with the competition, which eventually will harm the bottom line. If a company spends too much and runs up too much debt, it can go out of business. In the public sector, managers overspend on salaries and benefits and then whine that taxpayers need to pay more if they don't want to see their service levels cut. When there's not enough money to do both things, the public suffers or is forced to pay more in taxes or bonds. City governments on rare occasions go bankrupt, but they can't go out of business. The public always foots the bill.

Given these priorities and the huge pay and benefit packages firefighters receive these days, it's no wonder that fire departments receive thousands of applications for every spot that becomes available. Fire departments will sometimes hold recruiting sessions at auditoriums to deal with the large number of people who want to get on that gravy train. If firefighter salaries better matched true market demand for firefighters, more people deeply committed to this career would pursue it, whereas now the money is so good that people who might prefer to do other things seek out such jobs. If a person really wants to be a firefighter, that person will have a hard time getting such a job because the waiting list is so long. Throwing public money at things, as always, distorts the market and causes unforeseen problems. Yet these realities never get much public policy discussion. That's another consequence of public union dominance—serious policy issues are off the table if they conflict with the thinking of union leaders.

If only firefighters were so lavishly compensated, many cities, counties and states wouldn't be in such difficult financial straits. But for years now politicians have been dramatically increasing the pay and especially the benefits for all categories of government workers. The pay structure also has a sort of multiplier effect. Because they receive such generous pensions, public-safety workers are encouraged to retire at an early age, thus leading to "shortages" in law enforcement in particular. The taxpayer gets hammered twice, as he pays nearly full freight for retired employees and then has to pay for a full-time replacement. The artificially created shortages are used by unions to lobby for even higher pay and benefit packages ... for recruitment purposes, of course. This all adds up to an enormous drain on the public till, and it reinforces the dangerous idea that government workers are a specially treated class of citizen. They are paid like an elite group, and their contracts are treated as inviolate by the courts. Private employees must, in a down economy, work far later into life before retiring, while public employees retire far earlier—15 to 20 years earlier in many cases. And the taxpayers will ultimately have to pay more to clean up the mess, which only adds insult to injury. Public employees should earn reasonable pay and benefits, but it's nothing short of outrageous that they receive far more than the people for whom they supposedly work.

## KEYS TO THE RETIREMENT SCAM

The phrase, "3 percent at 50," is common during discussions about government pensions. It's a term almost designed to make one's eyes glaze over, but it's important to grasp the simple concept behind it. The term is applied to a pension formula for public-safety officials, especially in the more generous states and municipalities. It's a type of *defined-benefit* retirement system, as opposed to the *defined-contribution* systems that are more common in non-unionized private-sector workplaces.[36]

With a defined-benefit system, the employer guarantees a set retirement amount based on a formula. In many cases, the employee contributes to the plan, and the money is invested in a retirement system. In other cases, the agency pays the full contribution to the system, which is often the case with public-safety employees. In all cases, the employee knows exactly what he or she will receive from the employer once retirement arrives. With defined-contribution systems, the employer (and employee) contributes a specific amount of money in a fund, such as a 401(k), and the eventual payout is determined by the success of the investments and the amount of dollars put into it over the years.

As the stock market has tanked in recent months, most private employees have lost large portions of their retirement savings, whereas public employees with defined-benefits plans have fared well even though their retirement plans also have taken enormous hits. When investments in public-employee retirement systems fall below projections, the taxpayer, rather than the employee, picks up the slack or a large unfunded liability (debt) accrues. Indeed, many critics argue that the defined-benefit system encourages public employee retirement funds to take unreasonable risks. Take a look at the absurdly risky leveraged investments in the housing market that went south for CalPERS, the California Public Employees'

Retirement System. If the risks pay off, the retirees get the benefit. If the risks don't, it's the taxpayers' problem. Public employees have no real stake in the stock market or the overall economy, given that their retirement is a contract, etched in stone that must be paid no matter what. This also has an impact on political debates, given the skewed incentives.

This is from an *Orange County Register* blog post of mine in December 2008:

"Orange County Supervisor John Moorlach has long predicted that the public employee retirement systems could not sustain their high rates of return. These union-dominated boards take high risks to keep the returns high so that their members can continue to get higher and higher levels of benefits. CalPERS amortizes its costs over unusually long periods, which is like taking a 15-year loan on a Ford Focus. They've got every reason to play these games. If their strategies create good returns then it's easier to get increases in pay and benefits. If they don't, their current absurd level of benefits is guaranteed by taxpayers anyway. It's a good example of the economic principle of 'moral hazard,' which explains why those protected from risks will act in riskier ways. This is the ultimate in privatizing gain and socializing risk. Most people are focused on financial frauds on Wall Street, which is understandable, but some of these legal scams are bigger problems."[37]

I went on to explain about those risky CalPERS investments that went bad—often using as much as 80 percent of borrowed money to invest in new housing developments in strange places at the height of the housing boom. The *Wall Street Journal* featured a front-page article on this craziness: "CalPERS has said in recent weeks that it expects to report paper losses of 103 percent on its housing investments in the fiscal year that ended June 30. That's because CalPERS invested not only its own money, but billions of dollars of borrowed money that must be repaid even if the investment fails."[38]

In a November 9, 2008 *Sacramento Bee* article, however, CalPERS President Rob Feckner defended the soundness of these pensions: "It seems that every time the stock market suffers a major setback, those who don't fully understand how government pensions work begin sounding alarm bells that it will absolutely drive up the cost of government pensions. A close examination of history and the facts suggests it's way too early to make such assumptions. First, the California Public Employees' Retirement System employs a long-term investment strategy designed to weather periodic financial storms. This strategy, along with professional investment management, has produced an average annual investment return of nearly 10 percent over the past 20 years—which included two market downturns—well above our target of a 7.75 percent average annual return to fund benefits."[39]

Moorlach is best known because as a candidate for county treasurer in 1994 he blew the whistle on the leveraged investment schemes that ultimately caused Orange County to become the largest municipality to go bankrupt. He rebutted Feckner in an *Orange County Register* column: "What Mr. Feckner fails to mention are two critical concerns in his effort to calm state employees and the public is that nearly a decade ago CalPERS was fully funded. Consequently, with the great yields that he touts, CalPERS should be more than fully funded. The reason it is not is the second small concern that he failed to mention: Ten years ago he supported formula enhancements that increased benefits by some 50 percent! Changing retirement formulas in the middle of the game is a recipe for disaster. It shows a severe case of not fully understanding how government pensions work. They are not there to be plundered and pillaged by their employees."[40]

But plunder and pillage are the key words here. Moorlach, who has tried to rein in some of the excessive retirement benefits for public employees, relayed to me a conversation he had with a financial planner, who had just met with a public employee. The employee had to do absolutely no financial planning. His retirement was guaranteed, period. Come hell or a stock market crash, it didn't matter. He understood the defined benefits he was promised, which freed up a large portion of his workaday budget for vacation homes, RVs, fancy vacations and home remodeling. Only now is it becoming obvious that such obscene benefit levels cannot be afforded by the public at large. And even if this is affordable, do we really want a society where there are such large disparities in retirement living between government workers and the people who pay their salaries?

Because of its importance in understanding the plundering, I'll review how these retirement formulas work. Those who receive "3 percent at 50" are promised three percent of the final salary (either the final year or an average of the final two or three years, depending on the jurisdiction, but it's usually the final year for public safety officials in California) times the number of years worked available at age 50. So if a police officer began working at an agency at age 20, he could retire at 50 with 30 years on the job. If he earned a slightly above-average California police salary of $100,000 a year (base, not counting overtime, which is not calculated in the retirement formula), he would receive $90,000 a year until he dies, after which his spouse would receive it until she dies. That's 3 percent times years worked, which is 90 percent of the final salary calculation, or $90K. Non-safety employees receive less-generous formulas, but 2.7 percent at 55 is a common one in some counties, in which an employee will receive 81 percent of final pay after 30 years of work, available at age 55 (2.7 times 30 equals 81 percent of whatever the final pay happens to be). Now compare that to your own retirement plan and weep.

These amounts are absurd, but the story doesn't end there. There are many legal ways that government employees can spike their pensions. Here's a portion of an enlightening column by *Contra Costa Times* columnist Daniel Borenstein, who looks at one East Bay public pensioner: "Craig Bowen's salary during his final year as chief of the San Ramon Valley Fire Protection District was about $221,000 a year. So how did he end up retiring in December with a tax-advantaged annual pension of $284,000? The answer provides an amazing case study that highlights problems with public employee compensation and reveals tricks that allow workers to spike their pensions at the expense of their fellow employees and taxpayers ...

"Bowen was only 51 years old when he retired at the end of 2008. If he or his wife lives another 30 years, that bump-up alone would add $2.7 million in today's dollars to his pension. His total retirement payout for the next 30 years would be worth about $8.5 million in today's dollars — far more than most taxpayers have in their 401(k)s when they hit the half-century mark. ... As he told a reporter in December, a medical condition influenced his decision to retire. In March, the board of the Contra Costa County Employees' Retirement Association, which administers the fire district's pension plan, approved Bowen's request for a service-connected disability. As a result, under state and federal laws, much of his pension payment is exempt from income tax. Moreover, under state rules, if his wife survives him, she will be entitled to 100 percent of his pension for the rest of her life. ..."[41]

In addition to the normal "3 percent at 50" calculation, Borenstein explains that Bowen gets an additional $10,700 a year for unused sick leave—something the writer describes as "generally peculiar to the public sector. It's a benefit public agencies could, and should, end. Sick leave is supposed to serve as insurance to provide compensation when a worker is ill; it shouldn't be a tool to bolster retirement." Bowen also receives an additional $14,500 a year in standby and management pay, which also is odd. As Borenstein put is, "This is for a manager to be . . .well, to be a manager. It seems odd that a fire chief would be paid extra to perform duties that are basic to his job."[42]

This is incredible. When someone throws around the banal term "3 percent at 50," realize that it is not some mind-numbing management formula, but the description of a system whereby government employees are granted literally millions of dollars in retirement benefits simply for performing a highly secure job for 25 or 30 years. Remember that those who receive these benefits will be retired, and pursuing some hobby or luxuriating on a Caribbean beach somewhere while you work later and later into life to pay for these excessive goodies and for the higher taxes that surely will be needed to bail out these upside-down systems. Remember that the payouts are propped up by union-dominated retiree systems that play every sort of game to delay the day of reckoning and to conceal the fiscal reality from the public. Indeed, government employees are made instant millionaires just for taking a job and sticking with it over their career. This certainly is easier than taking the more traditional American route to becoming a millionaire, through risk-taking and entrepreneurship.

"Don't let anyone tell you the American dream has faded," writes Stephane Fitch in a January 2009 *Forbes* article. "The truth is the U.S. is still minting lots of millionaires. Glenn Goss is one of them. Goss retired four years ago, at 42, from a $90,000 job as a police commander in Delray Beach, Fla. He immediately began drawing a $65,000 annual pension that is guaranteed for life, is indexed to keep up with inflation and comes with full health benefits. Goss promptly took a new job as police chief in nearby Highland Beach. ...Given that the average man his age will live to 78, Goss is already worth nearly $2 million, based on the present value of his vested retirement benefits. Looked at another way, he is a $2 million liability to Florida taxpayers."[43]

I wonder how many Florida taxpayers have such a great retirement deal?

"At all levels of government, the rate of compensation has gone up much more rapidly than it has in the private sector and, most importantly, faster than the personal income of the people who pay for this," Steven Frates, senior fellow at the Rose Institute in Claremont, Calif., told the Los Angeles *Daily News*, "There has been a wealth transfer. It has gone from the citizens to the people in government. You often hear people in government cry that there are going to be cuts and we're hurting the poor and the little children. The fact of the matter is the citizens of the state, county and city are making life better, not necessarily for schoolchildren or people in need, but for government employees."[44]

Union leaders often point to the fairly low average pension received by government workers, but that's a function simply of averages. Many people work a fairly short time for an agency and only get a small pension, which isn't because the pension is low but because of the individual's short working period. The average, of course, includes all the many government agencies. So, for instance, the nation's 6 million retired government employees averaged $17,640 in pension benefits in 2005. But private sector employees averaged only $7,692 a year. Keep in mind that 90 percent of government employees received lifetime pension benefits vs. 18 percent of private employees.[45]

It brings to mind that silly old country and western song, "She got the gold mine and I got the shaft."

## WE DIE YOUNG!

A key argument that public-safety officials use to justify their absurdly high pension benefits is this: We die soon after retirement because of all the stresses and difficulties of our jobs. This is such a common urban legend that virtually every officer who contacts me mentions this "fact." They never provide back-up evidence. Here is one article I've been sent by police to make their point. It was written in 1999 by Thomas Aveni of the Police Policy Council, a police advocacy organization. Here is the key segment: "Turning our attention back towards the forgotten police shift worker, sleep deprivation must be considered a serious component of another potential killer; job stress. The cumulative effect of sleep deprivation upon the shift-working policeman appears to aggravate job stress, and/or his ability to cope with it. Even more troubling is the prospect that the synergy of job stress and chronic sleep indebtedness contributes mightily to a diminished life expectancy. In the U.S., non-police males have a life-expectancy of 73 years. Policemen in the U.S. have a life expectancy of 53-66 years, depending on which research one decides to embrace. In addition, police submit workmen's compensation claims six times higher than the rate of other employees … "[46]

I don't doubt that police work can be very stressful, but many jobs are stressful, many have long hours, many are more dangerous, many involve sleep deprivation. As intelligent adults, we all need to weigh the risk and benefits of any career choice. Aveni uses the high amount of workers compensation claims as evidence of the dangers of the job, but given the tendency of police and firefighters to abuse the disability system—miraculously discovering a disabling injury exactly a year from retirement, thus getting an extra year off and protecting half the pension from taxes—I'm not convinced this proves anything. Given the number of officers who are retired based on knee injuries, back aches, irritable bowel syndrome, acid reflux, etc., this suggests that police game the system and know their fellows on the retirement board will approve virtually any disability claim. There are so many legal presumptions (if an officer develops various conditions or diseases it is legally presumed to be work related, whether or not it actually is work related) that bolster the scam. "Disabled" officers often go right out and get similar law enforcement jobs, which calls into question how disabling the injury really is. Regarding sleep deprivation, police and firefighters have secured schedules that minimize the long hours—but then the officers often *choose* to work overtime to double their salary, which perhaps is the real cause of sleep problems.

But the big whopper in the Aveni article is the claim that officers live to be 53-66. If that were so, there would be no unfunded liability problem because of pension benefits. Police officers would retire at 50-55, then live a few years at best. But according to the CalPERS actuary, police actually live longer than average these days, which isn't surprising given that the earlier people retire and the wealthier they are, the longer they tend to live. According to a 2006 report to the Oregon Public Employees Retirement System, these are the age-60 life expectancies for the system's workers (meaning how many years after 60 they will live):[47]

- Police and fire males: 22.6
- General service males: 23.4
- Police and fire females: 25.7
- General service females: 25.7

So we see that police and firefighters who retire at age 60 live, on average, well into their 80s. That's real data and not the hearsay used by apologists for enormous police pensions.

CalPERS actuary David Lamoureux sent me a CalPERS presentation called "Preparing for Tomorrow," from the retirement fund's 2008 educational forum. The presentation features various "pension myth busters." Here is Myth #4 (presented as part of a PowerPoint presentation): "Safety members do not live as long as miscellaneous members." CalPERS officials explain that "rumor has it that safety members only live a few years after retirement." Then they use actuarial data to answer the question: "Do they actually live for a shorter time?" The presentation considers the competing facts: "Safety members tend to have a more physically demanding job, this could lead to a shorter life expectancy. However, miscellaneous members sit at their desk and might be more at risk to accumulating table muscle!"[48]

Fire officials, by the way, make identical claims as police officials about dying early.

For answers, CalPERS looked at an experience study conducted by its actuarial office in 2004. It looked at post-retirement mortality data for public safety officials and compared it to mortality rates for miscellaneous government workers covered by the CalPERS system.

Here are the CalPERS life expectancy data for miscellaneous members:

- If the current age is 55, the retiree is expected to live to be 81.4 if male, and 85 if female.

- If the current age is 60, the retiree is expected to live to be age 82 if male, and 85.5 if female.

- If the current age is 65, the retiree is expected to live to be age 82.9 if male, and 86.1 if female.

Here are the CalPERS life expectancy data for public safety members (police and fire, which are grouped together by the pension fund):

- If the current age is 55, the retiree is expected to live to be 81.4 if male, and 85 if female.

- If the current age is 60, the retiree is expected to live to be age 82 if male, and 85.5 if female.

- If the current age is 65, the retiree is expected to live to be age 82.9 if male, and 86.1 if female.

That's no mistake. The numbers are identical for public safety retirees as for other government workers. As CalPERS notes, average public safety officials retire earlier than average miscellaneous members, so they receive their higher level of benefits for a much longer time.

Here is CalPERS again: "Verdict: Myth #4 Busted! Safety members do live as long as miscellaneous members."[49]

The next time you hear this "we die early" misinformation from a cop, firefighter or other public-safety union member (most of them probably believe it to be true, given how often they have read this in their union newsletters), send them to CalPERS for the truth.

I expected these numbers in recent years given the pension enhancements and earlier retirement ages, but it seemed plausible that police in particular might have had a point about mortality rates in earlier days. But even that's not true. A 1987 federal report from the National Criminal Justice Reference Center, "Police Officers Retirement: The Beginning of a Long Life," makes the following point:

"'The average police officer dies within five years after retirement and reportedly has a life expectancy of twelve years less than that of other people.' Still another author states, 'police officers do not retire well.' This fact is widely known within police departments. These statements (which are without supporting evidence) reflect a commonly held assumption among police officers. Yet, a search of the literature does not provide published studies in support. Two suggested sources, the Los Angeles City Police and Massachusetts State Police, have provided data which also appear to contradict these assumptions. Reported in this paper are results from a mortality study of retired Illinois State Police (ISP) officers. It suggests that ISP officers have as long, if not longer, life expectancy than the population as a whole. Similar results also arise when examining retirees from the Ohio Highway Patrol, Arizona Highway Patrol, and Kentucky State Police."[50]

The report also casts doubt on the commonly repeated statistic that police have higher rates of suicide and divorce than other people. The federal report found the divorce rates to be average and suicide rates to be below average. This is important information because it debunks a key rationale for the retirement expansions, although more recent data should to be examined on divorce/suicide rates. Police have an oftentimes tough job, but many Americans have oftentimes tough and sometimes dangerous jobs. This needs to be kept in perspective. Public officials need to deal in reality rather than emotionally laden fantasy when considering the public policy ramifications of pensions.

Now that we realize that retired public safety officers typically live into their 80s, you can understand the depth of the pension and benefits problem. A big problem is that retirement systems plan for the long term, but then officials come around and enhance the benefits mid-stream, which then increases the long-term debt load. Orange County Supervisor John Moorlach, writing in the FlashReport.org Web site, offers an analogy of how the government retirement system has been working. Moorlach starts with the assumption that you, a private-sector employer, decide to pay your 25 year-old worker a "2 percent at 50" retirement benefit and invest your money with the expectation of receiving a 7.75 annual rate of return. Then you decide to increase the benefit retroactively to "3 percent at 50," as many California government agencies had done during the last decade:

"Well, the new benefit at age 51 jumps from $71,978 to $107,966 (a 50 percent increase). If the funding level is not changed, instead of ending with zero funds at the 80th year of life, the funds would dry up at age 65. In year 66 someone would have to come up with $168,208 from somewhere to pay that year's benefit. To fund the extra 15 years, someone would have to fund $561,500 in the 26th year! This is approximately half of what you have earned over 25 years of methodical contributions and investments. Now you can appreciate why municipal employers are reeling from recent retroactive retirement benefit enhancements."[51]

Multiple this many times over and you understand the mess the state and the nation are facing. We see endless pension increases, but no commensurate increases in contributions from municipalities or the government workers themselves. In the private sector, the entire benefit package averages less than 30 percent of an employee's salary. In the public sector, the pension benefit alone costs 25 percent of salary for average workers and 40 percent to 50 percent for police and fire officials—and that doesn't include the unfunded liability portion of it. These are big numbers and explain why Americans will soon face higher taxes, degraded public services and higher levels of debt to pay for all the promises made to government workers who, despite the dishonest claims of their union representatives, will probably outlive the average American.

## CASE STUDIES IN SECRECY

Readers often demand to know how such plans can go forward. They never had a say in these matters and don't recall any public debates about them as city councils and legislators were passing such generous benefit enhancements. Many forces converge to keep these debates as quiet and non-controversial as possible. In fairness, when the stock market was soaring and home prices were rising, legislators—rarely capable of looking ahead beyond the next election—were happy enough to expand pay and benefit levels. They were warned about the ramifications by many accountants and good-government activists, but they didn't feel the need to ponder the matter too deeply. The public didn't think much about it, either. In 1999, the California bill that allowed municipalities to grant "3 percent at 50" retirements passed with widespread bipartisan approval. But you can see the deception inherent in the process. The law merely allowed the granting of the benefit. Supporters knew, however, that once a few municipalities approved the new benefit, everyone else would have to jump on board, lest they would claim to lose employees to other nearby departments. And so the cycle began. The Assemblyman who introduced "3 percent at 50" legislation, Democrat Lou Correa of Santa Ana, still excuses the action as a law that merely allowed localities to enhance the formula.[52] But that's a lame excuse. Supporters knew that by allowing it, it was only a matter of time before some municipalities increased the pensions—and most others would be sure to follow. This is like explaining that you didn't kill anyone—you merely handed a loaded revolver to a criminal!

"A turn-of-the-century bonanza for California public employees has become a fiscal nightmare for cities and counties attempting to dig themselves out of record budget deficits," wrote Bob Taylor in an April 2003 article in the California Taxpayers Association journal Cal-Tax Digest. Cal-Tax, by the way, was one of the few sane voices warning against the bill's passage in 1999. "Virtually every local government in the state is being squeezed by pension bills that have come due during a period of fiscal crisis made worse by a severe economic downturn."[53]

The problems of the 1999 pension increase already were becoming obvious in 2003, and Taylor detailed the pension shortfalls that were afflicting city and county budgets even in the early phases of the downturn. But the article's relevance here is its discussion of the inside-Capitol politics that allowed the increase to be approved:

"Shortsighted state legislators—spurred by public employee unions—in 1999 approved legislation (SB 400, Ortiz) that dramatically changed public retirement formulas. At the time, the financial world looked rosy, the economy was booming, budgets were bulging and everyone wanted in on the gravy train.... The bill nevertheless sailed through the Legislature with barely a whimper of protest in the closing hours of the 1999 session, and without the normal detailed analysis of the fiscal implications. The essential piece of independent scrutiny came nearly three months later from the Legislative Analyst's Office, which pegged the cost of SB 400's retirement package at over $400 million a year starting in 2001-02. Why the analysis of this important piece of legislation came after the fact has never been adequately explained.

"It is instructive to examine the environment during the 1999 economic boom period. At that time, greed was the unspoken watchword as employee unions demanded a share of bulging government treasuries fattened by increased dividends from a wildly successful investment period. And it has been suggested by some observers that CalPERS administrators—who also would benefit from the retirement boom—became advocates for a piece of the action. They worked in concert with employee unions crafting the legislation, and then urged its passage. However, CalPERS alone cannot be blamed for today's painful reality. Local government officials themselves would have to share in culpability. Many of those officials gazed at the horizon and saw that they too would be beneficiaries from the retirement largesse. Human nature and self-interest during the flush times leading to the 1999 legislation created a greased track for SB 400."[54]

Taylor got it right when he chalked up the vote to the greed and personal advantage of everyone involved—even the managers stood to gain the massive benefit increase if the legislation got through. This is a crucial point, and one repeated throughout this book: both sides of the table in these government agencies stand to gain from pension-increasing deals. It's a rigged system. Can you imagine how nice it would be to negotiate with a boss who would receive any percentage gain that you received? There are no real checks and balances here.

Everyone was in on the game. That kind of fix is in at the municipal level whenever benefit increases are proposed. At the municipal level, council members and board members take great pains to keep criticism to a minimum, especially as financial problems and unfunded liabilities grow. I've found that some of the most controversial governance issues are discussed in the most banal terms by officials looking to avoid public scrutiny. Typically, if a city council is debating a topic that would generate widespread community debate or outrage (i.e., redevelopment plans that require subsidies or eminent domain, generous new contracts for public employees or retroactive pension increases) the agenda item gets downplayed on the public meeting calendar and officials describe the discussion in ways that won't generate attention. Officials tend to meet the letter of open-meeting laws, but frequently violate the spirit of them.

The real work is done outside public view. Public employee unions even have the audacity to argue that the deals they cut behind closed doors with elected officials are done deals that must be honored, even though the public rarely has even the slightest glimpse of what elected officials are negotiating.

"When people see the board of supervisors vote on a labor deal, what they don't know is that most often, an agreement has already been reached in private," explained *Orange County Register* reporter Norberto Santana in an article examining a controversial labor deal from 2006. After one supervisor complained about one aspect of the proposal, "Union officials, however, argue they already have a deal under the state's collective bargaining law because the Board of Supervisors authorized county negotiators to make an offer and union members voted for it."[55]

What a rigged system! It's even worse when you consider the point raised earlier—that everyone involved in the negotiations has a financial interest to see the deal go through. And Santana's article explains how a 2004 retroactive pension increase on the board was negotiated behind closed doors and then unveiled on a Friday afternoon with a vote scheduled for Tuesday. There was no chance for debate on that increase, nor for the county's "3 percent at 50" plan granted to deputy sheriffs retroactively in 2001. This is completely typical, in my experience.

"It gives no time for public input or review, which means that the unions only have to influence three people," the majority on the five-member board, then-Treasurer John Moorlach told Santana. Writes Santana: "He notes that there have been longstanding concerns that the county's labor negotiators are too close to union officials. This month, one supervisor relayed concerns to county CEO Tom Mauk after seeing the county's chief negotiator sharing lunch and champagne with a sheriff's union official at an upscale Santa Ana bistro." That scene has to epitomize the situation: a labor negotiator who supposedly represents taxpayers having a celebratory champagne lunch with the union official who supposedly sits on the other side of the negotiations table. A San Francisco grand jury found that "everyone involved in pension negotiations as well as implementing and monitoring the systems, is a member of the pension system. There is an apparent conflict of interest in nearly any effort on the part of public employees to reform pension practices."[56]

No wonder the public treasury repeatedly gets plundered.

One local story sheds light on how closely public employees work in tandem with elected officials, how both sides conspire to keep negotiations in private to avoid any public scrutiny of their deals, and how viciously the assembled forces come down on those who break the rules of the game and try to alert the public to the goings-on. It also shows how oblivious officials can be to the financial maelstroms swirling around them. It's worth going into this local story in some detail, because it is completely reflective of what good-government activists and the public are up against. What happened below happens at every locality, and you need to pay attention to these secrecy tricks if you hope to stop the plundering.

In the heart of the 2009 financial meltdown, with the impact of pension increases frequently covered in the media, the city of Fullerton, Calif., nevertheless sought to retroactively increase the defined-benefit retirement plan for its city employees by 25 percent—a last-ditch attempt for city workers to jump on the bandwagon right before it headed over the cliff.

The City Council had negotiated the increase in closed session. Four of the five council members—two Republicans, two Democrats —were clearly behind the deal. The Fullerton deal was negotiated in closed session, outside public view. Even though contract negotiations are legitimate closed-session items under California's open meetings law, known as the Brown Act, council members are supposed to give the public a clear idea of the content of the behind-closed-doors negotiations. In Fullerton, the agenda vaguely referenced labor negotiations. But as one California court put it, citizens should not need to be "clairvoyant" to have an idea of what public officials are doing in such meetings.

This is how these types of negotiations go: The union makes its demand to the council in private, and the council has staff negotiate a deal with the union. Most city council members are sympathetic to the demands of city workers for starters, and those that aren't full-on union allies are fearful of union political campaigns. The staff members doing the negotiating stand to benefit from any new deal. So they come up with a generous proposal. It's never discussed publicly—indeed, city officials claim that it *cannot* be discussed publicly lest it undermine the sanctity of labor negotiations and violate state law. The negotiated deal is then sent to the union members for approval and, if passed, gets slipped onto the open council agenda in a manner that leaves as little time for debate and opposition as legally possible. Usually, it gets placed on the agenda late Friday with a vote scheduled the coming Tuesday. Sometimes a taxpayer or citizens group gets wind of what's going on, but the union—which has

long known about the deal and has been working to assure its passage—
musters its forces on meeting night and creates the impression that the
vast majority of city residents are supportive, or at least not opposed,
to the deal. Opponents have not had time or sufficient details to rebut
the debatable numbers often used to support the proposal. Council
members, staff and public speakers—and often the local, civic-booster-
oriented media—are all in favor of the plan, so it then gets approved, often
unanimously.

In Fullerton, however, one council member was the proverbial skunk
at the garden party. Republican Councilman Shawn Nelson, a principled
advocate for limited government, didn't appreciate the way the council
was obscuring not only the legitimate details of the negotiations, but even
the basic subject matter. He called me and, without revealing details of the
closed session, shared his concerns about the way the public was not being
alerted about the subject of the closed-door negotiations. The establishment
came down on him in a hurry. Expectedly, the liberal council members
were furious that the public was now informed about what was going on.
But some conservative Republicans, including a prominent state senator,
were furious also, because Nelson's willingness to talk to me embarrassed
a Republican councilman that the GOP was backing for re-election. After
bumping into that senator at the Republican National Convention in St.
Paul, Minn., he laid into me about Nelson's supposed violation of the
Brown Act. Some officials and bloggers were actually calling for Nelson to
be prosecuted for revealing the details of the closed session.[57] Local union
mouthpieces and fellow council members portrayed Nelson as a criminal
even though he seemed to be the only one who was acting in the spirit of
the state open-meetings law.[58]

Nelson never provided the details—they came from another source.
Even if he had, it wouldn't have been different from what the other
side had been doing. Union members already knew the details of the
negotiations and indeed had the opportunity to vote on the contract.
They had been discussing it among themselves for weeks. Furthermore,
Nelson, according to open-government activists, was arguably the one
in conformity with state law, which is supposed to give the maximum
amount of information possible to the public, not game the system to
conceal everything. Under the Brown Act, governments are supposed to

provide enough information so that the public can comprehend what's being discussed, Jim Ewert, legal counsel for the California Newspaper Publishers Association, explained. The council was concealing proper information and Nelson called them on it.

Orange County Supervisor Chris Norby, a former Fullerton council member, captured the essence of what happened in a column reprinted on the Red County Web site:

"Thank you, City Councilman Shawn Nelson, for letting Fullerton taxpayers know about the ongoing closed door city pension proposals. Recent public employee pensions at the state, county and local levels have added billions in unfunded liabilities. They lure away our most experienced employees into early retirement and burden younger workers with added costs.

"Yet, the City Council has apparently been negotiating a new pension boost in closed doors for months. State law permits closed door negotiations, but doesn't require them. City employees were kept fully informed of all details and have already voted to approve the contract. All 430 employees have voted on a contract that has been kept from public view. The retroactive part of the proposal is particularly onerous. Employees may retire almost immediately and receive enhanced pension benefits for which they've paid virtually nothing. Younger workers must forgo raises and pay more to support the payouts to the newly retired.

"Nelson's disclosure led to several editorials in the *Register*, which in turn sparked a council firestorm. Nelson's council colleagues called him both a lawbreaker and a backstabber. He was told to be a 'team player.' Whose back is he stabbing? The city staff who advises the council? (all of whom will benefit by the new pension). Team player? The council is not a team with pre-rehearsed plays and a coach telling them all what to do. All must express their individual concerns.

"Typically, agendas go public Friday for meetings held on Tuesday. That's barely two working days, hardly enough for the pubic to respond to a complex pension-laden contract that was months in the making. The council can negotiate a fair contract while informing the public of the stakes involved. When this does come to a public vote, all of us will be forewarned—thanks to Councilman Nelson.

"I can personally relate to Nelson's frustration. When I first attended closed session labor negotiations as a supervisor, I was appalled that the board received no information in advance. I tried to absorb complex presentations, but was prevented by staff and fellow board members from taking any information out of the room to discuss with my staff. 'It's confidential—not to be discussed outside the room,' I was initially told by three of my colleagues. Yet, the union representatives passed all the information on to their members. The only people kept in the dark were the public. I made it clear I would never support any deals that I could not fully analyze with my own staff.

"A new board majority finally demanded back-up materials in advance and now regularly discusses all proposals with our own staffs. But most OC council members have no staff of their own, so they rely on city staffs, which often are the beneficiaries of the very proposals they bring to a council. ..."[59]

In their embarrassment, the council voted against the deal at the last minute, but only after council members publicly chastised Nelson, accused this editorial writer of slander and basically vowed to come back again when the timing was right. One Republican councilman couldn't figure out what the fuss was all about, given that they enhance public employee pay and pensions all the time. CNPA proposed legislation that would have required cities to provide more details about closed-door meetings, but that was dead on arrival in the union-dominated Legislature. This story, though local, provides insight into how hard it is for anyone to stand up to the forces allied on behalf of local public-sector unions. It shows how thoroughly the game is rigged. How can the public stand up to these forces?

Orange County remains a conservative county. And the pension issue had been on the radar screen for quite a while thanks to the Fullerton brouhaha, the 2004 pension increase, pension troubles in nearby San Diego, a county supervisor who has made this his cause celebre and a newspaper editorial board that has been focused on the matter. But in August 2009, the city of Costa Mesa voted to expand retirement benefits for the city's firefighters by granting them a "3 percent at 50" retirement package, upping it from the "3 percent at 55" package firefighters had previously enjoyed. Two of the supporters were conservative Republicans, which shows just how difficult it is to rein in these abuses when public safety officials are involved. Ironically, at the same meeting the City Council voted to cut the pay of non-unionized city workers and impose mandatory furloughs for union workers. The new budget had all sorts of cuts, but the council nevertheless managed to increase benefits for the firefighters' union. The deal produced savings over four years, mainly because the firefighters gave up a number of positions through attrition— which shows how unions will gladly choose to cut future jobs as long as their senior members get bigger pension checks at earlier ages. But those savings evaporate over the long-term, given that the new pension costs go on for 30 or more years (the life expectancy after retirement of firefighters and their spouses).[60]

Part of the problem in Costa Mesa and elsewhere is that cities face an unfair disadvantage when they enter contract negotiations. Typically, the unions will have in the past secured provisions stipulating that the old contract stays in place if a new one is not agreed upon. In the private sector, even in unionized companies, the old contract expires and workers might continue working under the old contract, but both sides have an incentive to come up with a new deal. In the public sector, the old contracts come with clauses that state that if a new contract deal isn't struck the old one stays in place—and those old ones come with mandated salary and benefit increases. These "evergreen" contracts make it nearly impossible to extract meaningful concessions from unions. The contract mandates pay increases based on the level of increases granted in other cities. In Costa Mesa, sticking to the old contract would have meant unaffordable pay hikes, so the city granted long-term pension increases to get some short-term concessions on pay and staffing levels. Furthermore, the staffing levels were determined in previous contracts and were basically featherbedding provisions requiring a far higher number of firefighters than would really be needed to do the job. The firefighters union was forced to admit as much when it gave up those positions and assured the public that there would be no impact on response times. It's absurd allowing staffing levels to be determined by contract—those levels should be determined by city management in response to the legitimate needs of the public. But, again, public service and the public's needs are not the focus of these negotiations. It's all about what the union wants.

The Costa Mesa deal got much attention in Orange County and

throughout Southern California, just as the Fullerton deal received much attention in the local media. But even before this book went to press, yet another agency in the region—the Metropolitan Water District of Southern California—came up with its plan to significantly increase pay and pensions for its workers, even as MWD had been pushing ahead rate hikes. As the *Register's* Terri Sforza reported, "At a time when generous public employee pensions are generating enormous heat (among the less-well-pensioned populace, at least), the giant Metropolitan Water District of Southern California is poised to increase employee pensions by 25 percent... It could cost Met some $70 million, and comes at a time when water rates are rising significantly, and when Met's pension investments in CalPERS have tanked at least $405 million, bringing Met's 'unfunded liability' to something very close to a half-billion dollars. Met's unions have approved the change."[61]

Notice the last sentence—the unions had already examined the deal in detail and voted to approve it before the public got any wind of what was happening. This is so brazen; the plan was halted amid terrible publicity surrounding pension hikes and at a time of falling investments and 20 percent rate increases for the district's water customers. Public sector greed knows no bounds, however.

## MANY MORE SCAMS

The public is scammed in other ways, also. As public-safety workers get new, more-generous retirement formulas, the other categories of government workers lobby to receive the old public-safety formulas, which are still far more lucrative than what any non-CEO, non-unionized private workers will receive. They claim it's only fair given the new enhancements for public-safety workers. Meanwhile, the unions always expand the categories of workers eligible for the higher class of benefits.

Liz Pulliam Weston explains the situation for MSN's Money Central: "The California Public Employees' Retirement System uses a multiplier of 2% for most workers, who also participate in Social Security, said spokesman Brad Pacheco. As a result, employees with 30 years' service can retire at 55 with pensions equal to 60% of their pay, although their benefit is reduced by whatever they get from Social Security. (These workers contribute 5% of their pay to the CalPERS system in addition to paying Social Security taxes.) One in three workers, though, really hit the jackpot. Prison guards and highway patrol officers get a 3% multiplier (the cops get it at age 50, the guards at 55). That means they can retire early with 90% of pay after 30 years' service.

"The state also has gradually increased the categories of workers considered public safety employees who qualify for a 2.5% multiplier. As a result, this group—which for a long time consisted mostly of prison cooks, plumbers and others with at least some inmate contact—now includes a much wider variety of non-prison jobs, including Department of Motor Vehicle driving examiners and public-health inspectors. These folks can retire at 55 with 75% of their pay. Like cops and prison guards, the public-safety jobholders don't participate in the Social Security system."[62]

Community college police are now pushing for the public-safety benefit. It's the old theory of concentrated benefits and dispersed costs— the cooks, plumbers and their unions have great incentive to lobby for the new expanded benefit formula, but no one else has much incentive to stand up against it, given that no one in particular will face enormous new costs. The costs will be spread out among the saps who pay the taxes and foot the bills.

Unions play a never-ending game of round-robin, by using every possible argument to increase pay and benefit levels. When benefit packages come before elected boards for votes, union leaders and supportive politicians often argue that the new packages won't cost taxpayers anything additional because returns on investment from the retirement funds will pay for the increases. In some cases, the employees have to increase their payroll deductions to pay for it, and pro-union politicians are very proud of the fact that these increases came at no cost to the taxpayer. But taxpayer contributions usually also go up, especially for public safety pension increases, and the public is responsible for the unfunded liability portions of the new benefit hike. Furthermore, these retroactive deals have many unforeseen consequences: shortages caused by large numbers of retirements, unhappy younger workers who must pay far more to subsidize the unearned early retirements of the older workers (in those cases where employees are forced to make contributions), who tend to dominate the union negotiating process, etc.

When Orange County retroactively increased retirement benefits for most of its workers in 2004, it was based on an 8.25 percent rate of return, something the treasurer compared to betting that the Angels baseball team would win the World Series every year for the next 30 years. Politicians who accepted those promises seem awfully gullible right now—although some of them are off to higher political office and are blithely ignoring the mess they made.

Another common ploy: those unions who represent workers in municipalities that pay below the state average go to city councils and demand to be brought up at least to the midpoint of other cities, lest they lose workers to more generous locations. There's little evidence that significant numbers of such workers jump ship for a little more money, and even less evidence that the agency couldn't find good workers to fill their place if they did—especially in a down economy causing double-digit unemployment rates in many states. But the scare tactics often work. Consider that half of the localities will always be below average, so as soon as one of the lower-paying agencies moves its pay scales upward, another agency falls below the mean, and that agency's union starts lobbying elected officials to move up the scale. It's like Garrison Keilor's world, where no one is below average.[63] This creates constant pressure for more.

Worse, some governments pass contracts that guarantee that, say, their police are the top-paid in the county, or are no lower than, say, the eighth-highest paid in the state. When other jurisdictions give raises, these government employees get them automatically, thanks to the generosity of unwitting taxpayers and the foolishness of politicians who sign off on such contracts. These types of deals take budget control away from elected officials, who must follow the lead of other localities in the state. If a city 400 miles away decides to increase pay and benefits for police, and that pushes the city's cops down a comparative notch, then a raise kicks in automatically, whether city officials budgeted for it or not and whether or not this is needed for recruitment or other public policy reasons.

## THE LOW-PAY MYTH

When public employees or their union officials are put on the spot to defend the high level of benefits that have increasingly drawn the public's ire, they offer a stock refrain that, in the past, was largely true: "We receive a better pension, for sure, but that's in exchange for lower pay." Yes, that pretty much was the deal in the past. Go to work in the public sector and you sacrifice high pay and prestige for an easier work schedule, more holidays and a secure retirement. That deal is long gone. Thanks largely to the political power of public-sector unions, government workers now, on average, get higher pay, a much higher level of benefits, far fewer working hours and even a good bit of prestige. The government workers I know boast about the indispensability of their professions — "we are here to help you," "we put our lives on the line," "we protect your freedoms," etc. — in a way I never hear from truly indispensable private-sector workers. And public-sector employees continue to thrive even in a down economy. As the private sector slashes and burns during a tough recession, public agencies continue to hire and public workers continue to get pay raises despite overblown reports of coming cuts in Sacramento and elsewhere.

Sure, there have been some furloughs and cuts in government to deal with a particularly bad deficit, in California in particular. But most of this is for show. For instance, by California state law school systems must send layoff notices to any teacher who potentially could be laid off, which means that every year, as the budget is being debated in Sacramento, school districts send out thousands of layoff notices. This scares the teachers, who scare the students, who scare their parents. It creates a political constituency to lobby for a budget fix. It leads to sad newspaper stories about that beloved, award-winning teacher who faces the budget axe and letters sent home from principals to parents urging them to contact the school board and legislators. But rarely are any of those teachers who receive layoff notices ever actually laid off. Indeed, many agencies continue to hire new workers.

As the *Sacramento Bee* reported on March 16, 2009, "California state government's full-time work force continues to grow despite Gov. Arnold Schwarzenegger's order to freeze hiring amid a historic budget shortfall. From June 2008 to February 2009, most state agencies either increased or kept the same number of full-time employees, according to a *Bee* analysis of personnel data. The state also failed to lay off as many part-time employees during the crisis as promised by the governor. While legislators and Schwarzenegger debated how to close a $40 billion budget deficit, 66 state agencies saw a net gain of full-time employees, 35 kept the same number of employees and 55 lost employees, data from the state controller's office show."[64]

So much for sharing the pain, yet the government and government-worker unions have held their rallies on the Capitol steps and have been pitching their sob stories to willing newspaper reporters. At a time when the state's unemployment rate topped 10 percent, and businesses are shedding a record number of jobs, with a reported nationwide loss of a half-million jobs in June 2009 alone, the California state government continues to hire, albeit at a slower-than-usual rate. That's reality.

The *New York Times* reported in February 2008, "It is not exactly a distinction that he had in mind, but seven years into his presidency, George W. Bush is in line to be the first president since World War II to preside over an economy in which federal government employment rose more rapidly than employment in the private sector."[65] The Obama administration is trying to out-hire the Bush folks.

A CBS News blog explained in May 2009 that "President Obama's call for 'shared sacrifice' doesn't extend to federal employees, at least based on the details of his administration's 2010 budget released last week. At a time when the official unemployment rate is nearing double digits, and 6.35 million people are receiving unemployment benefits, the U.S. government is on a hiring binge. Executive branch employment—1.98 million in 2009, excluding the Postal Service and the Defense Department—is set to increase by 15.6 percent for the 2010 fiscal year. Most of that is thanks to the Census Bureau hiring 102,000 temporary workers, but not counting them still yields a net increase of 2 percent in one year. There's little belt-tightening in Washington, D.C.: Counting benefits, the average pay per federal worker will leap from $72,800 in 2008 to $75,419 next year."[66]

CBS reported on 558,000 public layoffs over the year, but noted that such layoffs amount to a "sliver" of national layoffs. It pointed to massive job increases in some government agencies, such as Homeland Security, which grew by 22 percent, and the Nuclear Regulatory Commission, which grew by 25 percent in the period of 2006 to 2010. "The final evidence that it's a good time to have .gov e-mail address? Civilian government employees are set to enjoy a 2 percent raise. Not only are private sector workers struggling to keep their jobs, but their earnings are stagnating and pay cuts are no longer uncommon."[67]

In July 2009, the *Los Angeles Times* reported that there were a total of 6.2 million jobs lost nationwide, with the manufacturing sector topping the list with losses of 1.8 million jobs. In the public sector, employment had actually increased by 300,000 jobs. Clearly, government workers enjoy a higher level of job security, especially in a struggling economic situation. We all know how hard it is to fire government employees, even those accused of the most grievous offenses—a subject in later chapters.

And the statistics prove that government employees receive a better overall compensation package than private employees. "The pay gap between government workers and lower-compensated private employees is growing as public employees enjoy sizable benefit growth even in a distressed economy," according to a *USA Today* article. "Public employees earned benefits worth an average of $13.38 an hour in December 2008, the latest available data, the Bureau of Labor Statistics says. Private-sector workers got $7.98 an hour. Overall, total compensation for state and local workers was $39.25 an hour—$11.90 more than in private business. In 2007, the gap in wages and benefits was $11.31."[68] The article reports that public-employee benefits have increased at three times the pace of private-sector benefits. "For every $1-an-hour pay increase, public employees have gotten $1.17 in new benefits. Private workers have gotten just 58 cents in benefits for every $1 raise."

In salary alone, public employees earn more on average than private employees. Also using 2008 Bureau of Labor Statistics data, the *North County Times* (Escondido, Calif.) reported that "state and local government wages and salaries averaged $25.77 per hour, with benefits adding another 50 percent to the load. By comparison, private industry employer wages and salaries averaged $19.14 per hour, while benefits averaged another 41 percent on top. And lest you think that private sector managers somehow do better: Surprise, compensation is close, with private sector managers earning an average of $34 an hour against public sector managers at $32 an hour."[69] The San Francisco grand jury compared private salaries with public salaries within the city and found the following: "Supporters of government pension benefit increases routinely argue that public employees are underpaid compared to private-sector counterparts, so retirement benefits must be sweetened to compensate. However, recent surveys used by the City's Department of Human Resources to benchmark compensation disclose that in nearly all job classifications the City pays more in wages and salaries than the other governmental agencies and more than most private-sector employers."[70]

Writing for the Cato Institute on Aug. 24, 2009 in response to newly released Bureau of Labor Statistics data, Chris Edwards notes: "The George W. Bush years were very lucrative for federal workers. In 2000, the average compensation (wages and benefits) of federal workers was 66 percent higher than the average compensation in the U.S. private sector. The new data show that average federal compensation is now more than double the average in the private sector... In 2008, the average wage for 1.9 million federal civilian workers was $79,197, which compared to an average $49,935 for the nation's 108 million private sector workers (measured in full-time equivalents). The figure shows that the federal pay advantage (the gap between the lines) is steadily increasing."[71]

Government workers also have many ways to increase their pay that are typically not as readily available to private workers. The *Investigative Voice* reported that "Even as Baltimore struggled to cover a $37 million deficit last year and contemplated lay-offs, city employees ran up more than $60 million in overtime costs." The OT money "helped some employees more than double their base pay in 2008 as the city faced a fiscal crisis and job seekers were turned away."[72]

Government unions downplay those statistics by saying that more government workers have higher education. But think anecdotally about how much better lower-level clerical and blue-collar jobs pay in the public sector than in the private sector. Even back in 1996, before the most ferocious growth in government compensation, the *Monthly Labor Review* reported that low-level clerical workers and laborers were better paid in the public rather than private sector. One Michigan analysis found that a salary-and-benefit package for a receptionist at the Michigan state bureaucracy received a compensation package of between $42,200 and $59,700 compared to a similar private-sector receptionist in Lansing who would earn $30,200 to $34,400 a year in total compensation.[73]

I frequently look at salary schedules for public agencies. The salaries are, again, unbelievable. In California, community colleges typically pay their professors $100,000 and more and these professionals get all sorts of extra pay for things that private-sector professionals would assume to be part of the job—such as holding office hours and teaching extra classes. Police salaries are usually in the six-figures (including overtime), with many police earning more than $200,000 in salary and overtime alone. Top city administrators often earn nearly $300,000 a year, plus benefits in many instances. The government managers who enjoy these absurdly high salaries fancy themselves the equivalent of top managers in Fortune 500 companies, and indeed they earn less than CEOs and higher-level managers in many major private firms. That's a typical justification used by city managers, community development officials and police chiefs who compare their city budgets to the budgets in large companies. But in my experience, few if any of these government managers would be able to get a top-ranking private-sector job. City officials rarely are involved in managing an enterprise that involves risk-taking and entrepreneurship. Even at the management level public jobs are, in essence, bureaucratic jobs. And these jobs come with far more security than private-sector management jobs.

I've watched city development officials, for instance, as they try to manage large-scale development projects promoted or subsidized by cities. They almost always are outmatched by the developers, which is why cities so frequently cut bad deals with private developers. This reality is something of a joke among developers. Yet city officials—unskilled outside the world of dictates and bureaucracy—fancy themselves the equivalent of big-shot corporate players who deserve salaries north of $200,000 a year. Deserving or not, these are the common salaries they receive.

Not surprisingly, according to a *Las Vegas Review-Journal* analysis, California is leading this trend toward extremely high government salaries. Local government officials, of all categories, in California are paid on average $58,365 a year, with Washington, D.C. a close second at $58,260. Others in the top 10 list are New Jersey ($54,384), New York ($53,841), Rhode Island ($52,272), Connecticut ($52,247), Washington ($51,975), Nevada ($51,332), Maryland ($51,202) and Hawaii ($50,318).[74]

The top 10 list for average annual salaries for firefighters features California ($106,765), Nevada ($94,956), Alaska ($78,707), New Jersey ($77,842), Washington ($76,137), Washington, D.C. ($74,533), Oregon ($72,121), Arizona ($69,311), Connecticut ($69,087) and Maryland ($67,529).[75]

The top 10 list for average annual salaries for police features California ($91,392), New Jersey ($84,275), Washington, D.C. ($81,598), Nevada ($80,121), Washington ($73,830), Arizona ($71,679), Alaska ($70,977), Delaware ($69,831), Connecticut ($69,707) and New York ($68,860).[76]

These are high salaries, but they become astronomical when other factors are included. Keep in mind the many overtime enhancements, especially for police and fire workers. And here are some others, many of which are so absurd I'm left wondering who had the audacity to suggest them, and what officials would actually approve them without reacting in disbelief. Then again, I've worked in the private sector, where my boss often jokes, "How long have you worked here, Steve, not counting tomorrow?"

## CHIEF'S DISEASE

One would think that a "3 percent at 50" retirement would be a good enough deal for most people. Anyone in the private sector would jump at the opportunity at such a deal. But greed is a powerful emotion, so many public-safety officials aren't happy enough with a system that allows them to retire with 90 percent or more of their final year's pay at extremely young ages. They feel compelled to game the system, in ways that stretch and even break the law. Heck, everyone else is doing it! A large percentage of public-safety officials—more than two-thirds of management-level officials at the California Highway Patrol, for instance—come down with something widely known as "Chief's Disease" around a year away from their scheduled retirement.

"High-ranking [CHP] officers, nearing the end of their careers, routinely pursued disability claims that awarded them workers' comp settlements," according to a December 2004 *Sacramento Bee* report. "That, in turn, led in many cases to disability retirements. As they collected their disability pensions, some of these former CHP chiefs embarked on rigorous second careers—one as assistant sheriff of Yolo County, for example, another as the security director for San Francisco International Airport."[77]

The *Bee* investigations led CHP to identify 15 medical pensions that "warrant investigation for abuse or fraud, and some could result in criminal charges, according to a CHP report." But this isn't a problem of a handful of police engaging in allegedly criminal behavior. This is a story of vast numbers of public safety workers who game the system for huge financial reward, and get away with it because their agencies allow such disreputable behavior and the boards that determine whether a disability claim is warranted are dominated by fellow union members.

Consider this fact from the *Bee* series:

- "The percentage of CHP officers taking disability retirements increased from 47 percent in 1996 to a high of 82 percent in 2002."[78]

Think about that number. At that point more than eight in 10 CHP officers discovered a work-related disability—not just an injury, but a disabling injury or disability!—just in time to take early retirement and to shield half of the already-generous retirement income from taxes. The unions give the idea that their guys are taking bullets and getting beaten up by bad guys, but those are the rare instances. The disability retirements mainly are for back injuries, knee issues, stress, heart problems (remember, these automatically are considered to be work related, even if they are more related to weight problems and poor eating habits and a bad smoking habit) and even, in one case, acid reflux disease.

If 82 percent of your employees became disabled because of their work, you would have to assume that there is a problem. Police work, like all work, has its stresses and dangers and can be physically demanding, but these disability numbers have little to do with actual disabilities and everything to do with a system that rewards a form of legal thievery. According to the *Bee*, "The number of disability retirements spiked in the late 1990s when the patrol's fraud investigation team was disbanded." We know what a police chief would say if a member of the media wondered why certain crimes went up after the police department disbanded a crime-investigation unit. He would say that the criminals knew they wouldn't get caught. The same theory should be applied to this disgraceful pattern of disability abuse.

It's not just CHP that has these problems. The disability retirement scam is one perpetrated throughout the ranks of public safety employment. This book previously mentioned the local law enforcement official who retired after coming down with a severe form of acid reflux disease.

For instance, the official was declared disabled from one job only—but was free to pursue other stressful law-enforcement and political jobs as a replacement. The man, Mike Clesceri, was mayor of Fullerton (a part-time position) and was an investigator for the district attorney's office. He believed that his boss, the district attorney, was corrupt, so he wore a wire and recorded conversations as part of a state attorney's general investigation. The sting operation provided nothing of substance and the AG pursued no charges against the DA. Clesceri then claimed a disability, based on Barrett's Esophagus, a condition that results from excessive acid reflux. While he waited for his $58,000-a-year tax-free disability pension with cost-of-living adjustments, he pursued a local police chief's job and remained on the job as mayor and ran a tough re-election campaign. He even had the time to have his brother-in-law attorney send threatening letters to members of the community who commented on the absurdity of his disability pension. As he explained in a newspaper column, the disability only applies to his job at the DA's office. He's free to pursue his career at other agencies. This is an abuse, and its exposure ultimately galvanized the public to boot Clesceri off the Fullerton council. Most of these situations never get aired publicly.[79]

Of course, the fire guys are in on the scam also. This is from a July 2004 editorial from the Los Angeles *Daily News*:

"A firefighter faces great danger and earns the community's respect and admiration by putting his or her life and limb at risk to protect the lives and property of others. That said, it's outrageous that many retiring Los Angeles County firefighters could have gotten away with exploiting the goodwill of the public by scamming the pension and workers' compensation systems... Called 'chief's disease' for the prevalence of this scam in the upper echelons of public safety agencies, the pension-spiking scam has siphoned off millions of taxpayer funds, just to make a healthy retirement package for county firefighters that much more lucrative. The cost to Los Angeles County taxpayers has doubled in the past six years to about $50 million this year.

"The reason this affects the public treasury is because if a firefighter goes out on disability in his or her final year, the salary is tax-free. This creates an artificial boost in take-home pay, which is how the final pensions are tabulated. The injury also paves the way for a disability retirement with half the income being tax-free. The bottom line is more money for firefighters during their lifetime pension at the expense of a public that will be lucky to retire on a paltry Social Security check. And it's not just a few firefighters taking advantage of this. County records show that most retiring firefighters, an average of 63 percent, between 2001 and 2003 claimed a disabling injury during their final year of service."

Apparently, plenty is never enough for some groups of Americans. Keep in mind that chief's disease is most common among management at these agencies—among those who should be protecting the public dime.

## OVERTIME ABUSE

Public employees, especially those in public safety jobs, have convinced legislators to grant them greatly reduced work schedules. The rationale for public consumption: these are such tough, stressful jobs that the public is at risk if police or firefighters have to work excessive hours. But once the reduced work schedules are approved, the employees don't have that much to do so they end up—you guessed it—working on their days off. Now, however, they get overtime pay for these additional hours. The overtime system has become yet another scam to greatly increase pay packages for government workers, even though government workers claim that it's cheaper to spend money on overtime than to hire more people.

As a *San Francisco Examiner* article explained: "The legislation stipulates that no appointing officer shall permit any employee to work overtime hours that exceed, in any fiscal year, 30 percent of the numbers of hours for which the employee is regularly scheduled. In addition, employees would be limited to working no more than 80 hours in a regular work week. In the first six months of 2008, several public-safety employees have surpassed that number already with two firefighters in the Fire Department's Bureau of Equipment racking up more than 900 hours in six months. One firefighter, as the *Examiner* revealed, worked 19 straight 24-hour shifts before taking a day off."[80]

How does one work 19 straight 24-hour shifts without it sparking some kind of notice from supervisors?

A June 13, 2009 *Orange County Register* article explained how "officials transformed the post of sheriff's deputy into a six-figure job based on the belief that overtime was cheaper than hiring new officers."[81] Those cost savings were debatable, but what isn't debatable is that union policies embraced by the department led to the current situation: "Policies allowing deputies to work a three-day workweek and to retire early have dramatically boosted overtime costs. After enhanced pensions led to a large number of retirements, deputies with four days a week off were happy to fill up the empty shifts with overtime."[82] Here we see how one public giveaway leads to a cascade of other public giveaways. This is what happens when the public employee foxes guard the taxpayer henhouse.

And the *Register* found that all this overtime, rather than improving morale, has actually created new discipline problems: "The huge amount of extra hours and the large payouts have contributed to culture and discipline problems in the department, especially at county jails. Despite the six-figure earnings, some deputies slacked off on the job. Now, efforts by sheriff's officials to transfer deputies out of jail assignments and into patrol jobs have fueled union grievances and lawsuits."[83] Yet these deals were promoted as a way to fix problems.

When people have an entitlement mentality, enough is never enough. In Orange County, like some other locales, deputies must spend seven years patrolling the jail before getting an assignment to patrol a city. In the past, jail duty was viewed poorly and deputies eagerly waited to be transferred out into the community. Thanks in part to the overtime entitlement, deputies increasingly prefer to spend their entire career in the jails, where the work is easy, predictable and lucrative. One interim sheriff was shocked at how hard it was to get deputies to leave the unpleasant jail surroundings and head out onto the not-so-mean streets of suburban South Orange County.[84]

As a result, departmental top earners were not just high-ranking assistant sheriffs. There were lower-ranking investigators earning more than $220,000 a year, with more than half the money coming in OT. Quite a few jailers and lower-level deputies earned $190,000 or more in pay and overtime alone. Indeed, more than 100 deputies earned more than $150,000 a year and almost all of them earned more than $100,000 a year.

The need for such large amounts of overtime was driven by the "3 percent at 50" retirement plan, which created a wave of sudden retirements. And by something called a 3/12 workweek, approved by the county sheriff (Mike Carona, who has since been sentenced to 5-½ years of prison after a federal witness-tampering conviction) in 2000 at the urging of the deputies union. As the *Register* explained it, "Every two-week pay period deputies work six 12-hour shifts and one eight-hour shift. That leaves them seven days off every two weeks."[85]

One of the funniest rules is the "donning and doffing rule," by which police unions insist that police officers are paid for the time they get dressed and undressed.

Here's a March 9, 2009 blog from the *Buffalo News'* Susan Schulman: "Buffalo's fire department has been downsized in recent years as city officials attempted to reduce costs and bring the department into the 21st century. Fire companies were shut down. Manpower was sliced. But in the end, total payroll went up, because of skyrocketing overtime associated in large part with short-staffing. But the overtime money isn't distributed evenly.

"Firefighters on the verge of retirement gobble up big chunks of the extra $10 million. Sometimes the amounts are so large it's hard to understand how one person could have gotten so much under the existing system for doling out OT. However it's done, New York State counts overtime payments in pension calculations. As a result, many firefighters are retiring with pensions bigger than the base pay they earned while on the job."[86]

So New York is even crazier than California, in that it allows overtime to be figured into a public employee's final pension, whereas only some California systems allow that. This is a nationwide problem. One Southern official talks about the local police department, where virtually everyone gets promoted to captain over the last five years of work. It became so ridiculous that it was difficult to know who the actual captains were when work needed to get done!

A 2009 San Francisco grand jury found that "The legacy of pension spiking in police and fire departments combined with extraordinary future obligations to fund health care benefits should cause serious concerns by public officials."[87] The grand jury found that police officers and firefighters sometimes received more than their original retirement amount thanks to various pension-spiking games.

Here are some of the other scams:

- **Moving on up:** Because California allows government employees to lock in their permanent retirement based on their final year's pay, many employees will go to great lengths to find the highest-possible-paying job in their final year. The *Sacramento Bee* told the story of Sharon McCraw, a Sacramento-area accounting manager for the state who moved from her suburban home to a tiny apartment in the San Francisco Bay Area so that she could temporarily take a high-paying job that would increase her pension benefit by $18,000 a year. As the article explains, the law that granted pensions based on the single highest annual pay—unique to California—was quietly pushed through the Legislature in 1990 as a way to get organized labor's support for a budget deal. "Short-term relief meant long-term fiscal pain," the *Bee* reported. "A *Bee* analysis of current retirement data suggests that in a decade the cost has ballooned to more than $100 million a year."[88]

- **A terminal problem:** As many as 111 former San Diego city employees continued to receive taxpayer-funded health insurance, holiday pay and pension benefits for several weeks after being terminated from their jobs, something that cost the city $660,000, according to a city audit. "We are scraping for every nickel and looking for ways to save money and be efficient," the head of the city's audit committee told the *San Diego Union-Tribune*. "To know that $660,000 could have been saved, when I read that, my eyes jumped to that figure immediately."[89]

- **Just like the Mafia:** Even when officials are involved in grievous wrongdoing, they continue to get their pensions. In New York, the state pays out pensions to 450 corrupt officials. Some of them are in jail, but their families still enjoy the taxpayer-funded windfall. Consider that these are ill-gotten gains—in the case of Stephen Cracappa and Louis Eppolito, they spent their careers as police officers working for the mob, and actually carried out murders for the mafia. The Gothamist blogger quotes City Councilman David Yassky: "It's a world that rewards people who lie, cheat, steal, take bribes, betray the public trust and embezzle public funds."[90] The blog notes that efforts in the city to stop this practice "have gone nowhere." Chalk it up to the power of government unions, which are perfectly happy protecting their most degenerate members. One New York school district superintendent receives more than $173,000 a year as a pension even though he was convicted of stealing $2.2 million from the district.[91]

- **More vacation, bigger retirement:** Some public employees who max out on their vacation time can receive cash in exchange for the additional hours. The extra money also is used to increase their retirement benefit. The *Sacramento Bee* used an example of an average Sacramento County sheriff's deputy who pulls in an extra $7,000 a year in vacation pay. That can result in an extra several thousand dollars a year in retirement pay.

- **Golden handshakes:** As governments face budget crises, an increasing number of them are offering their long-time employees golden handshakes to get them off the payroll. The *San Leandro Times* reported in May 2009 that the East Bay city offered nearly 10 percent of its workforce a package that includes an extra two years of retirement credit in exchange for leaving right away. In June 2009, the city of Los Angeles offered early retirement to 2,400 city employees, even though the city's retirement liability is expected to triple to $1.6 billion in the next four years.[92] Often governments will give massive payouts to employees accused of misbehavior, just to get rid of them. The city of Yorba Linda, Calif., in 1999 allowed its city manager, Art Simonian, to resign and take $200,000 in severance pay and a $173,000 annual retirement after he was accused of granting himself and others unapproved bonuses. He was taking the city's motto a bit too literally: "The land of gracious living."[93]

- **DROP kicking taxpayers:** Many governments offer something known as DROP, which stands for Deferred Retirement Option Plans. Some critics refer to them as "sham retirements" because they allow a public employee to retire for a short time, then head back to work and collect both the retirement pay and the salary. The WHYY blog in Philadelphia explains that in that city, even elected council members are allowed to "retire" for a day and then head back to work.[94] In San Diego, the *Union-Tribune* reports, 1,788 city employees are part of a DROP program that allows them "to collect pension payments in a special account while still employed."[95] The key point, made by *Governing* magazine's Girard Miller, is "The mere existence of a DROP plan should signal that something is wrong with the pension plan. The idea of providing incentives to seniority workers to keep them in service—because their pension plan encourages a life of leisure well before age 60—is a signal that the pension plan benefit is simply too rich."[96] It also shows that these plans are designed purely for the benefit of the workers and are not designed for what's best for the public or for the proper functioning of the agency. Whether we're talking about DROP plans or "3 percent at 50" retirements, we are looking at systems that encourage employees to retire at young ages—and then the agencies, courtesy of taxpayers, must come up with other lucrative payouts to assure that people keep working. Often, the public employees want to keep working, given that it's a bit odd for someone to want to spend 25 years involved in nothing more than the pursuit of golf or other leisure activities. The Employee Benefits Legal Resource Site explains, in matter-of-fact style, "To the extent that employers are initiating DROP plans, the major reason is a concern about the ability to retain valued employees who are eligible to retire. Many governmental plans, either as a matter of plan design or due to inadvertence, contain substantial incentives for employees to retire early."[97] Now think about the logic in this. The employer offers a retirement plan so generous that it causes the employees to retire early. Then the employer realizes that it needs the employees and the employees realize they would like to work longer. So it comes up with a plan to keep them on the job by paying them a salary in addition to the retirement pay. Is that insane? Only in government would such scams become an accepted and even encouraged in practice.

- **Large loopholes:** You know the problem is bad when Massachusetts lawmakers actually debated closing some pension loopholes. The *Boston Herald* reported that in Massachusetts, government employees can combine the salaries from two jobs to hike their final pension benefit. The *Herald* also pointed to "The so-called king for a day rule, which allows employees who fill in for higher-paying positions to apply the higher salary towards one year of their creditable service."[98]

- **Volunteer "service":** The *Boston Globe* reported on a brouhaha whereby a former state senator claimed $22,000 in retirement pay for 19 years of service on a volunteer library board. In the face of embarrassment, John Brennan Jr. gave up on the benefit, but this was common practice until a *Globe* story spotlighted a 1998 law that gave library trustees pension credit if the local council approved of the deal.[99]

- **Extended leave:** Combine the abuse of the system with slow-moving bureaucracy and the level of waste is incomprehensible. In Massachusetts, it takes years to move injured officers off of the payroll and into a retirement system and given how common disabilities are, this becomes a costly problem. "At a time when Boston police are letting go of cadets and considering the layoffs of uniformed officers, the department is paying full, tax-free salaries to 21 sergeants, detectives and patrol officers who are on injured leave and not expected to return," according to a March 21, 2009 *Boston Globe* article.[100] Some of these officers have been out for as many as six years. It costs the department $1.7 million in salaries and the newspaper reports that it also costs the department in overtime as other officers have to fill in their slots.

- **Political pay-offs:** In Maryland, apparently, it's common for officials to gain full retirements after only a relatively small number of years on the job. The *Investigative Voice* reported on Deputy Police Commissioner Marcus Brown, who left Baltimore city police for a job with the Maryland Transportation Authority police. As the Web site explains it, "Brown had only 14 years on the job when the pension was granted, not enough time to qualify for a full pension. But then-Police Commissioner Leonard Hamm sent a letter to the pension board… stating that Brown had been laid off—three days after he accepted the MdTA police job—triggering a clause in Brown's contract that guaranteed his pension if he was terminated and setting off a storm of controversy that Brown's pension was a political pay-off."[101]

- **Up, up and away:** Even as pension funds lose money and the economy struggles and the unemployment rate goes up and the budget deficit increases, public employees still get their cost of living increases. The *Marin Independent Journal* reported in March 2009 that the Marin County Employees Retirement Association approved raises ranging from 2 percent to 4 percent for retired government employees.[102] So much for shared pain.

- **Expensive presumptions:** On May 8, 2009 Iowa Governor Chet Culver sent out a press release boasting about an increase in benefits for Iowa's police and firefighters: "Senate File 226 states that firefighters and police officers covered under the 411 Municipal Fire and Police Retirement System, who are stricken with cancer or certain infectious diseases, will now benefit from a presumption that their disease is work related, and therefore ensure appropriate disability retirement or death benefits are provided under the 411 system."[103] When average citizens get common diseases such as heart attacks or cancer, they are lucky if they have health insurance to cover the costs of the medical bills. There are no special presumptions that unleash additional benefits.

- **Ahead of her class:** The *Republican* (Springfield, Mass.) reported that the state's commissioner of the Department of Corrections "retired early at 54 in November with an annual pension of $106,212. She greatly increased her pension by shifting into a different job classification at the end of her state career, capturing the pension bonus given to police officers and prison guards."[104]

- **Politics is profitable:** Ohio lawmakers have figured out a lucrative way to received six-figure salaries after they are done in the Statehouse by serving in commissions where they don't actually have to do anything and those salaries are then used to boost their retirement pay, according to a *Dayton Daily News* investigation.[105] The newspaper found 75 former lawmakers who used their political connections to secure such deals.

- **Double-dipping elected officials:** It's common in the public sector for employees to retire from their job, receive a nearly full-pay pension and then to go on to work at the same agency or somewhere else for full pay. Such generous pensions also apply to elected officials. "Margaret Orrange served 30 years as North Collins town clerk before retiring," the *Buffalo News* reported. "Well, sort of retiring. She filed her retirement papers in December 2007, at 62, even though she had won re-election to another four-year term the month before. So Orrange was in Town Hall for the January 2008 swearing-in ceremony, and back on the job the next day—never missing a day's work although she began collecting a pension from a job she still holds today."[106]

- **Airheads for "air time":** In San Diego, where a pension crisis caused tumult in the city's government in the mid-2000s, city employees were allowed to buy something called air time. Employees would pay for additional years of work credit (up to five years). The Reason Public Policy Institute explains that such benefits are common across the United States, but that in San Diego employees were not required to pay the "full actuarial cost of the benefits."[107] RPPI gave the example of former Mayor Dick Murphy—dubbed one of the nation's worst mayors by *Time* magazine in 2005 for his complicity in that city's devastating pension scandal—who purchased credit at a cost of $71,760 spread across five years, for an annual cost of $14,352. "Assuming he finishes out his term in office, the benefit will increase his pension from $42,000 per year to $59,500 a year, a difference of $17,500 per year. Thus, his costs will be recovered in just over four years in retirement and he will continue to reap the extra $17,500 a year for the rest of his life." If he lives 20 years, that will cost the city $350,000 because of that one small pension-spiking benefit applied to one official.

- **Paying for incompetence and corruption:** The *Orange County Register* looked at the pensions of some controversial employees. It found that Bryan Speegle, who oversaw a department that had descended into anarchy, per a "scathing audit," took retirement amidst the brewing scandal and receives one valued at about $2.3 million. Former Sheriff Mike Carona, convicted on federal corruption charges, receives $207,979 in retirement benefits a year despite the conviction. One of his chief assistants, Charles Walters, receives $223,218 a year. The county's former treasurer, Bob Citron, whose bizarre investments led to the largest municipal bankruptcy in America in 1994, receives $92,900 a year in retirement benefits, despite his own felony conviction on financial improprieties with public funds.[108]

- **Overtime counts:** "Overtime is included in final pay for some California systems, but not most," according to CFFR's Marcia Fritz. "Nationwide it is common that OT is included, but no other system outside California's includes the single highest year pay in their formula."[109]

## 'THE ULTIMATE PENSION SPIKE'

I'll finish this chapter with the bizarre story of Armando Ruiz, a part-time trustee on the Coast Community College District in Southern California. Ruiz also worked full time as an administrator with the South Orange County Community College District. Ruiz wanted to run for re-election as a trustee and use the "incumbent" label on his ballot, but he also wanted to take advantage of a strange California law that dramatically increases the employee's pension payout if the person retires from two jobs on the same day.

*Orange County Register* columnist Frank Mickadeit called it "the ultimate pension spike": "Ruiz 'retired,' effective Oct. 31, as a part-time trustee of the Coast district and as a full-time counselor at Irvine Valley College. Even though the trustee gig pays just a $9,800 annual stipend, he was able to calculate his state pension as if he had been paid $106K a year for that 'job' plus the $106K a year he got for his real job at Irvine. So, based on a $212K salary he never really made, his pension will work out to about $108K a year for life. Otherwise, the pension would have been $59K—$54K for the real job; $5K for the trustee job. Even though Ruiz was officially retired from the Coast district board, he was still listed on Tuesday's ballot as an incumbent. A cynical person might say that by waiting to 'retire,' just days before the election Ruiz knew it would be too late to change the ballots. And incumbents rarely lose such elections."[110]

The only good news from that scam: the state did pass a law banning that particular and incomprehensible pension-spiking rule after people became outraged at the Ruiz maneuver. That perhaps is the best hope we have right now: that Americans will get outraged at these abuses—so much so that they adopt some of the reforms detailed in Chapter 8 of this book.

But our next step is to look at the way pension abuses in particular are harming and even destroying the budgets of various governments.

## CHAPTER THREE

# THE PENSION TSUNAMI

There are 10^11 stars in the galaxy. That used to be a huge number. But it's only a hundred billion. It's less than the national deficit! We used to call them astronomical numbers. Now we should call them economical numbers.
— RICHARD FEYNMAN

The term tsunami is the appropriate one to describe the potential disaster looming because of the massive pension and other benefit increases granted to public employees in the last decade. With tsunamis, residents rarely have more than an inkling of a disturbance out at sea, and then the enormous crashing waves descend upon the shore. Currently, most Americans have no idea what's about to hit them. They might have a vague sense that the nation has run up a great deal of debt in a variety of areas, but the public-employee benefit problem is not well known despite an increasing amount of media coverage of the subject.

Quite simply, the wave of benefit promises will wash away local and state governmental budgets and large portions of the incomes of most Americans. Remember that most of these benefits are vested, meaning that they have the standing of a legal contract. They cannot be reduced. And union backers, such as California's legislative Democrats, are cleverly stopping some of the more obvious exit strategies. For instance, when the city of Vallejo went bankrupt after coughing up 75 percent of its budget to police and firefighters, the Assembly pushed forward legislation that would only allow cities to use bankruptcy as an option if they get approval from a commission. And such a commission would of course be dominated by labor-friendly members. The result: cities would be stuck making good on contracts they cannot afford to fulfill. That legislation was stalled as this book is being written, but be certain that whatever its fate, the unions are working overtime to prevent governments from doing anything whatsoever to reduce the public's debt burden—anything except for raising taxes and floating taxpayer-backed bonds to pay for the mess.

So expect unfunded liabilities to continue to soar. Expect governments and pension funds to engage in questionable practices to push the debt further out into the future or to hide it from the public. One such practice is called smoothing, by which the retirement funds spread out their stock market losses over 30 years as a way to avoid dealing with the mess now. This keeps local and state governments from having to contribute more to retirement funds and thus avoids a growing public backlash. Notice the nice-sounding term to describe this rip-off—*smoothing*. It sounds so pleasant. This was, of course, CalPERS' approach, something Gov. Arnold Schwarzenegger rightly called a "pass-the-buck-to-our-kids idea." CalPERS is the nation's largest retirement fund and it is completely dominated by union advocates who use their investing power to influence the political process; and they use their control of the retirement funds to hide any problems that could undermine this benefit-enhancement game.

But at the end of the day, there are three things to expect as debt loads become unsustainable: cuts in governmental services, massive tax increases and pension-obligation bonds, or some combination of all three. When the economy was booming, these structural problems could be hidden. But the nation's economic problems are bringing attention to the pension situation. At some point, localities will simply run out of money to pay for rich pensioners and for soon-to-be rich pensioners.

On July 8, 2009, the *New York Times* reported that local governments throughout New York might have to triple their contributions to the state pension system in the coming six years as pension costs borne by local governments have soared from $2.6 billion to $8 billion in a single year. The information, based on an analysis from the state comptroller, predicted that counties will have to contribute "an amount equal to nearly one-third of their civilian payrolls to the state pension system and more than 40 percent of their payrolls for police and fire departments." The *Times* quotes Steven Acquario, executive director of the New York State Association of Counties: "It's alarming, eye-popping and unthinkable. To manage that liability in the face of this deep decline in government revenues is going to be a challenge. Where is this money going to come from?"[111]

You know where the money will come from. It will come from New York taxpayers in the form of massive property-tax and other hikes. The average New York taxpayer, who enjoys a lower salary and far lower retirement benefits than New York government workers, will have to work longer, retire later and pay more so that his public-employee neighbors can enjoy the lifestyle to which they have become accustomed. New Yorkers will also have to deal with worsening public services. If governments have to spend most of their money paying for their retired workers, that obviously leaves a lot less money to pay for those things that might actually benefit the public. The head of the New York Conference of Mayors told the *Times* the obvious: "The only way they're going to deal with it is through property taxes and reductions in the work force."[112]

## WASHINGTON MONUMENT SYNDROME

Now's a good time to remind readers of something known as the Washington Monument Syndrome or, alternately, the Mount Rushmore Syndrome. Here, Wikipedia offers a succinct explanation of it as, "a political tactic used by bureaucrats when faced with reductions in the rate of projected increases in budget or actual budget cuts. The most visible and most appreciated service that is provided by that entity is the first to be put on the chopping block. The name derives from the National Park Service's habit of saying that any cuts to its projected increases would lead to an immediate closure of the wildly popular (and not very expensive to maintain) Washington Monument. A recent example is the Massachusetts Turnpike Authority act of turning off the lights on the Zakim Bridge in Boston."[113]

In Southern California, officials have turned off some of the showers at the beach, even though these public showers cost virtually nothing to operate.

So, government officials through greed and craveness have promised their own workers pay and benefit levels that are quickly consuming majorities of their already large budgets as well as making a claim on the future through unfunded liabilities. When the pension bill hits the fan, and they can't pay their bills, these same officials will blame the greedy taxpayer who gets agitated at watching property taxes increase or annoyed at paying additional sales and income taxes. In order to create the impression that everything is cut to the bone and nothing can be done short of such tax increases, the bureaucrats will cut out the most obvious services—the things most likely to annoy the largest number of people. The Park Service shuts down the Washington Monument or Mount Rushmore, as if the service isn't awash in wasteful spending or has no less noticeable areas to cut. Or it will just neglect its core responsibilities, usually those things that affect the public.

"Crumbling sidewalks near the Jefferson Memorial are sinking into the Tidal Basin," the *Associated Press* reported. "Reflecting pools are filled with green, smelly water. And millions of visitors have trampled the oil into virtual concrete where grass can't grow. The National Mall is in danger of becoming a national disgrace."[114]

That's government for you. As the federal government was busy handing out billions of dollars in welfare to car buyers and car dealers through the "cash for clunkers" program, the National Mall—the home of the Washington Monument and other grand symbols of the American nation—was becoming unkempt and seedy. AP reported that "dozens of ducks and ducklings died of avian botulism because the water in a mall pool near the Capitol was fetid, as urgent repairs were needed to stop the Jefferson Memorial's sea wall from sinking into the mud."[115] Officials squander public resources on bureaucracy, war and pensions, but when times get tough they tighten up on those expenditures that directly benefit the public and the most basic services —i.e., maintaining the seawall around a magnificent monument—go by the wayside.

Huntington Beach, Calif., officials had a reputation for being rather generous with public dollars. City Hall is a high rise, home to many highly paid bureaucrats. Police there typically earn six-figure salaries and they have the "3 percent at 50" retirement plan. The city has ladled corporate welfare on downtown developers and spent millions to fight development plans on land surrounding a wetland. But when it came to handling one of the city's most fundamental services—maintaining the sewer system—officials there were AWOL. The City Council was dominated by environmentalists who used their platform and tax dollars to fight for various ocean-related environmental causes. But they somehow ignored an environmental disaster right under the city. As the *Los Angeles Times* reported in April 2001, "Huntington Beach, which last week took the extraordinary step of admitting criminal culpability for allowing massive amounts of sewage to leak from aging pipes, is poised to make another dramatic step: imposing property fees to fix the city's sewer system."[116] It took the district attorney to file criminal charges to force city officials—in my newspaper column I called them sewer criminals—to take care of the aging pipes. And, of course, the taxpayer gets stuck paying higher taxes to make up for the negligence of city officials.

In reality, government worker unions have a loud voice in City Hall. That's why City Hall often operates for the benefit of the people who work there—note the preponderance of city governments that are closed every other Friday or, in some cases, every Friday. The customer be damned. If you need a permit or help from the city on a Friday, you'll just have to wait because officials want to make sure their employees have an extra day off—a seemingly cost-free concession to the unions, albeit one that denigrates the service the public receives. The sewers have no one to speak for them. Officials have spent lavishly on pensions to satiate the unions and have ignored the unseen problems, such as crumbling sewers, bridges and other infrastructure. These are vital services, yet the public must put up with deteriorating and at times unsafe conditions. Politicians also purposefully shut down beach showers and national monuments as a way to show the public just how tough times have gotten and to lobby for more tax dollars. Expect more of this as pension liabilities mount. Be sure to understand the game officials are playing.

I worked for years in the newspaper business, and newspapers have been struggling with declining revenues and circulation over the past few years. Journalists have watched as managers struggle to make cuts with the least impact on the public. The reason is obvious: If they take it out on newspaper customers (and some of that has happened, of course) there will be fewer of them, and the downward spiral will continue. Newspapers that continue to make poor decisions do in fact go out of business or lose money. In government, there are only subjects. There are no real customers. In the mind of bureaucrats, it's best to inflict the most pain on the public as a leveraging tactic. As mentioned in Chapter 1, when the city of Vallejo overspent on public safety benefits and salaries, officials cut back on public safety services and warned the public against using the 911 system. The city cut back its libraries and stopped investing in infrastructure. This will be the model for the nation.

## 'PENSIONS: BEYOND OUR ABILITY TO PAY'

The subhead above is the name of the 2009 report from the San Francisco Civil Grand Jury. In California, grand juries not only have criminal indictment power, but the power to review how government agencies and programs function with an eye toward creating reform. San Francisco has the well-deserved reputation as being a liberal hothouse, so casual observers might conclude that pension problems there are the result of years of particularly bad policy making. Actually, San Francisco has long been a model for responsible pensions, and had long boasted of its fully funded pension system. "The thing that seemed to set the San Francisco system apart was the requirement for voter approval of pension benefit increases, a 'home rule' provision that had been in the charter of the unique consolidated city and county since 1889," wrote Ed Mendell, a Calpensions blogger and former Sacramento reporter for the *San Diego Union-Tribune*. "San Francisco, a hotbed of community activism, likes direct democracy. Voters rejected three attempts in recent decades to let the board of supervisors set pension benefits, each time by a wider margin."[117]

In fact, two conservative counties, Orange and San Diego, emulated San Francisco when they passed measures requiring a public vote for pension increases in 2009. San Francisco, however, had required such votes for more than a century, whereas the Southern California counties had approved this good-government measure to close the pension barn door long after all the horses fled the stable. In California's pension community, the San Francisco grand jury report was a stunner. Even San Francisco, the most responsible big city (it's also a county) in the state with regard to pensions, is having problems. This must be really bad!

First, the report found that the pension situation puts the entire fiscal health of the city at risk:[118]

"By fiscal year 2011-2012 the Controller estimates that San Francisco's pension contribution will be approximately $544 million. The estimated 200% increase in just 6 years is compounded by the fact that 40% of the active employees are currently eligible for retirement and another 15% will be eligible in the next 5 years. A dramatic increase in the retirement rate for some unforeseen circumstance will present an incredible risk to the City in terms of funding and cash flow. In the past month, the Controller stated to the Jury that the rising pension cost is a serious concern to the financial health of the City."[119]

Second, the grand jury assessed the blame correctly:

"The escalation of pension costs can be attributed to many factors not the least of which being the relationship of public officials and unions who have negotiated extraordinary pension and retirement benefits today, without consideration of the unfair financial burden placed on future generations."[120]

Third, the grand jury explained why even San Francisco's conservative approach to pension increases can only go so far:

"Unfortunately, the San Francisco electorate is as guilty as the politicians for approving measures that push out obligations to pay retirement and health benefits into future years."[121]

Members of the public, in other words, can easily be prodded into approving billions of dollars in pension hikes following union public-relations campaigns. Direct democracy can be as much of a problem as a solution—something discussed in Chapter 8, which outlines possible fixes for the problem. In California, voters statewide have approved some good, tax-limiting measures such as Proposition 13, but they also tend to approve massive taxpayer-spending items, such as Proposition 98, which guaranteed that 40 percent of the state's general fund budget would go to public schools. It's a mixed bag. Direct democracy is only as good as the voters, and in California special interests have the money and skill to dominate the initiative game. In many cases, unions run such dishonest ads that it's impossible to know what the particular initiatives are about. It takes so much money to run a statewide campaign in a 37 million population state with some of the most costly media markets in the nation that usually only the unions are the ones who can afford all the TV advertisements. Still, countywide initiatives can put the brake on some of this stuff. It's far better to ask voters to approve a pension increase than to simply let the Board of Supervisors do it quietly.

Fourth, the San Francisco grand jury found that police agencies in particular gamed the system and engaged in dubious pension-spiking activities:

"Significant time has been spent by law enforcement organizations, examining practices that can be used to dramatically increase the employee's final pension benefits, many of which have been determined to be abuses. Ultimately the public will bear the cost of these increasing pension benefits, via increases in taxes and loss of vital services. ... The Jury found a significant number of individuals whose retirement pay increased dramatically as a result of an unusual salary increase during the last year(s) of service."[122]

Chapter 2 looked primarily at the way public employees have enriched themselves, but this chapter is concerned with the impact of such greed on the public and on government agencies. The San Francisco grand jury confirmed that a fiscal crisis is looming, and one that goes beyond pensions. The city's health benefits debt is estimated at $4 billion and that the cost of living adjustment alone on pensions has imposed a $750 million future obligation on just this one city. These numbers are astronomical, and it's admittedly difficult for any average person to get a handle on such large amounts of money. But they surely will be able to understand it better when their taxes go up and the services they expect from government get scaled back.

## CUTTING SERVICES

In Orange County, Calif., Sheriff Sandra Hutchens proposed in July 2009 more than $20 million in cuts necessary to fill the gap caused by falling tax revenue. Her department slashed 40 percent of its command staff, cut a total of about 30 positions and made changes that affected about 200 positions through reassignments, demotions, changes to overtime and so forth. "These are services that we believe are quite important to maintaining public safety, that we're just not going to be able to continue," sheriff spokesman John MacDonald told the *Los Angeles Times*.[123] The sheriff, who strongly resisted the cuts, had also warned the Board of Supervisors that the cuts would make the county a less-safe place.

What the sheriff didn't say is that another reason for tight budget times is the Board of Supervisors' passage in 2001 of a retroactive pension increase for sheriff's deputies. That policy, advocated by the previous sheriff and the deputies union, caused pension costs to soar. The costs nearly doubled from the last year before the increase (2000) to the current year (2009), where pensions cost nearly $95 million, or 20 percent of the sheriff's budget. So the sheriff decries an economic downturn that is costing her department about $20 million, but doesn't mention that a previous pension increase is costing her department more than double that amount. It's safe to say that had the pension increase not passed, the department would have money to keep the officers on the streets and to avoid the cuts the sheriff claims are threatening public safety.

These are the real costs of absurd pension generosity by government officials. It's the public that pays the price as usual.

"As you all know, skyrocketing public pension costs are a huge drain on public budgets," Orange County Supervisor Chris Norby wrote to the head of the sheriff's advisory council. "The 3% at 50 formula for law enforcement approved by a prior board requires an annual $94.7 million county contribution (this represents 20% of the Sheriff's entire budget). Unlike non-sworn County employees, deputies make no contribution toward their pensions. I ask for your support in reining in pension costs and creating a second tier for new hires."[124]

Norby also points out that crime has been falling, despite the economic downturn, which suggests that the cuts are not necessarily dire. I've never bought the argument that declining police budgets always threaten public safety. Many factors contribute to crime rates, and law enforcement staffing is only one of them. The Santa Ana police chief once complained to me that his staffing level hadn't significantly changed over two decades even though the city's population had nearly doubled. He thought that was a case for hiring more cops. But crime rates over that period had gone down. In my view, that's an argument against necessarily needing more police. That's a complex criminal-justice and sociological argument that is better made in other contexts.

Police have an important job to perform and can affect crime rates. But budgets and police hiring should be determined by public-safety needs and serious analysis of crime data and policing strategies. The more we pay for pensions, the less we can address those needs correctly. It is clear that by vastly expanding retirement benefits, officials have greatly increased the costs of such retirements. And those increased costs are eating into law-enforcement budgets. That means that there's far less money to pay for current salaries and equipment or to use for other services or to return to hard-pressed taxpayers. Clearly, pension increases are taking a toll on the services the public expects from its governments.

## IMPACT ON SCHOOLS

A trillion here, a trillion there and soon we're talking real money. Well, *Business Week*, in a June 2005 article (before the crisis was full blown, by the way), explained that "Excluding federal workers, more than 14 million public servants and 6 million retirees are owed $2.37 trillion by more than 2,000 different states, cities and agencies, according to recent studies." The article found that in 2004, pension plan payouts had increased 50 percent in five years. That was the height of the market. In 2009, major pension plans had lost 20 percent or more of their value.

These are big numbers. But *Business Week* did a fabulous job explaining what those numbers mean to the average person. It focused on the public school system in Jenison, Mich., which it pointed to as a model of high achievement and fiscal responsibility, a system renowned across the country for its special programs and high quality of education: "But underneath all that success is a looming fiscal crisis. In the past three years, Superintendent Thomas M. TenBrink has surgically cut $4.2 million out of his $39 million budget in a quest to keep Jenison the fiscally responsible district it has long been. He has instituted fees for participating in after-school sports and field trips. He eliminated 30 teaching spots, leaving the district with 287. He hasn't bought a new textbook in three years. He saved $550,000 by turning an elementary school into a self-financing preschool and day-care center. But TenBrink is running out of options. ... School funds from the state are capped by law at $6,700 per student, a figure that has been frozen for the past three years, but costs are zooming. The fastest-growing outlay of all: contributions to pensions and retiree health care. This year the bill is $1 million. Next year it will jump to $1.5 million. An expense that for years hovered at 12.99% of payroll is now eating up 14.87% of it, and state finance experts predict it will hit 20% within three years."[125]

Expect fewer programs, more fees for parents and a declining school system so that these districts can pay for all the retired teachers and administrators, many of whom are retired early in life and who earn far more than the parents of the kids. Our system is turned on its head. It operates for the benefit of the workers, not the public. And the public will pay more and get less.

The government does a poor job providing all services. The nature of government, explained in the Chapter 1, is such that agencies will always put the needs of the bureaucracy above the needs of the public. Government decisions are by nature political decisions—resources are diverted to the places preferred by politicians and bureaucrats. In the marketplace, those companies that do the best job serving the consumer have the best success. Those that don't do a good job serving customers go out of business or struggle along or remain dependent on subsidies. That's why Americans should have little faith that General Motors will ever be a dominant player again in the automobile industry. The post-bankruptcy GM is owned by the U.S. and Canadian governments and the union health-care plans. Governments and unions will assure that the company produces the types of vehicles that appeal to those groups and they will make sure that union wages are kept higher than the market will allow.

Meanwhile, Toyota, and even Ford, will be driven by stockholders to serve the public. The profit-and-loss formula is the best way to create quality products. That's a long explanation for why school choice and true free markets in education are the best approach. As a newspaper writer in Ohio, I had written about the public schools there, which had just gone through a decade of increasing tax expenditures. Most of the new resources, however, ended up building state and local education bureaucracies rather than serving the students who are, after all, captive to the system and aren't really customers. The pension scandal reflects this.

GM embraced many of the same policies as the government, which is one of the main reasons GM had a "value gap"—the difference between the cost to produce the company's cars and the amount the public was willing to pay for them. As MetroWest reported, "The *Associated Press* reported Monday that higher health care costs alone accounted for a $1,500-per-car cost gap between GM and Japanese vehicles."[126] Private companies, in other words, can operate the same way as the government, but there is eventually a day of reckoning for them. Unfortunately, taxpayers—

through the Pension Benefit Guaranty Corp.—pick up the tab for those companies that modeled their business operations on government agencies or regulated utilities.

Another book, perhaps, is the right place to argue that schools ought to be produced in a true free market. Then most of the money would go to the classroom. Under such a system, students and parents would be customers who would shop around for the best deal. My childless neighbors wouldn't be forced to subsidize the education of my three children. People would be more willing to move into older, inner city neighborhoods because they would no longer have to worry about the quality of the local monopoly school system. We would have to evaluate the ways to assure that poor people would be able to send their kids to quality schools, but my sense is the poor would do far better under a free system. They are the ones whose kids currently endure the nation's poorest-performing schools.

There's a desperate need for competition in the school system through charter schools and vouchers. Mainly, this is a full disclosure about my philosophical views of education. But even within the context of the current public school system, it's important to recognize the degree to which outsized pensions and bureaucratic priorities are consuming resources that would be better spent in the classroom. The pension tsunami and the dominance of public-sector unions are degrading the education that students receive. This book deals with the Education Racket in Chapter 6, but the point here is that pension problems are not just theoretical. When school resources are diverted to pay for unreasonable pension benefits, those resources cannot go to current teachers and current classroom activities. The pension tsunami has many victims, and some of those include kids who are being deprived of educational resources.

The interesting thing about the above *Business Week* article is it outlined the effect of these policies on good school districts. Americans are used to hearing the bad news about the poor-performing and even dangerous urban school districts that have long been destroyed by the teachers unions. These urban districts could verge on collapse as the pension bills come due. One July 11, 2009 article explained that the Detroit Public Schools are on the verge of bankruptcy given that they would have to cut about 50 percent of their budget to fix its $259 million deficit. Given that salaries and benefits make up more than 80 percent of the school system's budget, there doesn't seem to be any obvious solution. Of course, we know how the unions would "solve" such problems.

A July 12, 2009 article in the Allentown (Pa.) *Morning Call* reported that Pennsylvania school districts are "already bracing for a huge increase in employee pension fund payments that could cost local taxpayers millions in 2012."[127] The state is mandating "deep cuts or substantial tax increases" to make up for substantial losses in the state's retirement fund. The Pennsylvania School Employee Retirement System, consistent with other retirement systems nationwide, had lost 25 percent of its value over a six-month period in 2008. In one Allentown area school district, property owners will have to pay $200 a year—up $140—just to cover pension costs.

Let's remember what caused this problem. *USA Today* reported as far back as January 2006 that the major pension funds in all 50 states "continued to enhance benefit formulas, ease early retirement and improve other benefits from 2000 through 2004 despite states' financial problems." It pointed out that 1996 to 2000 was also a period of benefit growth. One state in particular, New Jersey, "approved 17 benefit enhancements since 2000 that increased the unfunded obligations of public pensions in the state by $6.8 billion... ."[128]

But we're not dealing with some theoretical loss of money. Government agencies of all sorts will have fewer resources, people will pay more for additional fees and taxpayers will look at increasing tax payments. And the same influential lobby that created the mess will continue the drumbeat for its same-old tired solution: more taxes. If you think this is an exaggeration about union tax solutions for the problem, consider the American Federation of State, County and Municipal Employees' (AFSCME) solution for dealing with California's 2009 budget crisis. The union pointed to research calling for increasing tobacco taxes, imposing an oil-extraction tax on oil companies, eliminating property tax protections (Prop. 13) for commercial real estate owners, raising the state's already highest-in-the-nation income tax and getting rid of most corporate tax credits. The union also would like to get rid of the two-thirds vote requirement that allows Republicans to hold back an endless sea of tax increases. Such an approach would destroy California's already struggling economy and send tax-producing Californians out of state in droves. But that epitomizes the approach the unions want to take toward all budget issues, including pension-related matters. Just keep spending and taxing and spending and taxing.

Writing in the *New York Times*, David Kocieniewski complains that New York governments are making up for revenue shortfalls with a variety of "microcharges" — "with escalating fees for things like tanning bed inspections, pistol permits and marriage certificates, daily life can start to seem like a labyrinth of public-sector panhandlers."[129]

Get used to it as the pension tsunami hits the shore.

All the taxing in the world can't cover up this debt problem, even if one put aside union ignorance about the effect on productivity when taxes are increased to confiscatory levels. A *Standard & Poor's* analysis of state pension liabilities from 2007 found that per-capita debt and unfunded liabilities for the states' various pension systems ranged from a few hundred dollars ($414) in South Dakota to $6,341 in New Jersey. Perhaps it would get the public's attention if, say, the state of New Jersey sent the average four-person family in that state a bill for more than $25,000 to pay for all the promises New Jersey politicians made to government employees.[130] That bill would come with a note: "Given that we refuse to fix this problem, expect other bills like this one in the future."

The bills are coming due and they are real bills that will require Americans to pay up with real money.

## STOCK MARKET CRASH

Government officials blame the market downturn for their current predicament, and pretend that they merely are victims of an unforeseen bad economy. But they knew better. When times were good, government agencies expanded pensions and other benefits and based their increases on exceedingly optimistic predictions — predictions that could not possibly be sustained for 30 years or more. There were plenty of people who warned about the fruits of their decisions. The town criers were mocked and ridiculed. Now the officials who created the mess and ignored sensible good-government advice shrug their shoulders and play victim and look for ways to offload the costs onto taxpayers.

Sure, the economy went bad, as it does periodically. But the pension liabilities shot up because government officials kept increasing benefit levels for employees and assuring everyone these deals would pay for themselves. It's worth repeating that under the current system, whereby the union members get the rewards of particularly good investment returns and the taxpayers shoulder the risks of any shortfalls, it behooves the pension plans to take outrageous chances. It is the ultimate in privatizing gains and socializing risks. If you were given the same parameters—you benefit from a big score, but won't pay the price for your losses—you too would be tempted to take absurd chances. Maybe it would make sense to invest in a roll of the dice at a Vegas craps table. You might win big, and if you lose someone else gets to shoulder the losses.

And so now consider the fate of CalPERS, the nation's largest public retirement system. As the *Wall Street Journal* reported in December 2008, CalPERS made a decision at the height of the real estate bubble to invest massively into property holdings, including some highly risky deals involving vacant land. The bubble burst and CalPERS lost 103 percent of the value of its housing investments in one fiscal year. Here's the kicker: CalPERS not only blew its investments on some shady deals, it borrowed money to leverage those deals. So it has to pay back the borrowed cash as well. This is the type of scheme that caused Orange County's municipal government to go bankrupt in 1994, as referred to in an earlier chapter. CalPERS is telling California cities and school districts that they will have to pay far more in fees to make up for these losses, even though CalPERS already extracts one of the highest fee levels in the nation, according to the *Journal*. In some cases, CalPERS used 80 percent in borrowed money to finance these deals and the system foolishly guaranteed the debts, even though it's more typical, the *Journal* reported, for the home builder partners to be the ones to shoulder the risk.[131]

Why not? It's only taxpayers who will have to clean up the mess.

The *Journal* touched on the sheer idiocy of the CalPERS investment strategy: "A massive block of land with room for about 8,000 units near the small town of Mountain House, Calif., the nation's most 'underwater' housing market by one measure. (Nearly 90 percent of homeowners there owe more on their mortgages than their homes are worth, according to mortgage-research firm FirstAmerica Corelogic.) As of June 30, CalPERS valued the investment at negative $305 million, reflecting the fact that it has repaid borrowed money used in the deal."[132]

"In the past 24 months, the state of California Public Employee Retirement System has lost over $128 billion, which is almost equal to the entire 2009 state budget," reported Mark Hill of the *Marin Republican Examiner.* That puts the losses in perspective.[133]

*Bloomberg News* reported in July 2009 that Moody's Investors Services placed Illinois' long-term credit rating on watch "after lawmakers adopted a budget that includes $3.5 billion in short-term notes to meet pension expenses."[134] The state's pension fund was only 46 percent funded, so legislators borrowed $10 billion in pension obligation bonds to pay for the annual pension payments. This is not much different than borrowing thousands of dollars to make monthly mortgage payments. Something has to eventually give. Note that as part of this Illinois budget deal, the state is postponing $3.2 billion in payments to vendors. That number is close to the amount owed to state pensioners, so in a way the vendors are being compelled to float the state the money to make good on its debts to its special class of retired workers.

The loss of 26 percent of the value of New York's pension system —or $45 billion—is actually worse than it seems, according to E.J. McMahon, director of the Manhattan Institute's Empire Center for New York State Policy. "It's actually worse—when you realize that New York, like most other government employers across the country, systematically understates the true value of its long-term pension promises."[135]

This understatement problem is widespread. It serves as a reminder. Whenever government officials say that their systems are OK, you know that they are concealing problems. When they tell you they have a slight problem, you know they have a massive problem. When they say it's a crisis, then you better head far inland to avoid the coming tsunami waves.

The *Economist*, reporting that U.S. government pension funds have lost $1 trillion in value since October 2007, found that in Britain the pension costs might be double the amount claimed by the government. The magazine pegs the U.S. unfunded pension liability at more than $3 trillion—an amount that is inconceivable. It rightly compares the unfunded liability situation to a Ponzi scheme, where new investors or taxpayers must fund the claims made by older ones. Advocates for bigger government always point to problems in private-sector entities and investments, but the private sector is held to high standards and must conform with myriad regulations. As the *Economist* notes, "public-sector pension schemes are generally exempt from the same accounting and regulatory pressures as their private-sector counterparts."[136]

This is happening even in the more fiscally prudent states. Reported the *Denver Post* on July 14, 2009: "Following the loss of more than $10 billion last year, Colorado's largest employee retirement system now can meet only 51.8 percent of its obligations to retirees, a development that could mean higher deductions from government workers' paychecks and greater taxpayer subsidies."[137]

Union members of course are whining about the higher deductions. In Virginia, which has experienced similar losses in its retirement fund, legislators are balking at this possibility: "[P]ublic employees could be asked to pay a share of their own contributions for the first time since 1983, possibly a 2 percent share," according to the *Daily Press* (Newport News, Va.).[138] Will the outrages never cease? Government workers sometimes don't even have to pay their own share of their retirement contribution. The government agency, via the taxpayer, pays for that also! While Virginia public employees contemplate the horrors of having to pitch in 2 percent toward their own lush, guaranteed retirements, consider what is happening in the private sector. Employees and retirees are the ones losing the 25 percent to 40 percent in account values. They are the ones who deal with the losses. They have to work longer or delay retirement or save more. By contrast, some government employees might have to pony up a few pennies to help out.

Eventually, the stock market bust will be felt at the local level. The *Boston Globe* interviewed New Bedford, Mass., Mayor Scott Lang, who gave some straight-up explanations of what's going on: "He says current pension and health insurance systems for city employees have to go, period. If not, they will destroy the city and its ability to maintain the services people expect like public safety… 'The question is… How much does it cost a household to pay for these pensions? You have to make a choice… If you're not going to change, then no road repairs, no keeping the city beautiful, no infrastructure work. You'll end up with unfunded levels that begin to suck the air out of every expendable dollar we have. If you put your ear to the tracks, you can hear it coming.'"[139]

Or you can see the wave cresting a mile away from shore.

## THE POWER OF DELUSION

What if the stock market revives? That appears to be the hope of many public officials, who want to ride out the current downturn. "A combination of public unions, mass retirements and horrible performance won't easily be solved merely by stabilization of the economy, or a modest rebound," wrote Joe Weisenthal of the *Business Insider*.[140] It's like the housing bust, which will subside. Home prices will start to head upward again, but it's unlikely that we'll be looking at 30 percent annual value gains in hot markets anytime soon. Some fundamental economic models have to change. Likewise, the nation should not miss this opportunity to make fundamental changes to public pension systems and to rein in union power so that these mistakes are not soon repeated. People have short memories. Once the economy is on sound footing, the unions will start demanding things again. Indeed, even as the pension mess spirals out of control, public sector unions are still demanding higher levels of benefits. The city of Vacaville, not that far from bankrupt Vallejo, in July increased pension levels for police officers despite the warnings, despite the news, despite the nearby bankruptcy.

Perhaps the scariest article that I've read on the subject comes from Ed Mendel, writing in the *Capitol Weekly*, which includes this gem: "The CalPERS chief actuary says pension costs are 'unsustainable'..." When the CalPERS actuary says as much, and explains that pension fund's smoothing practices won't fix things, you know there is trouble. "I don't want to sugarcoat anything," CalPERS actuary Ron Seeling said at a retirement seminar. "We are facing decades without significant turnarounds in assets, decades of—what I, my personal words, nobody else's—unsustainable pension costs of between 25 percent of pay for a miscellaneous plan and 40 to 50 percent of pay for a safety plan (police and firefighters) ... unsustainable pension costs. We've got to find some other solutions."[141]

But Seeling's words aren't enough, as public unions gear up to fight against meaningful reform. Indeed, CalPERS itself is trying to spin what Seeling said. This is from Daniel Borenstein's *Contra Costa Times* column: "At CalPERS, my request to talk to Seeling about his comments was denied. Instead, public information officers told me that he misspoke—

that he reversed his clauses. What he meant to say, I was told, was 'Without significant turnarounds in assets, we are facing decades of unsustainable pension costs ...' In other words, they were suggesting, he wasn't predicting long-run shortfalls, he was hypothetically speculating on what would happen if markets fail to rebound. Moreover, they emphasized, it was his personal comments, not the official CalPERS position."[142]

But all the spin in the world cannot put that genie back in the bottle. What Seeling said originally was the truth.

I mentioned how California unions are working to make it nearly impossible for localities to declare bankruptcy. In New Hampshire, "Groups representing municipal, county and public school employees plan to file a lawsuit against the state of New Hampshire for shifting more of the financial burden of the state retirement system onto cities and towns," according to a July 17, 2009 article in Fosters.com.[143] The public employee unions are offering virtually nothing. They are gearing up to stop any possible fix short of tax increases. It is delusional. Surely, even some union officials need to realize that massive tax increases will further destroy state economies, and such destruction will only create a downward cycle of unfunded liabilities. Here's where some basic understanding of economic principles would come in handy, but just as private-sector unions bled the Big Three automakers dry and helped destroy many private businesses, so, too, will government unions remain bitter-enders who will destroy the country to save their cushy pensions.

This can't work. The bigger problem, though, is the effort by pension funds and government officials to conceal the depth of the pension and benefit problem, as a way to delay the day of reckoning. This book mentioned earlier the disreputable process called smoothing, where CalPERS and other pension funds spread out the losses over inordinately long time frames. And there are pension bonds, which amount to borrowing money to pay off additional amounts of borrowed money. That sort of thing can't go on forever. In some states, including the pension obligation poster child of California, it's fortunately rather difficult to float pension bonds.

In 2002, California's then-Gov. Gray Davis tried to paper over the $38 billion deficit by floating $2 billion in pension-obligation bonds, which seemed clearly in violation of the state's prohibition on amassing debt of

$300,000 or more without voter approval. The Pacific Legal Foundation filed a lawsuit on behalf of the Fullerton Association of Concerned Taxpayers (FACT) and prevailed. Wrote Jon Coupal, president of the Howard Jarvis Taxpayers Association, "The state wanted to borrow money at up to 15 percent interest by issuing bonds to make this year's annual payment to [CalPERS].... That would free up money from the special fund that is earmarked for CalPERS, allowing the state to spend it on other things. In court, the state argued that the Constitution should be construed to allow an exception for 'obligations imposed by law'.... " Fortunately, that idea was rejected but expect governments to try such maneuvers as much as possible. Coupal argued that the court sent "a message to Sacramento that the proper way to balance the budget is by living within the state's means, not shifting today's expenses onto the backs of tomorrow's taxpayers."[144]

Six years later, the state of California continues to run up massive debt. It doesn't appear likely to ever learn the lesson the court gave it. As pension liabilities soar, it remains to be seen whether the court system will continue to put a brake on efforts by governments to "fix" current problems by floating future debt.

## ENRON-BY-THE-SEA

The city of San Diego faced a political crisis caused by its mishandling of pension liabilities. In its "The Gathering Pension Storm" report from 2005, the Reason Public Policy Institute focused on the city of San Diego, which was one of the first municipalities nationwide to experience crisis-level problems caused largely by its pension obligations. Ironically, as Reason pointed out, "the city of San Diego was touted as one of the best-run cities in the country. In just a few short years, however, 'America's Finest City' has gone from being touted as one of the most efficiently run large cities in America and the most efficient of California's largest cities to being dubbed the 'Enron-by-the-Sea.'"[145]

What happened?

The San Diego story is long, sordid and incomplete, but James Kelleher at the *Orange County Register* on April 26, 2005 captured its essence in this short paragraph: "San Diego finds itself in deep fiscal trouble ... . In 1996, after a vote by the City Council, it purposely began under-funding its municipal pension system even as it increased retiree benefits... For years, above-average returns on Wall Street permitted the city to convince the trustees of the retirement system that this approach was less dangerous than it sounded. When the financial markets went down beginning in 2000, city officials kept the trustees on board by increasing pension benefits yet again and by creating special benefit enhancements that seemed targeted toward the trustees and the leaders of key municipal unions."[146] The result: $1.4 billion pension deficit as of that article's writing and various federal and local criminal investigations.

It's incredible. City officials knew that there was a problem. But, thanks to undue union influence—and indeed top union members controlled the pension system and city government—officials actually increased the pension benefits for workers and gave special benefits for trustees. The *Los Angeles Times* noted that every council member won election with major labor-union support. Pension board trustees worked for the city and benefited from the pension deals. Before the City Council OK'd the under-funding deal, RPPI reported, the council approved a special benefit that allowed the leaders of labor unions to include their union salaries in addition to their city salaries in calculating their taxpayer-funded retirement benefit, thus enabling them to more than double their retirement pay. The firefighters union chief, Ron Saathoff, for instance, was able to turn his $84,000 city salary into a $173,268 a year pension, according to the RPPI report.[147]

Saathoff eventually was indicted by federal prosecutors and as of July 2009 was, along with four other retirement and city officials, facing 30 counts of conspiracy and fraud. These officials are seeking dismissal in the case by arguing a technicality—that prosecutors have changed the theory by which they are prosecuting these former pension system officials. But the case goes on, and serves as one of the most sordid reminders of the way the taxpayer is abused by greedy insiders who know how to play the system for personal benefit.

As *CityBeat*'s Daniel Strumpf explained in the 2005 article, "San Diego's Pension Scandal for Dummies": The scandal started in the early 1990s when the city faced an economic downturn and officials did not want to make additional payments into the retirement system, as required by the city's actuary and city charter. A city auditor proposed some accounting tricks that would allow the city to put in less money to the retirement system than mandated by the actuary and required by the city charter. The city's lawyers balked. But then-City Manager Jack McGrory came up with a plan that increased pension benefits for the trustees and city workers in exchange for under-funding the pension system.[148]

The city would make lower payments and those payments would increase in the future, eventually mandating a lump sump payment by future boards. To buy off political support, the city plan created a DROP (Deferred Retirement Option Plan) program allowing employees to collect retirement benefits in an account before they actually retired and it shifted health-care benefits for city workers to the retirement plan. The deal also allowed retirement pay to top an employee's salary while working. As part of the deal, Strumpf explained that the city approved a trigger that would require lump-sum payments to the retirement system if the funding level dropped below 82.3 percent.[149]

So the city reduced its pension payments and increased pension benefits. This was hidden from the public because the stock market was booming, and that provided all the cover that the union-owned politicians needed.

An auditor and some others noticed that the funding level had become dangerously low—well below the 82.3 percent level. So, as Strumpf again explained, the city did an end-run around the trigger by giving the city "a five-year grace period to pay a balloon payment …." Problems mounted, exacerbated by a class-action lawsuit by city workers irked that the city was under-funding their pension plan. This effectively eliminated the under-funding schemes and exposed a deeper problem—a pension hole that was about to consume 20 percent of the city's general-fund budget.[150]

As RPPI explained, "The public remained in the dark about the city's pension system machinations, and likely would have remained so, if not for pension board trustee Diann Shipione … . Shipione blew the whistle on the pension scheme and shook the foundation of City Hall."[151] She told the City Council that the benefit enhancements appeared to be conditioned on approval of the agreement, something that "appears to be corrupt." She helped kill a city bond deal by pointing out that the city had not leveled with people about its pension liabilities. Although she eventually received a Chamber of Commerce award for her whistleblower efforts, she was at the time mocked and vilified by the entire city establishment.

Here's RPPI again: "City officials responded to Shipione's insights not by undertaking serious introspection to see if there really was a serious problem with the pension system, but rather by lashing out at her." The assistant city manager accused her of misrepresenting the facts and the pension board "purchased an ad in the *San Diego Union-Tribune* that sneered, 'Chicken Little Would Be Proud.'" The city banned her from the pension board meetings and planned to arrest her if she showed up and tried to take part in them.[152]

Now think back to my story in Chapter 2 regarding Shawn Nelson, the lone Fullerton council member who alerted the public to the back-door plan to retroactively increase pensions for government workers even after it was clear that the city could not afford such taxpayer-funded generosity. Republicans and Democrats ridiculed Nelson and prominent officials called for his prosecution for allegedly violating the state's open-meetings law even though it was clear that they were the ones who were circumventing the spirit of open government, not Nelson. After the dust cleared, Nelson was granted the Orange County Republican Party's Elected Official of the Year Award, just as Shipione was widely honored. But what's needed is a lot more support and courage while a crisis is unfolding rather than the presentation of awards after the fact.

Still, this reminds me, ironically, of the quotation from a speech at the 1914 convention of the Amalgamated Clothing Workers of America: "And, my friends, in this story you have a history of this entire movement. First they ignore you. Then they ridicule you. And then they attack you and want to burn you. And then they build monuments to you." Or at least they give you meaningless awards.

Although San Diego was forced to make some changes and clean up its act, the city, as of this writing, still faces a $2.7 billion pension liability. Its credit rating has been upgraded and criminal trials against the five former pension bosses continue. But most significantly, for the purpose of this chapter, is the lasting effect on traditional municipal services. In a July 9 column for the *San Diego News Network*, political columnist Steve Francis details the many things the city cannot do because of its crushing financial burdens stemming from pensions and health-care costs for retirees.

Francis bemoans the inability of the city to build a new library. There's no money in the general fund to do so. "And, as everyone also knows, the reason for this is that the general fund simply does not have enough money to cover the projected pension deficit or retiree health care obligations," Francis wrote.[153] He pointed to the need for the replacement of City Hall, "a building riddled with asbestos, which is inefficient to operate and which needs tens of millions of dollars just to make it safe." He points to the lack of money to construct a new convention center, reductions in police and fire funding and decrepit neighborhood streets throughout the city.

I might disagree with him about whether the city should fund big capital projects such as a convention center, but we can all argue over those proposed plans. What's clear is that such plans are not even possible—short of the passage of tax-increasing bond measures to fund them—as long as municipalities are crushed under the burden of retiree-related benefit costs.

One would think that San Diego, of all places, would have learned its lesson about under-funding pensions and increasing benefits. But institutional prerogatives die hard, and there's no changing the reality that almost all of the people making almost all of the retirement-pay related decisions stand to benefit personally from them. Almost all the politicians are dependent on government unions for their political future. A sort of groupthink takes hold, the modern example of the emperor without any clothes.

A July 17, 2009 *San Diego Union-Tribune* editorial warned the city's pension board against jiggering the numbers in the face of financial losses to the pension fund caused by bad investments and a sinking economy: "Is the San Diego retirement board poised to repeat the folly of deliberately under-funding the pension system and piling up a crushing multibillion-dollar debt for future generations to pay?"[154] Frankly, after what San Diego has been through, no one should even have to ask that question. But the newspaper pointed to an agenda item that would "manipulate actuarial assumptions in order to artificially reduce the city's annual required contribution to the pension system." But with required annual contributions expected to jump as much as $70 million, officials are again looking for gimmicks—in this case by avoiding "corridor" limits that would require larger payments when income is down. The *U-T* also pointed to the city's use of smoothing, that CalPERS trick to hide the real cost of the losses.

San Diego City Councilman Carl DeMaio, writing in the newspaper, blasted those accounting tricks as a repeat of past mistakes and reminded readers that "the city's current financial practices are still unsustainable." He noted that city officials continue to raid reserves to pay for these costs and pointed to the $3 billion in pension and health-care liabilities in addition to a $1 billion maintenance backlog. "When you include all of these liabilities, city debt stands at $17,800 for each San Diego household — and that's not counting debt issued by the city's Redevelopment Agency."[155] No wonder the city is falling back to its old debt-masking ways.

*Voice of San Diego* columnist Scott Lewis wrote that, as of July 2009, the city remains close to bankruptcy: "San Diego City Hall has finally admitted that it can't pay what it owes to the pension fund that is holding and investing assets to pay retired city workers. The city has concluded that if its pension fund doesn't change the rules and they don't lessen the city's burden, the city will be insolvent."[156] This gets back to the discussion about "corridor" limits. Lewis does a great job explaining how this smoothing system works: "The pension system knows what its assets are worth. And it compares those assets to how much it owes current and future city retirees. But the assets fluctuate in value every day. In order to keep from sending the city a wildly fluctuating bill, the pension system 'smoothes' those market peaks and valleys. But the pension system doesn't want to let that smoothing get out of hand — or at least it didn't. It put into place a 'corridor' that limits how high and low the actuarial valuation can be compared to the real or market value of the stocks, bonds and property it owns on a given day." But now the folks who run the pension fund want to get rid of those limits and allow themselves the latitude to "pretend like it has far more assets than it does." In other words, officials want to hide how much the funds have been losing so that no one gets too concerned and city employees still receive their generous payments without any undue criticism.

Lewis points out a letter from a former retirement board official defending the current board's plan to reduce the corridor limits. In it, the writer, Tom Hebrank, argues against those who would use the current economic situation to force the city into bankruptcy. Hebrank explains that bankruptcy "would jeopardize, not protect, SDCERS' [San Diego City Employees Retirement System] members."[157] Columnist Lewis has

it exactly right: the letter reveals the mindset of pension trustees. They
are not concerned about taxpayers and protecting the interests of the city
so much as they are about protecting the interests of their fellow union
members, who could lose some of their out-sized benefits if the city
declares bankruptcy. The system protects its own even though bankruptcy
might be what's in the best interest of San Diego residents. No wonder
these pension officials want to conceal the truth about the size of the
pension deficit problem.

## FULL DISCLOSURE NEEDED

American Enterprise Institute scholar Andrew Biggs, writing for the
*Wall Street Journal*, describes the current pension tsunami as the result of
"overgenerous benefits, chronic under-funding and now trillion dollar
stock-market losses"—something that some experts say results in a $2
trillion nationwide pension liability based on the same market-based
valuation methods used by private companies.[158] Biggs points to the
approach taken by administrators of two Montana pension plans, who
are selecting actuaries based on their willingness to use methods that
downplay the pension debt. The difference in approaches is enormous.
Public pension plans now use a method that discounts "future liabilities
based on high but uncertain returns projected for investments." That
would put the nationwide liability at around $310 billion. The more
sensible, private-sector approach discounts "pension liabilities at lower
interest rates to reflect the chance that the expected returns won't be
realized."

The Government Accounting Standards Board, Biggs explains, doesn't
require pension funds to adopt market valuation methods, but is taking a
look at the matter now. In 2004, the board adopted what is known as GASB
45, which, as Wikipedia explains, "is an accounting and financial reporting
provision requiring government employers to measure and report the
liabilities associated with other (than pension) post-employment benefits
(or OPEB)."[159] The result of GASB 45: Local governments could no longer
hide $1.5 trillion in non-pension benefit liabilities.

As Credit Suisse explained in an investor's report on the impact of
GASB 45, the revelation of the once-hidden OPEB liabilities will have

major effects on state and local governments, including higher tax burdens and cuts in other services.[160] Once governments must adopt more realistic market-based measures for their retirement plans, I'd expect similar pressures for higher taxes and service cuts. These are the real-world results of giving away the store to government unions. But in the meantime the agencies and retirement systems will continue to hide their true liabilities. One such effort, reported on by Peter Cohan in the Daily Finance Web site, is a lawsuit filed by CalPERS against rating agencies that gave AAA status to controversial Structured Investment Vehicles—a relatively new form of security that took a hard hit during the sub-prime crisis, given that these non-transparent funds were heavily invested in the junk mortgages that went bad. CalPERS is blaming the agencies, but as Cohan wrote, "the simple fact remains that a pension fund owes a fiduciary duty to those who depend on it to know a huge amount about its investments. And CalPERS failed miserably in fulfilling that fiduciary duty when it came to investing in those SIVs."[161] A successful lawsuit will only allow the fund to continue along its merry way.

These measures will only hide and delay the problem for so long. "If unprecedented increases in state pension contributions made by local governments are implemented, the private sector may soon find it difficult to afford the public sector's retirement plan," reported the *Post-Journal* of Jamestown, N.Y., writing on a New York state comptroller analysis predicting that "local governments might be forced to more than triple their contributions to the state pension system over the next six years."[162]

*USA Today* reported on major pension funds that are woefully underfunded, ranging from the one for Indiana teachers (45.1 percent) to the one for Illinois state employees (46.1 percent) to the one for Oklahoma teachers (50.5 percent).[163] How long before we see a wave of tax increases, service cuts and municipal bankruptcies?

These are the fruits of excessive government spending and union dominance. As the *Wall Street Journal* noted in its "The Albany-Trenton-Sacramento Disease" editorial, the states that have embraced this big-government philosophy are the ones that have the largest budget deficits, the highest taxes and the lowest economic growth. They also have the highest rates of out-migration.[164] The fact is, another result of the pension crisis is long-term stagnation and decline. Although pension problems are nationwide, those states with the biggest burdens will be the states least able to build sustainable and growing economies with entrepreneurial cultures.

Do we really want a situation where cities have no room to maneuver because they must spend the bulk of their budgets on pension obligations? Do we really want all services to suffer so that an entire caste of 50-something former employees can live like royalty on salaries that often top what they earned at their peak working years? No one is suggesting that public employees be stripped of decent pay and decent retirements, but it's absurd that everything else must suffer so that they can live with guaranteed pay and benefits at young ages.

And as good as government workers have it, they continue to get preferential treatment at the expense of average Americans. As Congress and the White House debated the $900 billion proposed federal health care plan in August 2009, senators talked about various tax increases "including a tax on health insurers that offer high-cost plans...," according to an *Associated Press* report. "Negotiators are considering exempting plans for police, firefighters and teachers from the tax."[165] That proposal, of course, plays on the "they are heroes" line of argument. But these government workers have fabulous health-care benefits of the sort that most Americans do not have. Yet thanks to union pressure, the government wants to exempt the folks with the gold-plated plans from any taxes, while they impose taxes on others.

Government workers always tell me that they need these retirement benefits because they don't receive Social Security. Yet any person would trade their paltry Social Security promise for the generous public-pension guarantees enjoyed by government workers. It's true that government workers generally don't receive Social Security, but they don't have to pay for it through payroll taxes, either. Given the precarious long-term situation with Social Security, many Americans don't even expect to get their full benefits. Clearly, there are the haves and the have-nots, and Social Security is the system for the latter group.

# A SPENDING PROBLEM, NOT A REVENUE PROBLEM

Before we look at solutions, let's remember the source of the problem. This is not caused by the economic conditions, bad as they might be. It is not a revenue problem, as California Rep. Tom McClintock would often say.[166] It is a spending problem, plain and simple. "Overall, the average person's state tax burden has risen by 42 percent since 1999—nearly 50 percent beyond what the state would have needed just to keep spending constant, with allowances for inflation," according to *Chicago Tribune* columnist Steve Chapman.[167] "All that growth should have been enough to pay for essential programs and furnish ample reserves, allowing state governments to weather a downturn without major adjustments. But the states put a priority on burning through all the cash they could get. Last year, they spent about 77 percent more than they did 10 years before."

We've seen a massive transfer in wealth from the private sector to the public sector, from taxpayers to tax consumers. The result is a class of coddled, overpaid and under-worked public "servants" whose pay and retirement levels cannot be sustained without cutbacks in public services and higher taxes. This uncontrolled spending, mostly to the benefit of government workers and not for the benefit of the public, is the real cause of the fiscal problems facing state and local government. The pension tsunami, in particular, is about to hit the shore. But there's more to this story than money and budgets. Government officials have also gained special protections for themselves that exempt them from many of the rules and standards that apply to everybody else. That is the subject of Chapter 4.

CHAPTER FOUR

# AMERICA'S POWERFUL
# AND PRIVILEGED ELITE

All animals are equal, but some animals are more equal than others.
— GEORGE ORWELL, *Animal Farm*

Orwell's great novella was, quite obviously, a critique of the totalitarian systems that elevated the rulers above the people—and particularly the Soviet system that did so while espousing the virtues of equality. I'm not suggesting that America has become an authoritarian or totalitarian nation, but it has increasingly been elevating the prerogatives of its government workers over others. They have become members of a powerful and elite group. Earlier chapters document the growth in pay and especially benefit levels for these folks, and have looked at the impact of this spending on public services and public budgets. But one of the worst problems with the elevation of government workers has been the special powers and protections they have grabbed for themselves. We're all equal in America, but some people are more equal than others.

"[*Animal Farm's*] brilliance lies in the fact that it's able to specifically allegorize *Stalin's* Russia while, somehow, it also manages to remain so universal that it can be applied to almost any tyrannical regime either preceding or following the novel," wrote book reviewer Andrew Cotlov on the Culturazzi Web site.[168] "In some ways, *Animal Farm's* commentary on the corruptive nature of political power and the power of language as a tool of ideology and control rings so true that it continues to play out in the political world as a sort of self-fulfilling prophecy."

I've noticed in particular how government workers have exploited language and imagery to achieve their goals. The 9/11 attacks have been used far and wide by police and fire agencies to guilt the public into giving them more of everything they want, from higher pay and benefits to more special legal protections. Government workers of all categories have exaggerated their importance and the dangers they face to elevate themselves above the average folks they rule over.

The special license plate program discussed in Chapter 1 is a relatively minor thing, all things considered. But it speaks volumes about the attitudes of those who are supposed to serve us. So it's worth explaining a little more.

Drivers of one out of every 22 cars on California roads have special license plates whereby their addresses are kept secret from toll agencies and parking enforcement agencies. When an officer pulls over someone with one of these plates, the addresses are in a special database that alerts the officer that the driver is a government worker, or fellow police officer, or a family member of someone in law enforcement or government work. The result is a de facto pass on many, if not most traffic laws by the drivers.

"The addresses are kept secret," according to my *Register* column, "so toll-road operators and parking enforcement cannot easily track down violators. The Transportation Corridor Agencies, which runs the toll roads, does not legally have access to the confidential addresses. The Orange County Transportation Authority has to go through additional hoops to get the addresses and admittedly doesn't pursue toll violations too zealously."[169]

After the *Register* broke this story, the Legislature responded by expanding the number of categories of government workers covered by this protection! This is what we call at work a "desk-pounder"—an anger-inducing situation, even if it doesn't rate high on the list of overall injustices. It's reflective of an attitude and the way the government unions have masterfully used language ("we put our lives on the line", "we are heroes", "we are in danger", "we serve the public") to get what they want. Everyone in politics is afraid to question the presumptions here. You'll never hear a politician question whether these public servants really do behave in a sacrificial manner or whether they really do face dangers beyond what other Americans face.

In reality, we see the emergence of an arrogant group that knows that it doesn't have to follow the laws the rest of us follow. The other day, I saw a man speed along in the HOV lanes on the freeway in his high-end, late-model Mercedes, while gabbing on a cell phone plastered against his ear—in obvious violation of California state traffic laws. He had a license-plate holder that identified him as a police officer (or retired one), and he was using a newspaper to block the sun from one of the windows. The newspaper was PERSpective (the publication of the Public Employees Retirement System). He knew there was no chance he would get a ticket.

I think it's dangerous to create a society where some people are legally more equal than other people.

## BACK TO BASICS

What makes a great society? That's a worthwhile foundational question to ask as we look at the way the government has enriched its own workers at the expense of everybody else. Certainly, we need to have some level of government to protect the rights embodied in the American Constitution. Our system of government—separation of powers, enumerated rights and other limits on government power—is what has enabled our nation to thrive and prosper for so very long. We need some government and some government workers. But few Americans would suggest that our large bureaucracies are the foundation of this great nation.

During the research for this book, I thought about the importance of entrepreneurship—of the risk-taking capitalism that has created our wealth. Some level of government, in enforcing the rule of law and a system of property rights and in maintaining the streets and other infrastructure, has enabled the free-market system to flourish. But it has been that system of freedom and capitalism that has created the nation's wealth. The growth in government and in government perks and pay comes at the expense of that wealth. Government is a consumer of wealth others create. It generates nothing of its own—a point even big-government advocates must accept. You need some of it to handle some core functions, but as it grows too large and meddlesome, it saps the dynamism of the economy.

"At the root of wealth-creation is entrepreneurship, and entrepreneurship is impossible unless we are ready to risk testing new ideas, products, and services in the market-place," writes the Acton Institute's Samuel Gregg.[170] "It is a given that most new enterprises in free economies fail. This underlines how much we all rely upon people being willing to take risks, be it entrepreneurs starting new businesses, banks extending credit, or financiers investing in venture-capital schemes."

I read interviews with entrepreneurs. They often go to great lengths to secure the funds needed to pursue their dreams. They mortgage their homes, tap their finances and borrow money from friends and investors. They believe in their ideas. If they are right, and their ideas best serve consumers and they develop a successful business, they can reap great rewards. If they are wrong, they can lose everything. But this isn't just about money. As Gregg adds, "Those willing to risk the expenditure of their capital, time, or labor in an enterprise, [Thomas] Aquinas argued, enjoyed a claim over the fruits that non-risk takers in that activity did not share."[171]

According to the Small Business Administration, 50 percent of new businesses fail within the first year and 90 percent of them fail within five years. Yet year in and year out Americans pursue these risky dreams. Even successful businesses have to be on their toes. I've watched businesses soar to initial success, and then the fickle consumer goes on to other things and the businesses go crashing to the ground. I'm a tough consumer. I might love a business and frequent it, but the moment I have a not-so-great experience, it's time for other choices. That's why the businesses that succeed for long periods of time are those that do their best serving others. It's that moral aspect of capitalism that animated author Ayn Rand.

Entrepreneurs are risk takers. They create wealth and jobs. They have no guaranteed income, no 9-5 schedule, no guaranteed retirement. In Wayne Root's book, referenced earlier, he starts his chapter on government by explaining that "As I sit writing this chapter on New Year's Day 2009, it occurs to me that I've worked all day. On a national holiday. From 6 a.m. until 10 p.m... These are the things you do when you have a private-sector job."[172]

It irks him that government employees enjoy such lavish pay and benefits and they get all sorts of time off. He's right. What is it about signing up for a government job—a job that may sometimes be necessary, but is funded through the fruits of others' labor—that creates such a sense of entitlement? Government workers, as I've documented in earlier chapters, earn high salaries and can retire at young ages with full pay or more. Their pay is guaranteed. The government keeps hiring even during the worst recession in decades. They are millionaires, when one considers their pension benefits, the day they accept their taxpayer-funded jobs (provided they stay on the job for two or more decades). As long as they show up, they are paid well for life. It's not just the money, then, or the benefits that are so frustrating, but the special privileges and protections they enjoy.

## YOU CAN'T FIRE US!

Chief among such privileges is a level of job security unheard of not just among entrepreneurs, but among average working folks who show up at private-sector companies. Most Americans can be let go from work for any reason at all—we are "at will" hires, which means we work at the pleasure of those who hired us. There are certain legal protections everyone has (protection against being fired for, say, discriminatory reasons), but every day at work could be our last one there. Government employees have no idea how the real world works. They function in a system where promotion is based on seniority, training and other factors, not on individual performance. In the private world, a new boss or a new set of priorities can mean changes in personnel. Such is life. And, of course, entrepreneurs are "employed" as long as they can sell products and services at enough of a profit to pay the utilities, rent and compensation for employees, not to mention paying the tax man and accountants and consultants who help them conform to the many regulations that will be enforced by workers who have never experienced anything but a secure existence. It doesn't seem fair, quite frankly.

It's long been a standing joke that one cannot fire a government employee. This is well known among government job-seekers, as well. *Washington Post* columnist Stephen Barr wrote about a Merit Systems Protection Board survey designed to help agencies lure Generation Y workers (those aged 18-29). The top strength of government employment, according to the survey, was job security, followed closely behind by benefits.[173]

This is no surprise. According to *U.S. News & World Report*, the "7 Jobs for Job Security in a Recession" include four government categories (air traffic controller, public-school teacher, government accountant and federal judge), two categories dominated by government jobs (nursing and college professor) and one category dependent on the government (lobbyist). In the real world, "It's no secret that 'job security' is the thing of yesteryear," according to an article on JibberJobber Blog. "The idea of having a job that is cradle-to-grave is an idea that only very old people can embrace. The current worker... knows there is no such thing as trusting the employer to keep you around, provide you pensions and health insurance, and all those other sweet perks..."[174]

Unless, of course, one works for the government. That's where one gets the pay, the perks and cradle-to-grave benefits. It's where it's nearly impossible to get fired even if you have engaged in some obvious misbehavior.

## EVEN ABUSERS CAN'T GET FIRED

Some of the most stunning articles I've read in a long while were in the *Los Angeles Times'* 2009 investigative series, "Failure gets a pass," which documents the near impossibility of firing unionized public school teachers in the massive Los Angeles Unified School District—even those teachers credibly accused of sexually molesting or assaulting their students. The *Times*, by the way, is no conservative journal, which made the front-page series all the more astounding.

The first article in the *Times* series, "Firing tenured teachers can be a costly and tortuous task," documented the case of teacher Carlos Polanco, who was accused by the school district of "immoral and unprofessional conduct" for making fun, in front of his class, of a student who had just returned after a suicide attempt.[175] Here is a summary of charges from the school board:

"On or about May 16, 2006, Mr. Polanco used poor judgment, engaged in conduct that jeopardized the health and welfare of an eighth grade student with a history of suicide attempts, demonstrated a lack of professionalism and failed to follow district policy regarding respectful treatment of others when he questioned the suicidal student, when he returned to school after being hospitalized for a suicide attempt, about the suicide attempt, looked at his cut wrists and remarked that the cuts were weak. Mr. Polonco added that the student should carve deeper next time. He stated to the student, 'Look you can't even kill yourself.' Mr. Polanco then engaged other students in the discussion of the suicidal student's attempted suicide, which prompted another student to engage in a detailed explanation of how to hit a main artery. Mr. Polanco then remarked to the suicidal student, 'See, even he knows how to commit suicide better than you.'"[176]

That's horrifying and a good reason to fire this cruel man, who obviously has little concern for the safety of his students and lacks common decency. The school board voted to fire him, but that's just the first part in the Rube Goldberg-like maze of the firing process in a district that, according to the *Times*, fires far fewer than one teacher per 1,000 a year. No wonder. The union-dominated Commission on Professional Competence overruled the Polanco firing. The commission found technical reasons why it could not rule on the unprofessional behavior accusations—the notice of dismissal wasn't provided by the proper deadline. And then the commission unanimously found that Polanco's behavior was not immoral because "it was not established that Javier was ever suicidal, that he ever intended to harm himself, or that he in fact had ever been hospitalized." After reading the commission's decision, I'm left with the clear impression that there is no possible way the commissioners would ever approve a firing.

The *Times* looked at every case (where records were still available) where the board fired a teacher and that firing was contested to the commission over the past 15 years, and concluded that "Building a case for dismissal is so time-consuming, costly and draining for principals and administrators that many say they don't make the effort except in the most egregious cases. The vast majority of firings stem from blatant misconduct, including sexual abuse, other immoral or illegal behavior, insubordination or repeated violation of rules such as showing up on time."

The investigation found that classroom performance is almost never a cause for firing. There's virtually no way of getting rid of a teacher who is a really bad teacher, as long as that teacher doesn't molest students or commit major crimes and shows up to class. Talk about the biggest special privilege of all: if you are a teacher, your job is virtually guaranteed as long as you don't commit the most egregious acts of misbehavior. You can be terrible at your job, even incompetent. But you can't be fired. How is that for an amazing perquisite? In California, teachers get these tenure protections after a mere two years on the job.

The investigation documented one absurd case after another. A teacher drank alcohol in front of kids and made offensive, sexual remarks to students, but he couldn't be fired. Nor could the teacher who was "spotted lying on top of a female colleague in the metal shop" because there was no proof they were having sex. Nor could the district fire the teacher who "kept a stash of pornography, marijuana and vials with cocaine residue at school," according to the *Times*.[177]

Think about this when school officials claim that public schools do such a great job teaching students. How great can any institution be if it is impossible to fire poor-performing workers and nearly impossible to fire downright degenerates and law-breakers?

In another series installment, the *Times* found that "About 160 instructors and others get salaries for doing nothing while their job fitness is reviewed. They collect roughly $10 million a year, even as layoffs are considered because of a budget gap."[178] The article focused on the case of Matthew Kim, who had repeated allegations of sexual harassment lodged against him. He was removed from the classroom seven years ago and has been collecting about $68,000 a year for doing nothing. The teachers union won't allow the 160 teachers in limbo to do other types of work (clerical, cleaning, chores, etc.), so they sit in a school building and wait for a ruling.

The commission concluded that Kim had improperly touched three female students, but decided against firing him and mainly criticized the school district for not giving Kim better documentation of the allegations against him. The *Times* article brought attention to the case, which ended up in Superior Court. In July 2009, according to the LA Now Blog, Judge David Yaffe finally granted the district permission to fire Kim: "Yaffe ruled that the state commission ignored evidence that Kim was sexually harassing co-workers and students and said the commission was changing 'the facts of the case to support it prior decision… '"[179]

So Kim is gone, but that doesn't fix a system that, as another *Times* article explained, puts accused sexual abusers back in the classroom where they can victimize students again and again. That article focused on teacher Ricardo Guevara. The district paid $1.6 million to sex-abuse victims in a civil lawsuit. "But there was something the jury—and the public—was never told: This was the third set of accusations that Guevara had molested students," according to the *Times*.[180] "Twice before, when law enforcement officials had decided they lacked the evidence to win a criminal conviction, L.A. Unified officials quietly put him back in the classroom." The district errs strongly on the side of protecting employee privacy and does not send along personnel files when teachers are transferred to other schools, so the new administrators have no idea, for instance, that their new hire has been plagued by molestation allegations.

Advocates for government always argue that the terrible abuses documented in the media, or by people within the system, are aberrations. But clearly the newspaper investigation found this to be a systemic problem. The numbers confirm the anecdotes and even public-school administrators, in Los Angeles and elsewhere, complain that they cannot get rid of bad apples. Consider the thousands of students who will be influenced and instructed by any given teacher over the course of a career. Think of all the damage done when students aren't learning, or have to deal with the disgusting behavior documented by the series. Government apologists also argue that the system can fix itself once abuses are revealed.

Well, the *Times* series was a blockbuster, published on the front page and over several days. The school board, under pressure after the series, took up the issue of reforming firing procedures.

Here's how the *Times* editorial board explained the backlash on June 15, 2009: "They put it off. They debated it at length and watered it down. And in the end, the Los Angeles Unified School Trustees barely passed a resolution asking the Legislature to make it a little easier to fire teachers accused of serious crimes. Mind you, not the ineffective teachers who sleep in the classroom, ignore the curriculum and pass their unprepared students to the next grade. Just the ones who stand accused of abusing or molesting students."[181]

The union hacks who control the commissions will virtually never allow the firing of a teacher. And the union hacks who control the school board—school unions, after all, are the ones with the money to run the board campaigns and almost always assure that their candidates are on the board—won't allow any serious reform. They won't even talk about getting rid of bad, lazy and incompetent teachers. They can barely bring themselves to make it easier to get alleged child rapists, molesters and drug addicts out of the classroom. This system cannot reform itself.

## RIGGED COMMISSIONS

There are many problems with the situation ably described in the *Times* series. It harms education, harms individual students and leads to the actual victimization of children. The impossibility of firing bad teachers is a fundamental impediment to the reform of school systems. This point is made in the context of this chapter for the obvious reason: these problems are driven by an absurd special privilege given to teachers and other government workers. Thanks to tenure, civil service protections and union activism, government workers are protected from firing as long as they show up on the job and don't commit any major crimes. Because of this protection, they also are protected from normal means of accountability. The bar is very low for them. In the private sector, one must perform well to keep a job. In the public sector, one need only show up to work.

Government officials always tell me that there are many forms of oversight of their behavior. Police, in particular, complain about the many levels of accountability they must endure. But the secret is that most of these are pro forma. Other government workers control most of the oversight bodies. We see with teachers that the various oversight mechanisms serve only to protect accused teachers and to drag out the disciplinary process over years. Any system that takes seven years and hundreds of thousands of dollars in costs to remove a teacher credibly accused of improperly touching several students is broken.

When I've written about police-abuse issues, I've found that the system also is designed at every level to protect the officer. Most records are secret. Police have few obligations to respond to complaints. The complaint process starts with an internal investigation, but at every level the process gives the benefit of the doubt to the accused officer. In one prominent case of jail abuse in Orange County, the district attorney found that the internal affairs investigators were coaching the witnesses and perjuring themselves. Outside commissions have limited powers and often are dominated by police advocates and apologists. In California, when the member of the public files a complaint against an officer, the only obligation the agency has is to either come back with a "sustained" or "not sustained" verdict. Any discipline is purely internal. And, even then, there's rarely if ever an instance where the public has gained a "sustained" verdict. But we always hear, "Don't worry, our internal affairs folks are tough." But then the public sees no sign of discipline and often the officers who were involved in bad activity end up getting high-visibility promotions. This has happened so often that I'm almost cynical enough to believe that police agencies do it on purpose, to prove to the public that they are accountable to no one.

When really atrocious things happen, grand juries might be empanelled. In Orange County, after the murder in the county jail of John Chamberlain, the DA did in fact call a grand jury to look at allegations that the deputies who patrol the jail instigated a beating that resulted in a 50-minute torture/murder. Deputies claimed to have been sleeping or watching a Dodgers game while this violent incident took place right in front of the guard station. The grand jury indicted the inmates who beat the prisoner to death, but did not indict any of the deputies who allegedly instigated the beating and participated in the cover-up. They got a pass.[182]

I always laugh at cops who tell me that the grand jury is an oversight body for their behavior. Grand juries are only empanelled on high-profile police-abuse cases. They provide no day-to-day oversight for routine allegations of misbehavior and excessive force. Grand juries are led around by the nose by district attorneys, who typically are so busy burnishing a tough-on-crime image that they almost never file charges against law enforcement for on-duty abuses (outside of sexual misconduct, theft or basic criminal activity). Internal affairs units are, well, internal, and the external review boards are run by DAs and others who are part of the law-enforcement community.

Yes, there are many oversight mechanisms for police, teachers and other government employees, but they mostly end up giving cover to the employees because the mechanisms are dominated by fellow union members. Consider also that the retirement boards that approve or deny disability claims also are dominated by the unions, as are the retirement funds. Often the city councils or boards of supervisors have been elected with the help of unions. This isn't a conspiracy, just the reality of the power of the government worker unions. It's very difficult for anyone to stand up against this tide. But don't let anyone convince you that the preponderance of commissions and panels amounts to real or transparent oversight.

The whole system works to protect government officials from accountability and to ensure that they have lifetime employment—well, not really a lifetime given how frequently they retire at young ages. The privileges documented in this chapter—special protections, shielding from real accountability, protection from firing—no doubt embolden the worst actors within the ranks of government and also encourage average government employees to behave in ways that might not be tolerated in the private sector.

## THE BROTHERHOOD

In reality, there are legal protections government employees enjoy and extra-legal ones—namely, a culture that values protecting one another and that punishes those who apply the laws to members of their own brotherhood. This culture is particularly well pronounced among law enforcement, given the paramilitary nature of these organizations and the out-sized sense of danger that the police culture inculcates within its membership.

These two paragraphs from the Nov. 29, 2006 *Wall Street Journal*, written by former San Jose and Kansas City Police Chief Joseph McNamara, a Hoover Institution scholar, are important for understanding the current attitudes that foster this brotherhood mentality:

"Simply put, the police culture in our country has changed. An emphasis on 'officer safety' and paramilitary training pervades today's policing, in contrast to the older culture, which held that cops didn't shoot until they were about to be shot or stabbed. Police in large cities formerly carried revolvers holding six .38-caliber rounds. Nowadays, police carry semi-automatic pistols with 16 high-caliber rounds, shotguns and military assault rifles, weapons once relegated to SWAT teams facing extraordinary circumstances. Concern about such firepower in densely populated areas hitting innocent citizens has given way to an attitude that the police are fighting a war against drugs and crime and must be heavily armed.

"Yes, police work is dangerous, and the police see a lot of violence. On the other hand, 51 officers were slain in the line of duty last year, out of some 700,000 to 800,000 American cops. That is far fewer than the police fatalities occurring when I patrolled New York's highest crime precincts, when the total number of cops in the country was half that of today. Each of these police deaths and numerous other police injuries is a tragedy and we owe support to those who protect us. On the other hand, this isn't Iraq. The need to give our officers what they require to protect themselves and us has to be balanced against the fact that the fundamental duty of the police is to protect human life and that law officers are only justified in taking a life as a last resort."[183]

The results of this new attitude are troubling.

Many Americans were aghast when they saw the YouTube video of an off-duty Chicago police officer, Anthony Abbate, who weighs 250 pounds, savagely beat a 125-pound female bartender who refused to continue serving drinks to the drunken off-duty cop. "It is one of the most brutal and savage attacks that I have seen caught on tape," a Cook County state's attorney told a local TV station. News reports suggest that Abbate had a troubled history with the department. He had a DUI arrest and was involved in a federal lawsuit after he beat to death a man in his custody. We know that all professions and institutions have bad actors among them, but what was so shocking in the Abbate case was the way fellow police officers handled the investigation and even tried to protect Abbate after charges were filed. Abbate eventually received a slap on the wrist of a sentence, which I've found typical whenever abusive police officers have to answer before judges and juries.[184]

*Los Angeles Examiner* writer J.D. Tucille captured the double standard after the June 24, 2009 verdict gave Abbate two years' probation and required him to attend anger management classes: "If you and I got so blind drunk and belligerent that we beat the stuffing out of a bartender half our size, we'd get buried in some deep, dark hole. And if the attack was captured on a video camera and played to public outrage on the news, they'd pour concrete over the top of that hole. But 250-pound Chicago police officer Anthony Abbate was gifted with a light sentence that includes no prison time after laying a brutal beating on 125-pound Karolina Obrycka that you can watch in all its brutal glory on YouTube."[185]

Another officer was suspected of threatening and trying to bribe the bartender into keeping silent about the beating. When Abbate appeared in court, "A dozen of his police pals blocked reporters and cameras, ticketed vehicles, threatened one news team with arrest and made sure Abbate was whisked in and out of the building through private entrances out of public sight," wrote *Chicago Sun-Times* columnist Carol Marin.[186] In the same column, Marin pointed to another video showing six off-duty police officers beating four businessmen at a downtown bar: "When police were called to investigate, the off-duty officers waved them off."

This is not just typical in Chicago, but virtually everywhere. Blogger Carlos Miller pointed to the *Miami Herald*'s belated reporting on a police officer, Sarah-Anne Hoyle, who had resigned from the Miami Police Department after she wrecked a squad car. Six hours after the crash, she had a blood-alcohol content of .047. (In Florida law, levels of 0.08 and higher are considered legally drunk.) "Police said they did not have enough 'probable cause' to demand a sobriety test at the time even though one sergeant said she reeked of alcohol. ... Instead, they fed her apples, allowing her to sober up for six hours before they administered the test."[187]

I hear stories all the time of regular citizens who are assumed to be drunk and given tests after being pulled over. But when one of their own might be drunk, police can't find any reason to administer the test and fellow cops spend hours trying to sober her up before checking her BAC. After the Orange County harbormaster was pulled over by another police agency and found to be drunk in a squad car, the department insisted that it had no policy on deputies who are drunk in squad cars after they are off the time clock. The same agencies that stretch every law to ensnare regular people stretch just as hard to excuse fellow officers caught in illegal acts. It's even worse than that. Officers who try to hold their coworkers to the same legal standards as other Americans are often victims of retaliation and abuse.

The *Victor Valley Press* (Victorville, Calif.) reported on June 13, 2008 on a former sheriff's deputy who sued the department after complaining of retaliation for arresting an officer for a DUI: "The complaint alleges that Holtz's coworkers ... then retaliated against him for the arrest by putting his name tag above a urinal, trashing his mailbox and mocking him... . The complaint further alleges that the defendants refused to perform a good faith investigation or prevent the harassment."[188]

## CODE OF SILENCE

I'd like to share some detail on a story I helped cover. In one case in Orange County on May 15, the district attorney had filed charges against a deputy accused of using a Taser to torture a handcuffed man. The trial ended with a hung jury. The D.A. was not going to retry the case out of frustration by the poor testimony from police officers. The D.A.'s office pointed to a code of silence. Rather than get upset that her deputies were allegedly lying under oath, the sheriff became enraged that anyone would question the veracity of her deputies' testimony.

Here I reprint a portion of my *Register* column on the code of silence because it carefully documents the way law enforcement officials cover up for one another and make it very difficult for their fellow officers to be held accountable for their alleged crimes and abuses. It's rare for district attorneys to even press these types of charges, but the code of silence offers an extra layer of protection from accountability:

"Sheriff Sandra Hutchens and Association of Orange County Deputy Sheriffs President Wayne Quint were both furious—Wayne had steam coming out of his ears, according to one associate—at District Attorney Tony Rackauckas, and more specifically at his press spokesperson, Susan Schroeder, for a few matter-of-fact comments she made after a recent mistrial. When asked why the office was not going to retry the excessive force case against a deputy who used a Taser on a handcuffed suspect, she gave an honest answer: 'We argued in closing arguments that we felt there was a code of silence—what is it? A thin blue line. We're very disappointed... It's very important for the District Attorney's Office to have ethical and law-abiding law enforcement officers.' The D.A. believes OC deputies had 'blue amnesia'—they lied, or conveniently 'forgot' critical facts—when testifying in a case involving one of their own. It's the latest incident in a string of cases involving sheriff's deputies who allegedly covered up for their misbehaving colleagues....

"Deputies painted a clear picture of [deputy] Hibbs and his Taser abuse in an internal investigation and before the grand jury. But they told differing accounts of the event once the trial got under way... On Sept. 13, 2007, Deputy Christopher Hibbs and Deputy J.C. Wicks observed a suspicious-looking man in a trench coat walking the streets at 2 a.m. in Anaheim. The suspect, a parolee named Ignacio Lares, ran away and, with the help of an off-duty Los Angeles officer who was in the area at the time, they caught him. Hibbs used a Taser on Lares, who was resisting being cuffed. Other officers show up. Wicks writes up the police report and includes the Taser incident in it, which is required under department policy. No problem.

"The cops catch a fleeing bad guy, use a Taser to subdue him and file a report.

"But then in December, Hibbs is about to be transferred to Villa Park. As part of that hiring process the higher-ups get wind of locker room banter about the possible misuse of a Taser. As it turns out, Hibbs didn't just use the Taser once on Lares that night, but he used it at least one other time while Lares was handcuffed in the back of the squad car. After an interview with Deputy Chris Thomas, an officer who arrived on the scene, the sheriff's department concluded in a memo: 'Thomas saw Hibbs attempting to question the subject, again, handcuffed in the back of the unit, and when the subject refused to answer or was belligerent, Hibbs used his Taser to 'drive stun' the suspect. According to Thomas, he used the Taser several times.'

"Or as the boys in the locker room jokingly mimicked the sound of a Taser (according to one deputy's testimony): 'What's your name, what's your name, clack, clack, clack, clack. Tell me your name, clack, clack, clack, clack.' Lares reportedly was crying and pleading for mercy. At the grand jury, deputies were clear about what happened that night. Thomas, for instance, said he did not see anything that justified the use of the Taser in the back seat of the car and explained that 'it was in my mind that this is enough, we have to stop this.'

"But as the case moved toward trial, the sheriff's department—which handed information about the Hibbs incident and cooperated with the D.A.—called the D.A. and said that the witnesses were going 'sideways.' According to an internal affairs interview, Thomas said he 'could only hear the sounds of a deployed Taser, but he did not actually see Hibbs deploy it.' At the grand jury, Thomas thought that the Taser use had gone too far and testified that there was no obvious reason for it, but in his new interview he suggested that 'there had to have been justification for it.'

"At the grand jury, Wicks said he could see Lares through the window and never heard him struggle or do anything that would justify the Taser use. At the trial, Wicks said he couldn't see Lares or inside the vehicle. At the grand jury, Sgt. Robert Long testified that department policy requires that the person who uses a stun gun must document it in the report, but at the trial he claims that there is no such requirement. 'The sergeant who wrote the memo explaining what Thomas saw, Robert Gunzel, testified at the trial that his report wasn't based on facts, but on assumptions. At the trial, the deputies even changed their minds about where they were standing when Hibbs used the Taser.'"[189]

Schroeder couldn't believe that the sheriff and the union were angry at her—for the truth that she spelled out—rather than for the behavior or their own employees. This shows exactly what people have to go up against when they point out the obvious code of silence or misbehavior within police agencies. The union, by the way, sent out a despicable e-mail to thousands of law enforcement officials across the state with an unflattering photo of Schroeder on it—an obvious act of intimidation that angered the D.A.'s office.

It's rare for a D.A. to react the way the Orange County D.A. reacted. He was angry at the way officers ruined one of his cases and at the overreaction by sheriff's officials. But even though his actions spotlighting this case were admirable, the D.A. still did not file charges against any of the cops whom he believed to have broken the law. They still got a pass, and the sheriff said she would deal with the matter internally—so the likelihood of serious punishment for law-breaking is rather slim. What if the case involved such abuse committed by regular citizens and not officers? Can you imagine anyone getting the same breaks that these deputies received?

I referred earlier to the John Chamberlain jail murder. The sheriff who protected his deputies was, eventually, convicted of witness tampering in a federal corruption probe unrelated to the jail death. But the entire sheriff's department structure closed ranks around its own deputies. The department cleaned up the evidence scene and refused to give a lie-detector test to the inmates who claimed that they were put up to the beating by jail guards. The savagery of the murder, and the blockbuster allegations aired in the media, led the D.A. to empanel a grand jury. The report documented a culture where deputies slept on the job, played video games, searched the Internet and didn't bother doing their required rounds (and where the deputies created signals to warn that supervisors were coming around). It found that deputies inflicted unauthorized discipline on inmates, fired pepper balls at inmates and allowed other inmates to use the department's public information resources to learn the names of fellow inmates accused of child molestation or abuse. (Chamberlain had been arrested for possession of child pornography.) The report found that deputies routinely let "shot callers" run the jail. Deputies were accused of falsifying the log book after Chamberlain was found dead by entering into the log that "Chamberlain had told deputies that he had not been in fear of his life."[190]

This is an obvious case of abusive behavior and corruption within a jail system, but then the D.A.'s investigation revealed the following points:

- "Subsequent to the discovery of Chamberlain's body, OCSD [Orange County Sheriff's Department] personnel prevented the OCDA [Orange County District Attorney] from conducting an independent investigation into the murder of Chamberlain. That was in violation of existing county protocol and historical precedent. When the sitting 2006-2007 grand jury requested information on this protocol, there was evidence that one OCSD official provided it with inaccurate information regarding an investigation of previous custodial deaths."

- "Some OCSD witnesses gave testimony that mischaracterized the protocol and history of custodial death investigations."

- "In addition, after testifying before the 2007 Special Criminal Grand Jury, some OCSD personnel violated the secrecy rules governing grand jury investigations by disclosing to other OCSD personnel the substance of their testimony, the nature of the questions they had been asked, and the evidence shown to them. These same individuals then knowingly testified falsely before the 2007 Special Criminal Grand Jury concerning their violations of grand jury rules."

- "OCSD records subpoenaed by the Special Grand Jury were either not produced, produced redacted or produced by unqualified witnesses. They had the effect of substantially delaying the grand jury's progress."[191]

Those were the conclusions of a district attorney who has traditionally been highly defensive of law enforcement. The allegations coincided with the stories that journalists routinely reported on regarding the local jail, yet the D.A. did not prosecute anyone in the sheriff's department, even though he believed that they purposely stalled the investigation, stonewalled the department, committed perjury, destroyed documents and evidence, and covered up for fellow officers who were involved in very serious misbehavior. The brotherhood protects its own.

## PROFESSIONAL COURTESY

Whenever it is revealed that legislators get special privileges, people get angry. The laws should apply to everyone equally, they explain. True enough. Yet many Americans shrug when they find out that law enforcement extends professional courtesy to other law enforcement officials and their family members. This seems like a bigger problem given the large numbers of people working for various police agencies and the large number of their family members. This creates dangers, also. In one Southern California case, an off-duty cop had killed his best friend in a high-speed reckless driving accident. The district attorney alleged that he had been let off the hook time and time again for dangerous driving after flashing his badge. Is it safe to have large numbers of people exempt from basic traffic laws?

A web site called abuseofpower.info points to a reality: "When a cop stops someone for a traffic violation or responds to a call about a disturbance, and that person flashes a police or firefighter ID, things usually relax. Responding officers and traffic cops have a great deal of leeway in choosing what laws to enforce, with whom to enforce them, and the manner in which they uphold the law. The symbol of the brotherhood entitles the offender to 'professional courtesy.' The responding officers usually apologize for the intrusion and any inconvenience, and it's understood that 'nothing happened here.'"[192]

When the D.A. filed charges against an eccentric ex-local official who had taken a half-empty bottle of ketchup from a university cafeteria, the D.A. spokesperson told me that officials can't pick and choose whom they decide to arrest and file charges against.[193] But we all know the reality. There is plenty of discretion, and indeed we should all be glad for it. Given the large number of laws on the books, we don't want everything prosecuted and everyone arrested every time some jot or tittle of a local, state or federal law is violated. But it is wrong that one class—law enforcement and certain other categories of government worker—routinely is not held accountable for the same laws that would definitely be applied to regular citizens.

Sometimes police agencies deny the obvious. But one need only peruse Web sites and publications for law enforcement officials to realize that this is the standard, even if occasionally an officer will sometimes have integrity and arrest a fellow off-duty officer who is driving drunk or assaulting a barmaid or taking kickbacks or some other egregious offense. This is from a Web site called NJLawman.com, which featured an article on professional courtesy:

"Several years ago during a trip up to Hoboken with some guys from work, we stopped off at the bar district which overlooks Manhattan. I forget the name of it. When we couldn't get a parking spot we asked some Hoboken cops for guidance. They put us in an unauthorized area behind their police car so we wouldn't have to walk and so they could watch our car for the night. The guys and girls at Newark Airport Port Authority PD will let you put your car in their lot and shuffle you to and fro when manpower allows. If your wife and kids break down in our town, we'll get them back to you in one piece even if it means setting up a three-county leap frog with the departments in between. The bottom line is that we go the extra mile for each other and extend courtesies that we couldn't normally do for the public. I may have never met you, but you know if you need a favor, just ask. I know the same."[194]

The NJLawman argues that today's professional courtesy is not "diplomatic immunity": "In the old days there were no limits to what cops were suppose to do for each other. Those guys though didn't make the salaries we do today. There aren't many readily available jobs with the money, benefits, and pensions we have, so risking your job to fix a traffic ticket is no longer part of the equation."[195]

In other words, there's some risk involved in letting fellow officers break the law and it's not worth going too far and risking that high salary and great pension! The limits are not based on any sense of public-spiritedness by police, but fear of getting in trouble for going too far.

It's one thing if people help out others using their personal resources, but quite another when public resources are used to help out fellow government workers. It's even more ridiculous to grant members of the brotherhood immunity from many types of misdemeanors and even felonies. Reacting to the *Register*'s article on special license plates, Jim Baxter of the National Motorists Association explains why this is such a bad idea: "Our system was based on the ideal that everyone is to be held to the same standard, be equally responsible for our actions and that there not be an anointed elite with privileged status. Granted, this is an 'ideal' and ideals are something we strive for knowing that perfection is usually not achievable. Still, when a glaring and pregnant contradiction to the ideal is so apparent and malignant, as is 'professional courtesy,' why is it so readily ignored?"[196]

The answer, I'm afraid, is that government unions have so much power and no one is willing to stand up to them.

## SPECIAL BILL OF RIGHTS

The Bill of Rights is an incredible document, one that details some the fundamental, God-given rights enjoyed by American citizens. The idea is to create boundaries around which the government cannot intrude. The Constitution affirms the right of each citizen to, in essence, be left alone. The document is about protecting individuals against intrusions by the state. That's why the idea of a Peace Officers Bill of Rights is so counterintuitive. Government officials should have special responsibilities as they conduct their core function of protecting our rights. Instead, as American liberties recede, the special rights afforded government officials expand. And so in California, and other states, peace officers have special rights as approved by the respective legislatures.

California's seven-page document is quite detailed and ironic. Police organizations often complain about the expansion of laws designed to protect criminal defendants, yet their bill of rights includes all sorts of detailed protections of the same sort. For example, "The public safety officer under interrogation shall not be subjected to offensive language or threatened with punitive action, except that an officer refusing to respond to questions or submit to interrogations shall be informed that failure to answer questions directly related to the investigation or interrogation may result in punitive action. No promise of reward shall be made as an inducement to answering any question. The employer shall not cause the public safety officer under interrogation to be subjected to visits by the press or news media...."[197] Suffice it to say that police organizations would be up in arms if they had to follow these procedures when interrogating members of the public who are under police scrutiny.

Thanks in large measure to the Maryland Law Officers Bill of Rights, Maryland officers almost never get punished. According to the *Washington Examiner*, "Montgomery County police officers caught breaking the rules almost always receive light punishments because of a disciplinary process tilted in favor of the police union, according to the assistant county attorney who handles police internal affairs cases. In 2008, one out of nine officers found by the department to have committed a serious offense received the punishment originally recommended by Police Chief J. Thomas Manger, according to Assistant County Attorney Chris Hinrichs."[198]

Even many law enforcement officials understand the problems with these bills of rights, which make it nearly impossible to discipline bad officers. "State lawmakers have passed a bill that enhances the rights of law enforcement officers, despite opposition by local police chiefs and sheriffs who say the proposal impedes investigations and disciplining cops," according to the *Tampa Tribune*.[199] The law was passed in reaction to the Tampa Police Department's efforts to clamp down on officers who were shopping and doing other non-work-related activities on company time. It imposes many more hurdles on departments that seek to punish officers who are misbehaving. "Opponents including Sen. Steve Oelrich of Gainesville, a former sheriff, said the bill would impede investigation and disciplining of police officers," the *Tribune* explained. "Sen. Gary Siplin, D-Orlando, cited the Tampa case and called the bill 'a cover-up bill, a fix for bad police officers.'"

Think back to the *Los Angeles Times* series on teachers. These types of laws, procedures and commissions work to make it impossible to get rid of really bad government workers. They also make it so difficult for managers to control their departments that it pushes the best civil servants out of the profession and into other endeavors. These protections also end up luring the worst sort of government workers—those who know how to game the system and who are looking for jobs where they can't be punished for their bad behaviors.

## PROTECTED BY SECRECY

In California, police officers gain a level of secrecy that also works against the public interest and amounts to a special privilege that ordinary citizens would love to enjoy. A state Supreme Court ruling on Aug. 29, 2006, in *Copley Press* v. *Superior Court*, "held that records of an administrative appeal of sustained misconduct charges are confidential and may not be disclosed to the public," according to the American Civil Liberties Union of Northern California.[200] "The decision prevents the public from learning the extent to which police officers have been disciplined as a result of misconduct." Police unions have used the ruling to shut down citizen oversight panels of law enforcement abuse and to shut out the public from knowing about any of the misdeeds of officers.

I've found that in covering cases of alleged excessive force, or when police are involved in deadly shootings, that it is no longer possible to find out if the officer has a history of abusive or violent behavior. As the ACLU explained, before *Copley* internal records were confidential, but they became public after matters were appealed to outside administrative appeals boards. Now it's all secret. And even a watered-down bill that would have restored some level of open records to the process was shut down thanks to the unified efforts of Republican and Democratic legislators. Police unions used the most heavy-handed and dishonest tactics to stop the legislation. Here is another one of my columns, from July 1, 2007, written after watching the circus of a hearing in the California Assembly, which gathered to consider a bill that would have overturned *Copley*:

Cop lobby flexes its muscle

"The Brotherhood"—members of California's various police and law enforcement unions—showed up in force at the California Assembly's Public Safety Committee hearing Tuesday morning in Sacramento. There were perhaps hundreds of them in attendance— mostly big, burly white men, dressed typically in sport coats that were emblazoned with pins from the cop agencies and government unions they represent. Quite frankly, they strutted around like they owned the place, which is pretty accurate given that they basically do own most of the legislators.

The front rows of seats in the audience at the committee are reserved for legislators and are occasionally used by their staff. But Tuesday, while the committee considered a Senate-passed proposal that would allow the public to learn about police officers who are disciplined for abusing their power or breaking the law, those seats each were reserved with a notebook piece of paper stating, "For guests of Chairman Solorio." Jose Solorio is the Santa Ana Democrat who chairs the committee and he held those seats for his special, invited guests—various law enforcement lobbyists.

The legislation at issue was Senate Bill 1019, which would overturn a state Supreme Court decision last year that destroyed the state's longtime policy of openness by granting all law enforcement a special layer of police-state-like secrecy when it comes to police wrongdoing. Previously, Speaker Fabian Nuñez—who, ironically, had made strong public comments criticizing police tactics and misbehavior after the Los Angeles Police Department thuggishly cleared MacArthur Park after immigration protests May 1—had removed from the committee Mark Leno, the San Francisco Democrat who supports police oversight, and failed to replace him. Perhaps symbolically, one member of a diverse group supporting the bill tried to sit in one of the reserved seats but was shooed away.

And, so, before the meeting even started, anyone paying close attention to the room's dynamics could see that the fix was in. Leno was gone, the cop lobbyists sat in the front as special guests. Solorio, at the behest of both parties' leadership, shoved public concerns out of the way for the benefit of one influential interest group. That group's members were cocky about this win, as the cops sitting around me laughed and joked as supporters of the bill told their stories. "Get a haircut," one of them said rather loudly to some laughter as a pony-tailed backer of the bill explained his support for it.

It wasn't funny to me, but this level of disrespect for the public summed up the entire meeting. This was as close an example in Sacramento of a vote as one will find pitting the public's interest against a particular interest group. Sacramento watchers shouldn't be surprised that the special interest won.

It's a hallmark of a free society that government officials, especially those who have life-and-death power over others, need to be held accountable. For decades, there was at least a system of open records in dealing with abusive officers. All government employees face public disclosure of their on-the-job misbehavior. All members of the public face public disclosure after they are, say, arrested—before a conviction or acquittal is granted. Yet law enforcement, after last year's decision, gets a pass. An officer can mistakenly arrest you, can beat you, can even take your life if you flee or resist him, and then the public (including victims and their families) will learn nothing about the investigation or whether that officer is disciplined. The public now is forbidden from learning about the background of officers who repeatedly use excessive force.

"Ultimately, this bill is about the public's right to know, about the public's ability to hold government accountable," said Senate Majority Leader Gloria Romero, a liberal Democrat and author of SB1019. In a previous statement, the conservative Sen. Tom McClintock, a Thousand Oaks Republican and a co-sponsor, agreed: "The police exercise the ultimate of official power—and that ought to be tempered by the ultimate of public scrutiny. Unfortunately, because of a combination of bad law and a bad court decision ... the police have the least public scrutiny."

Terry Francke, speaking briefly on behalf of his First Amendment organization called California Aware, said, appropriately, that "no other organization insists on total secrecy for the worst among them." At the hearing, the mother of a girl killed when a police chase went awry, explained: "Things should be found out. What they do wrong should be corrected. The way things are now, we will never know [what happened]." Exactly. Organizations cannot oversee themselves. Free societies err on the side of openness, because openness leads to justice and to improved policies. No one wants additional oversight for themselves—certainly not members of a government union—but that's where legislators need to step in and put the public first.

Solorio gave a bizarre, rambling speech complaining about the rapper Ice-T, about rap-music lyrics in general, worrying about the effect of open government on police recruitment efforts and claiming that police already are vilified by the public. (Actually, they seem to be treated like heroes and given every benefit of the doubt and every possible protection, but that's an argument for another day.)

He then offered Sen. Romero the chance to withdraw her bill. She defiantly refused and demanded a vote. None of the committee members had the guts to offer a motion to vote on the bill. They all sat around looking po-faced, and then the bill, for all intents and purposes, died. It was an act of cowardice by Solorio and his fellow members. "We come to Sacramento to vote, not remain silent," Romero rightly complained.

The arguments from Solorio and the cop lobby were mostly deceitful. Opponents claimed that the bill went too far. Yet Romero and her supporters amended the bill so it didn't go nearly as far as the original. SB1019 would let municipalities decide whether or not to have open disciplinary hearings, and it created a special protection by allowing a police chief to allow certain information to be secret because of its sensitive nature. The chairman claimed that he didn't like the bill because it allowed cities to set their own standards and that he preferred a statewide standard. Yet Solorio opposed the previous bill also, which included those exact standards he now said he wants. Welcome to Alice in Wonderland, where words don't mean anything in particular, but rather are spin to excuse a preordained conclusion.

As far as wanting more amendments, a frustrated Romero told the committee: "I introduced this bill months and months and months ago... Not one amendment has ever been offered to me. Not one paragraph, not one sentence, not one word, not one syllable." What was offered from two leading police organizations: a direct threat to legislators that the groups would oppose term-limits reform (that's hitting below the belt, given that legislators desperately want to stay in office longer) if this legislation ever becomes law.

Backers of the bill assembled a wide range of supporters. The list of opponents consisted entirely of police organizations, unions and government groups.

What is it they fear? The Orange County Sheriff's Department was represented at the hearing, and opposed the legislation, as was the Orange County District Attorney's Office. Ironically, opponents argued that SB1019 isn't needed because cities already have civilian oversight of law enforcement. Yet O.C.'s sheriff and D.A. also testified at the county Board of Supervisors meeting in opposition to civilian review.

They don't call it the Secrecy Lobby for nothing.

What a disgusting outcome. In a free society, the law should tilt in favor of oversight, in favor of the public's right to know. In all the discussions at the hearing, the voice missing from the debate, Romero pointed out, was the public's. "The people were absent."

Our voice is still missing, but it's never too late to raise it.[201]

## SOVEREIGN IMMUNITY

Government officials have forms of legal immunity not enjoyed by average Americans. Basically, under the doctrine of sovereign immunity—a British concept based on the idea that the sovereign, or monarch, can do no wrong—individuals cannot sue the government or its officials except in those specific instances where the government allows such lawsuits. In reality, this concept protects government officials from the harm they cause on the job. If a police officer wrongly kills someone, individuals can sue the agency (i.e., taxpayers), but the officer is protected from personal liability. He might be reprimanded based on internal disciplinary procedures or found guilty of a crime in certain limited circumstances (although that's very rare given that the law gives police officers in particular wide latitude to use deadly force), but he, as a representative of the sovereign, cannot be held accountable for his behavior. Such protections protect every sort of government worker.

Jarret Wollstein explains the ramifications of this doctrine in an International Society for Individual Liberty booklet from 1997: "This doctrine is a relic of ancient times, when the king or sovereign held absolute power and was above the law. Today, not only is sovereign immunity still the law of the land, it's been extended to virtually all government agents—from Child Protective Service caseworkers, to IRS agents, to local cops and judges.

"Making thousands of government agents legally immune to prosecution is an open invitation to abuse and corruption. Even when police or BATF agents or courts clearly harm innocent people, they usually end up investigating *themselves*. Not surprisingly, in the overwhelming majority of cases, they find themselves 'not guilty.' Of course, not all government agents are brutal or corrupt. Many act heroically, risking their lives to protect ours. And honest mistakes and self-defense should not be confused with criminal recklessness or corruption. But as the power of government has grown, so have abuses."[202]

The basic point here is obvious: If a private citizen caused harm as part of his on-the-duty job, he is still liable for that harm. That's a powerful check on his behavior. A private security guard is personally liable if he kills someone as part of the job. A government law enforcement official is not liable. When leftists complain about private companies, they forget that at least such companies are held to high standards of conduct. Enron executives get prosecuted. But government officials who squander other people's fortunes rarely are prosecuted for such behavior, although they of course often get prosecuted for acts of outright corruption.

Whatever one thinks about the necessity of this protection, there's no denying that it is a strong protection that government workers receive. Again, this works to reinforce the problem that's at the heart of this book: the creation of a society in which the rulers have more power and protections than the ruled. Writes author James Bovard, in a 2003 Future of Freedom Foundation article:

"Sovereign immunity creates a two-tiered society: those above the law and those below it; those whom the law fails to bind and those whom the law fails to protect. ... The fact that government can recklessly endanger people's lives with little or no financial responsibility for the resulting deaths means that the further government control extends, the more often citizens will be killed or injured. The doctrine of 'sovereign immunity' illustrates how power corrupts. If government officials did not already feel far superior to private citizens, they would not have the audacity to claim a right to injure them without compensation. That some government agents are punished on rare occasion merely shows that the power of contemporary governments is not absolute. Even tyrants occasionally find it in their interest to sacrifice one of their underlings to placate public wrath."[203]

Here's a final and ironic side element of sovereign immunity: the idea that governments are not responsible for the protection of the people they are sworn to protect. Police agencies have gone to court to uphold the idea that no officer is responsible for protecting any citizen. That's understandable in a way, but private companies that pledge to provide certain services certainly can be held liable if they do not perform under their contract. Government exempts itself.

## POWER CORRUPTS

I've written increasingly about excessive force and violations of civil liberties by government officials, ranging from local sheriff's deputies, to Child Protective Services officials, to federal agents. Government officials have an inordinate amount of power over average Americans.

The law is written in such a way that police can open fire as they see fit. After lethal shootings, D.A.s are charged only with looking at whether the officer committed a crime. But the way the law is written, that's almost an impossibility. If the officer believed his life was in danger, that's a good enough reason to shoot. And hence examples of questionable shootings become ever more widespread.

In Anaheim, a young newlywed named Julian Alexander heard a ruckus outside his home in the middle of the night. An officer had been chasing some burglary suspects and Alexander—not knowing who was outside his door—stepped outside with a large broom handle or dowel. The officer saw him and shot him to death. He could have stepped back or calmly defused the situation, but instead the officer decided to kill the young man. He had every right to do that under the law. The police chief expressed condolences to the family and told the newspapers that Alexander was innocent of any wrongdoing—and that simple act of compassion and honesty brought wrath from police and their defenders, who apparently have learned to dehumanize their victims. The department refused to release the name of the officer for months, and he returned to work as if nothing much had happened. The D.A. eventually exonerated him and the family pursued justice in the civil courtroom.[204]

In north San Diego County, a disgruntled neighbor called police to complain about noise coming from a congressional fund-raiser. A sheriff's helicopter and eight deputies showed up at the party. One deputy entered the house and was caught on video pepper-spraying the various, mostly elderly, guests who dared to speak back to him. The officer said he used pepper spray because he felt threatened and didn't like that guests were standing behind him. As often happens, two of the guests were arrested—typically, in any altercation with police, the civilians are charged with disorderly conduct or resisting arrest.[205]

In his LewRockwell.com column, Will Norman Grigg writes about a recent and increasingly typical police response: "In Virginia, police officers raid a baptismal party for two small boys. Without cause or provocation they assault the grandfather who owns the home, Tasering him three times while children and other guests look on in horror. When the pregnant daughter-in-law of the victim intervenes, she, too, is forced to perform the 'electron dance.' The grandfather is charged with disorderly conduct and public intoxication, despite the fact that Virginia state statues specify that such offenses cannot be committed on one's own property."[206]

The incidents go on and on. Because I've written about the subject, I get many calls from people who share highly credible stories about police abuse. In one instance, the Huntington Beach police, notorious for their crackdowns on drunken revelers in their city, planted a loaded weapon on a driver they had pulled to the side of the road. Scott Moxley of the *OCWeekly* explained what happened in a November 2006 report:

"With a horrified suspect watching, Huntington Beach police planted evidence—a loaded revolver—in the man's car during a DUI accident investigation in January, the *Weekly* has learned. The controversial revelation is not now in dispute although cops, prosecutors and city bureaucrats attempted to keep the incident a secret by sealing records and stalling discovery of related documents. Despite those efforts, the gun incident became an issue during an obscure misdemeanor trial last week at Orange County's West Court in Westminster. Police officers were forced to admit under oath that a snub-nosed handgun had been tossed like a Frisbee about four feet into the trunk of a Hyunda belonging to Tom Cox, the suspect. The loaded gun bounced twice and slammed up against the driver's side of the car's trunk. No bullets were discharged."[207]

Cox filed a complaint against the police for the weapons-planting, which is how the matter came to light. Police then claimed that—despite their laughter at the scene—this was a serious training exercise. The police chief said that he had never heard of and certainly wouldn't authorize any such training exercises with loaded weapons, but that he would institute new procedures banning such exercises in the future. Hmmm. The jury sided with the cops and convicted Cox of a DUI, Moxley reported. There's no indication anyone was punished for such horrible behavior. The police wouldn't release any details, arguing that this is a personnel matter, which just happens to be protected from any public release of documents.

It's very hard to get information about police shootings or questionable incidents. This is from my Dec. 17, 2006 column: "After Huntington Beach officers Shawn Randell and Read Parker fired 15 shots at Ashley MacDonald in September, killing the distraught teen as she held a ...knife in a nearly empty city park, I expressed shock in print: You mean two male officers could come up with no better way to subdue a young girl than to shoot her to death? In response, the usual suspects (the police chief, the police union, unthinking defenders of anything that police do) argued that I should not rush to judgment. I should not draw a conclusion before the official investigation, handled by the Sheriff's Department, is completed and the results released, they argued.

"So I went back to an incident in Huntington Beach 2-1/2 years ago in which Steven Hills, a distraught man who, according to police, had called 911 and made threatening statements, was shot by police 29 times and killed. The report of the investigation is done. Plenty of time has passed. Since the HBPD tells me that I shouldn't rush to judgment on the MacDonald case, but wait until the report is complete, I thought it only fair to look at the report about Hills. Well, the police department and the Sheriff's Department won't release that report. It is exempt from the public records act. That's quite a scam: Shut up until the investigation is done, but once it's done, it's none of your business."[208]

This is not a book concentrating on police abuse, but we see that the most powerful officials most anyone will come in contact with have life-and-death powers over us, and many means to cover up questionable shootings or beatings, or even downright misbehavior and abuse. The government official is the king and we are all subjects in these increasingly common police vs. public incidents. The whole system is rigged in favor of the government in these disputes.

I was at a party with a middle-class blue-collar suburban crowd. Someone talked about my recent column about police abuse. I expected that the group would be hostile to my ideas. This seemed like a typical law-and-order crowd. But one guest after another shared horrific stories about encounters with suburban police officers and sheriff's deputies. Some were about typical rudeness, but one person explained how SWAT officers busted into their home, pulled their guns and held one of the family members on the ground. It was a drug bust, but they had gotten the wrong address. After ransacking the house and scaring the kids, the officers abruptly and unapologetically left. One officer allegedly told the homeowner that bad things would happen if he mentioned the event to anyone.

This is from my article for the *Freeman* on "The Militarization of American Police": "There's plenty of anecdotal evidence that police are far from reluctant to pull their weapons or feel much remorse when they do. After Riverside police gunned down a sleeping girl named Tyisha Miller in a car in 1998 (she had a gun in her lap, was unconscious, and after police smashed her window, she moved and they immediately opened fire), the officers involved in the shooting stood around, joked and animatedly reenacted the shooting, according to *Los Angeles Times* reports. One of the officers commented, 'This is going to ruin their Kwanzaa,' after upset family members showed up at the scene. One local man arrived at the scene of another officer-involved shooting and reported that the police were high-fiving each other.

"In another recent local case, a Costa Mesa police officer admitted pulling a gun on a teenager after the officer noticed that the boy and his friends were riding their bikes without helmets. He chased the boy into the boy's backyard and drew his gun. After the boy's dog came to defend him, the officer shot the dog 15 times. The city paid the family a large sum of money, but the police department insists the officer's behavior was correct police policy. That's perhaps the scariest part of this whole disreputable incident."[209]

It's not just police officers. Everyone knows stories about abusive IRS agents and enforcers of the nation's environmental laws. Business owners live in fear of inspectors from the EPA and state environmental agencies.

Child Protective Services officials can tear apart a family on their whim. In one case, CPS investigated allegations of abuse after a family's young child scalded himself at the sink. The father got into an argument with the nurse at the hospital and, allegedly, she got back at him by calling the county CPS. A doctor's report concluded that the burn was the result of an accident, not abuse, yet the county worker changed the document to make it look like it was the result of abuse, according to the family. The family lost its children while the investigation proceeded. Eventually, the father—due largely to the stress of the situation—had a stroke and lost his eyesight. The children eventually were released but there was no apparent punishment for the social workers. The family filed a lawsuit, but didn't seek money. Instead, it sought changes so that such things wouldn't happen again. The county grudgingly signed a document requiring new training for its CPS officials and agreeing that employees wouldn't forge documents. What a concession!

Here's the portion of an article from the *Drug War Chronicle*:

"Ronnie Naulls never saw it coming. The church-going businessman, husband, and father of three young girls knew he was taking a risk when he opened a medical marijuana dispensary in Corona, a suburban community in the high desert of Riverside County east of Los Angeles.

"Although he had played by the rules, obeyed all state laws, and successfully battled the city in court to stay open, Naulls knew there was a chance of trouble with law enforcement. He knew there was a chance of the federal DEA coming down on him, as it has done with at least 40 other dispensaries this year alone.

"But when they did come down on him, it was far worse than he ever imagined. At 6:00 am on July 17, the quiet of Naulls' suburban neighborhood was disrupted by the whir of hovering helicopters as heavily armed DEA agents stormed his home and collective. They seized cash and marijuana, they seized his property, they seized his personal and business bank accounts. They arrested him on federal marijuana charges. But that wasn't enough for the DEA. The raiders also called Child Protective Services (CPS). With Naulls already hustled off to jail, his wife sitting handcuffed in a police car, and his home in a shambles after being tossed by the DEA, CPS social workers said his three children were endangered and seized them. Naulls and his wife were also charged with felony child endangerment."[210]

I wrote about a case where a young girl was taken from her loving grandmother's home and placed in the home of a foster parent who had been accused of swimming naked with other foster children. In another instance, an autistic boy was taken from his loving parents—parents who were never even accused of any wrongdoing—because the government preferred that he be treated with psychotropic drugs rather than cared for in a holistic manner that didn't require sedation.

"What kind of society rips a 17-year-old autistic boy from his loving home and places him in a state-run mental institution, where he is given heavy doses of drugs, kept physically restrained, kept away from his family, deprived of books and other mental stimulation and is left alone to rot?" I asked. The boy's parents used doctor-approved restraints that kept the boy from hurting himself. A teacher didn't like the constraints and called CPS. "After the complaint, social workers intervened and decided that the judgment of a psychologist who examined Nate's records but never even met the boy trumped a lifetime of treatment and experiences by his parents, Ilya and Riva Tseglin. Without prior notice, 'the San Diego Health and Human Services agency social worker, with the aid of law enforcement, forcibly removed a struggling and terrified autistic boy … from his home, while his mother and father, who are Russian Jewish immigrants, and Nate's younger brother stood by helplessly,' according to the complaint…."[211]

In a separate realm, developers often have deep fears about city officials and planning departments. They know that if they complain about policies that they are unlikely to get their projects approved. They are completely at the mercy of the officials who check and approve the plans for their developments. Homeowners tell me frequent stories of officious code inspectors who nit-pick their projects, of waiting weeks and months—while their project is on hold—for government inspectors to get out and do their jobs. The inspectors often are arrogant and bureaucratic. I've watched business owners propose their projects before planning commissions, where the commissioners use completely subjective reasoning to approve or disapprove of new businesses or who place absurd requirements on a business in exchange for getting the required Conditional Use Permit.

In Old Towne Orange, Calif., for instance, a group of appointed officials gets to determine whether a project conforms to the completely subjective historical standards. One couple was being forced to potentially remove a beautiful architect-designed walkway and staircase because the Planning Taliban didn't approve of the use of brick on the front of bungalows. Critics alleged that those homeowners who used the architectural services of some of the commissioners didn't have any problem getting approvals. Apparently, groups of nosy neighbor activists patrolled the neighborhood and turned in to the authorities unapproved additions and repairs. Government employees have a long reach into our personal lives, even in some areas that seem rather minor. In a lighthearted Aug. 16, 2009 article, "Please step away from the hose, sir," the Los Angeles Times reported on the city of Los Angeles' water cops, who "have been on the prowl in search of lawn-loving Angelenos who don't know or don't heed the city's tightened water restrictions." City officials have also encouraged "vigilantes" to snoop on their neighbors and report them for "mysterious puddles, broken sprinkler heads and after-hours hand-watering… ."[212]

A local Republican Assembly member, Jim Silva of Huntington Beach, in 2009 won the Legislator of the Year award presented by the California Association of Code Enforcement Officers for legislation that expanded the number of government workers who could arrest people. "Specifically, Silva is honored for sponsoring a noxious bill, AB1931, allowing 'illegal dumping officers' to join the long list of government officials who 'exercise the powers of arrest of a peace officer during the course and within the scope of their employment,'" I wrote on the Orange Punch blog.[213] Surprisingly, many categories of government regulators have the powers of police officers. Current law gives these powers to: cemetery guards, college security officers, health facility security officers, state fire officials who handle security, transit inspectors and supervisors, parole officers, science center security guards and some other categories. Given government bracket creep, how long before the water enforcers in Los Angeles can do more than simply write tickets to those illegally washing their Hondas?

I could go on and on with examples large and small. The number of laws is growing. The amount of regulatory control over our lives is rapidly increasing at all levels of government. Soon, perhaps, government will have ironclad control over private health-care decisions—beyond the immense control it already has. The more laws we have, the more regulators and police we'll have to enforce the laws. And the more of us will live subject to the authority and even the whims of those who enforce the laws. The more that happens, the more we'll experience the sort of abuses and questionable practices that have been detailed in the last few pages of this book.

Again, it would take an entire volume to deal with the abuses of government agents, or the failure of the Child Protective Services system (including a court system that gives parents no standing, is secretive and more reflective of what one would expect in Soviet society) and the militarization of police forces.

The purpose here is to remind you of the immense power that these officials have. We're not talking about special privileges and protections for some tiny group of inconsequential Americans. Instead, we're talking about amazing powers, privileges and financial rewards for a large and growing group that can have vast influence on every one of our lives.

We need to keep asking ourselves the question: What kind of society are we creating? It certainly isn't looking like a particularly free one, where government is limited and the individual is master of his future and has a set of rights that cannot easily be violated by the government.

Brown, former assemblyman, state controller and lieutenant governor. He was elected in 1998 as governor and was championed as a moderate with the potential to become a Democratic rising star and presidential contender. His personality matches his first name, yet as much of a laughingstock as he later became (losing a recall in a field with 135 candidates, including a pornographer, other bizarre personalities and an action-movie actor, who would win the election), it's easy to forget that Davis was championed as a potential presidential contender. *Time* magazine featured him in such a light. For a typical viewpoint, as he headed into his successful 2002 re-election against Republican Bill Simon, I turn to conservative columnist Joe Guzzardi, writing on the VDare Web site:

"Don't be surprised if, sometime in early 2003, Democratic eyes turn to Sacramento. Gray Davis is as plausible a candidate as anyone... Davis, as unappealing as he may be to most people, is a savvy, cutthroat politician who has plenty of money and an equal amount of drive. Look how Davis put the skids to Republican primary favorite Richard Riordan. In the beginning Riordan, the former Los Angeles Mayor, had a double-digit lead over [GOP primary candidate Bill] Simon. When Davis got through with him, Riordan lost by double-digits."[224] Guzzardi reminds us of Davis' highly unusual and especially cutthroat strategy during the Republican primary. He much preferred running against the conservative candidate, Simon, than the popular liberal/moderate, Dick Riordan, so Davis spent money during the GOP race trashing Riordan and helping Simon clinch the nomination. He handily defeated Simon as planned, winning by 5 percentage points.

Davis wasn't simply ruthless, but clever. He understood that the key impediment to Democratic statewide success in California was the perception that it was the soft-on-crime party. And California, largely a middle class and suburban state, remains fertile territory for tough-on-crime measures, especially among the older, white demographic that dominates on Election Day. Davis decided in 1998 to be the toughest guy on the block with regard to crime. He wasn't about to let the Republicans outflank him on the right on this issue. Here is the *New York Times'* explanation of this, from a May 23, 2000 article:

"It was the height of the bitterly fought 1998 campaign for governor of California, and Gray Davis, a Democrat, was trying to prove that he would be tougher on crime than the Republican attorney general, Dan Lungren, who was running on a record of two decades in law enforcement. As governor, Mr. Davis—then the state's lieutenant governor, with a record as a moderate—insisted he would be harder on crime than anybody. He would give judges discretion to sentence 14-year-olds to death; he would let them consider supporting non-unanimous jury verdicts. Indeed, Mr. Davis said in a televised debate, on issues of law and order, he considered Singapore—a country that executes drug offenders—'a good starting point.'

"No one took that remark literally. But these days, Democratic lawmakers say it sometimes seems as though Mr. Davis was only slightly exaggerating. Halfway into his second year in office, the governor is establishing himself as more of a conservative on criminal justice issues than his Republican predecessors, or any other elected official in California—if not the nation."[225]

The article, which correctly depicted California as the toughest law-and-order state in the nation given its three-strikes law and other measures, described Davis' close association with the law-enforcement unions, his support for an initiative that would lock up offenders as young as 14 in adult prisons, his siding with the unions rather than civil-libertarians on racial profiling issues, his appointment of law-enforcement supporters to various corrections boards, and his expansion of the state's prison-building frenzy despite drops in the crime rate. As the *Times* noted, "Both his supporters and critics regard the governor's stand as a political buffer against potential challengers who might fault him for being soft on crime."[226]

This dynamic—the coalition of conservative Republicans and pro-union Democrats who refuse to be outflanked on the issue—has led to the ironclad control of public safety policy by the law-enforcement and prison-guards unions. Leaders in both parties pander to the electorate, which is conservative on this issue, leading to a rapid expansion of power and perks for these union members. No one wants to be depicted as soft on crime in those campaign mailers, and everyone wants to have the blessing of law-enforcement unions. Obviously, law enforcement needs to be part of the discussion about crime policy, but the policy—especially since Gray Davis' tenure—is being driven by interested parties that are more concerned about enhancing pay and benefit levels, expanding the number of government jobs and shielding their members from accountability than they are about enhancing public safety.

What is really appalling, however, was Davis' close association with the prison guards, and the massive pay increases he granted them during a budget crisis. Davis was credibly accused of running a pay-for-play political operation and the CCPOA paid plenty to assure his election and got even more in return. The story of CCPOA's growth in power also is a story of how inextricably linked the growth in government policy is to the growth in the power of unions—and how those unions then become a permanent lobby always pushing for more government growth. It's a self-perpetuating system.

Soon after Gov. Schwarzenegger's election, *Sacramento Bee* columnist Dan Walters argued that the new governor's pledge to reform California politics ran straight into the power of the prison guards. He traces the CCPOA's move from "virtual invisibility to the state's most politically powerful union" to the massive growth in incarceration rates and the expansion of prisons. It is a chicken-and-egg debate—did the CCPOA's influence cause the growth in prison building or did the growth in prison building lead to the enhanced power of the union? What is not in contention is the union's power and the results of its use of such power. Walters explains that CCPOA helped Republican Pete Wilson win the governorship in 1990, then helped Davis win and not only secured "ever-fatter contracts and benefits—but the union's influence extended beyond such bread-and-butter matters to include, it's now evident, influence over the department's management."[227]

Basically, the prison guards successfully employed the same trick that other unions have been using throughout the nation; they dominate both sides of the negotiating table, the commissions that deal with investments and they control the management structure that oversees potential employee wrongdoing. "Time after time," Walters reported, "newspaper reporters and officials investigations have revealed such influence. Occasionally, the Legislature has even delved into it—mostly when cover-ups of bad or even illegal behavior behind prison walls are alleged. Another round of legislative hearings began Tuesday, this one sparked by allegations of a union-inspired cover-up of misconduct in a

2002 riot at Folsom Prison, and a federal judge's crackdown on the state's highest-security prison, Pelican Bay. ... Max Lemon, an associate warden at Folsom, tearfully told state senators that the union continues to wield massive influence in the department and noted that he's had to seek personal protection for fear that he would be injured or killed for breaking the code of silence."[228]

Although Schwarzenegger has taken a tougher line on this particularly thuggish union, doing so has done little to abridge its power. Prison guards insist that their salaries and benefits are necessary to attract a professional work force, but the reports suggest that the CCPOA operates in a way that is far from professional. It has resisted efforts to clean up the state's abusive prison system. Under Gray Davis, the guards became used to calling the shots. In July 2002, *Reason* magazine's Geoffrey Segal pointed to the $2.3 million the CCPOA spent to elect Davis, and then the payback: "Six months ago, California Governor Gray Davis signed a sweetheart deal with the California Correctional Peace Officers Association (CCPOA), giving them a 33.76 percent pay raise over the next five years and granting prison guards looser sick leave, even as the rest of the state is suffering a $24 billion deficit. ...A growing number of critics are calling foul on the contract, arguing that it is little more than a political payback."[229]

Working the prisons is no fun job. After a series of jail tours (and county jails typically are less odious than state prisons), I was emotionally exhausted after spending a couple hours in carefully guided tours of these awful places. Nevertheless, in many rural areas in particular these are viewed as plum jobs because of the high pay (often over $100,000 a year with overtime, with a 2006 average salary of $73,428) and generous retirement and health-care benefits. The jobs require little education and only a modest amount of training. A small city in Ohio where I used to live was home to several jails and prisons, and many people there eagerly pursued these jobs and viewed them as good, steady, high-paid work. If the people who performed these jobs hated them, they could take other jobs or spend less time working overtime shifts.

This is a diverse country and one man's dreaded job might be another's dream job. The market—the level of pay needed to attract the desired quality of applicant—should set the pay rate, not unions. Legislators should set law enforcement policy based on what's best for the public rather than on what creates the highest number of union jobs. And those who work in unions should not be exempt from oversight. A code of silence should not be tolerated. Granted, these sound like Pollyanna-type expectations, but they aren't. If you work in the private sector, think about your line of work. Are decisions made based on what's best for you or the customers? Is illegal behavior protected or punished? You get the idea.

Davis' efforts were attacked by the Left, and by those of us in the libertarian world, but that didn't change the policy. Van Jones, writing in the left-wing AlterNet Web site during the recall battle, made it clear that increasing pay and perks for workers decreases programs for the inmates: "With just a 1.8 percent overall reduction, the Department of Corrections' budget remains almost completely intact. Some areas of the prison budget even get a big boost—mostly luxuries for the department bureaucracy and for prison employees. Davis makes up the difference by gutting health care, educational and vocational programs, drug rehabilitation and other services for inmates."[230]

Maybe some readers aren't too concerned about the welfare of the state's prison inmates, many of whom assuredly deserve their fate. It's unclear whether these programs are helpful overall to inmates who eventually must re-enter society. But there is something noxious about shifting dollars from programs that potentially serve a public-policy purpose—many are designed, after all, to reduce California's alarming 80 percent recidivism rate—to money for already well-paid prison guards. Keep in mind, also, that a federal judge later took control of the state's troubled prison system and mandated billions of dollars in additional spending to deal primarily with health-care issues there.

"On Tuesday, U.S. District Judge Thelton Henderson rejected the state's request to end a court-appointed prison health care receivership," the California Healthline Web site reported on March 25, 2009. "Henderson removed the prison medical system from state control more than two years ago after concluding that care provided to inmates did not meet constitutional standards. Prison health care receiver J. Clark Kelso has submitted a plan seeking $8 billion to build seven new health centers for 10,000 prisoners and to improve some existing prison medical centers."[231]

Union dominance of the prison system is costly to the state. It has undermined state authority over the system and has led to multibillion-dollar federal mandates. Continuing budget deficits have led to calls to release large numbers of inmates, so the cost of expanding pay and benefits rather than improving prison conditions has a potential impact on public safety as well. These are in part the fruits of the CCPOA's political muscle.

## UNIONS BEAT SCHWARZENEGGER

After the recall, Gov. Schwarzenegger seemed serious about taking on vested interests and "blowing up the boxes" of government. But as Walters predicted, the governor ran into union power—and not just the prison guards' union—as he tried to tackle California's budget and other problems. The recall was a genuine grassroots revolt, as people were angry at the budget mess, at higher taxes and at the absurd electricity situation. But it's a lot easier to build a coalition of people who don't like the status quo than it is to build one for a positive agenda, especially an agenda that takes on the state's vested interests.

During the 2003 recall vote, conservatives were eager to elect as governor state Sen. Tom McClintock, a genuine conservative tax fighter and someone with a defiant libertarian streak. Tom is one of the most principled people I've ever met in politics, but the business community never liked him (they prefer moderate deal-cutters), so the opportunistic Schwarzenegger—who cut his teeth in politics by pushing a state-funded after-school program initiative that won approval in the November 2002 election—became the right-of-center choice. Many of us were happy enough when he won, despite our concerns that his free-market rhetoric was rather thin, given our fear that left-wing Democrat Cruz Bustamante would end up in the governor's seat if Republicans split their votes. Bustamante, then a lackluster lieutenant governor, bucked the Democratic Party's plan to keep big-name Democrats off the ballot and focus on stopping the recall altogether. As a side note, the election was a two-parter: voters decided whether or not to recall Davis, and the second part of the ballot included the names of replacement candidates should the recall vote be successful.

Schwarzenegger ran into unexpected (for him) resistance to his reform agenda during his first year and a half in office. He championed himself as a centrist, and did indeed push some left-leaning policies (stem-cell funding initiative, a transportation bond and the expansion of education funding), but he also was pretty good on some business concerns, such as reforming a workers' compensation system that—no surprise here—was so tilted in favor of "injured" workers and their attorneys that it was driving businesses out of the state. He repealed the car tax and managed to balance the budget without raising taxes.

Then in 2005 the governor decided to push ahead a series of reforms that would potentially improve things beyond the next election cycle. It was bold, and his agenda was decidedly conservative on those matters. McClintock was genuinely impressed by the scope of the proposals. The reforms of course went nowhere in the Democratic-dominated Legislature, which led the governor to craft a series of initiatives that would go to the voters. This is typical in California, which had embraced Progressive Era Gov. Hiram Johnson's direct-democracy reforms that have made it exceptionally easy to take matters to the ballot. Given the state's gerrymandered legislative districts—the politicians have chosen the voters, so to speak, assuring that there rarely is a change in party control of any seat—it's impossible to throw the bums out. Californians have become accustomed to deciding major matters at the polling place. Which means granting influence to the big-dollar and often-deceptive campaign ads surrounding voter initiatives.

The governor decided to tackle two significant reforms: shifting public employees to 401(k)-style defined-contribution plans, initiating merit pay for teachers and imposing a realistic spending cap on the state budgets. In a sane world, these measures would be considered obvious reforms in a state that is constantly overspending its budget. But in the world of Democratic-dominated and union-controlled California, these were considered radical reforms. Unfortunately, the business community thought these reforms to be too far-reaching. And Schwarzenegger wasn't prepared to deal with the dirty tricks of union-owned Democrats or to stand up to the oncoming union advertising onslaught.

First, the dirty tricks: Under state law, writing the official titles and summaries of initiatives is the job of the state attorney general, a post then held by Bill Lockyer (as of 2009 the state treasurer), a leftist with hopes at the time of becoming governor. He wrote titles and summaries that were designed to destroy the initiatives. This actually was one of the nastiest tricks

I've seen—something worthy of some Third World tin-pot dictatorship. The Democratic process is dependent, at some level, on politicians acting in a fair-minded manner. Instead of impartially describing one initiative, Lockyer "wrote a title and summary for the governor's planned overhaul of the public pension system [that] emphasized that the initiative would end death and disability benefits for police and firefighters," according to the *Los Angeles Times*.[232] That was a dubious claim—to the degree it had any merit, such language could have been tweaked given that it clearly wasn't the governor's intent to deny those benefits. But Lockyer did this to destroy the initiative, and his union allies pounced on it as expected and Schwarzenegger put an end to serious pension reform.

As *Bee* columnist Dan Walters explained, Schwarzenegger and the state's moderate-to-liberal business leaders and conservative activists spent so much time arguing over the nature of the spending cap, that it gave Lockyer the chance to also destroy Schwarzenegger's budget-controlling plan. Conservatives wanted a tight cap—spending growth tied to inflation and population growth—and the spineless Chamber of Commerce types wanted something less stringent, given that they like their business-oriented spending and infrastructure programs. In the official description, printed on petitions, Lockyer "dwells on the measure's potential effects on Proposition 98, the state school spending guarantee that voters enacted in 1988," Walters wrote. "Had Schwarzenegger and his allies settled on details of the measures earlier, as they intended, they would have had time to challenge Lockyer's actions in court. But by delaying, they gave Lockyer an opportunity to slant things the other way without leaving themselves time to go to court."

Lockyer deserves the scorn of anyone who believes in good government, but Schwarzenegger was clearly outmatched by the Democrats and the unions as he tried to implement real reform. The governor ran into deadline problems and a world of opposition to his merit-pay idea, which would have allowed teachers who meet objective standards to be paid better. The current system is based on seniority, but the teachers unions—which often protect the worst among them, as Chapter 4's discussion of Los Angeles Unified School District made clear—went ballistic. The governor scuttled that idea and came up with the idea for combat pay—a bonus for working in troubled school districts. That would seemingly be unobjectionable—giving extra money to public school teachers—yet the California Teachers Association was against that one also, embracing the "let no flower bloom" approach that has long typified its leadership.

I'm recounting this story so readers understand how difficult it is for anyone to take on the union interests to promote any sort of reform, no matter how small. My personal theory is that the unions will pull out the big guns to defeat a tiny reform they don't like given how easy it is for them to raise money. They take it from paychecks without approval and have big lines of credit secured by future dues payments, sometimes using their real estate as collateral. And they often will blast away just to prove to their membership that they are engaged in the process. One union official admitted that despite polling showing that he couldn't beat a particular candidate he spent big anyway or else the membership would have given him a hard time. Given that reality, politicians ought to think big, also. You get the full attack for a little reform, so you might as well go for the biggest-possible reforms. The governor didn't realize this. "Unfortunately, the governor has taken the worst of all approaches," I wrote in my April 24, 2005 column. "He has riled the politically powerful unions, but has backed away from reforms that would help Californians and chip away at union power."

Early in 2005, the governor also ran into resistance from the California Nurses Association, which held angry rallies and dogged the governor wherever he went. One thinks of nurses as kind, healing sorts, but this is California. The nurses were represented by a $175,000-a-year non-nurse, Rose Ann DeMoro—a brass-knuckled union activist known for her aggressive approach. The union was angry about the pension proposal, but its main anger was directed at the administration's attempt to deal with vast nursing shortages in the state's hospitals. Under Davis, the state passed a union-sponsored law that required one nurse for every five patients—an inflexible standard that required hospitals to hire more nurses. The problems, as any normal person would have observed, is that California and much of the country already was facing nursing shortages. At the time, many hospitals were shutting down their emergency rooms. One reason was the large number of uninsured patients who must be treated regardless of their ability to pay. But the most frequently cited reason for shutdowns was the nurse/patient law. They just couldn't afford to hire the additional nurses, so the hospitals reduced their service rather than try to live up to this nonsensical union job-creation edict. Yes, in an ideal world, more nurses are better than fewer ones, but this was a counterproductive way to advance better medical care.[233]

At the time, our editorial board interviewed Vicki Bradshaw, secretary of the California Labor and Workforce Agency, and she told me the state was producing 10,000 too-few nurses a year. There are 10,500 qualified applicants a year for state nursing school slots, she explained, but only 6,000 openings, which limited the state's ability to train the many potential nurses eager to enter the field.

My family learned firsthand the stupidity of California's nursing school situation when we shopped for universities for my oldest daughter who wanted to earn her BSN (Bachelor of Science in Nursing). At the state universities, a potential nursing student must get accepted in a regular program and take general courses for two years. At the end of two years, the top students would enter their names in a lottery—mandated as the result of the state's settlement of a discrimination lawsuit filed by the Mexican American Legal Defense Fund—and those randomly selected would get the few nursing slots available. We learned that my daughter had about a 10 percent to 20 percent chance of getting in such a program even if she had good grades. And then it could be another four years of study on top of the initial two years. She opted to pay more and go to a private four-year nursing program that selected students in the normal manner. This is typical California public-policy insanity. Hence, hospitals recruited 45 percent of their nurses from out of state or out of the country, often the Philippines.

Instead of dealing with these very real constraints, the nurses' union preferred to depict the governor as someone who was trying to destroy medical care and deprive nurses of a good living. The governor suspended the law but was overturned by a judge. So it goes.

Ultimately, the governor's package of reforms for the November special election included Propositions 74, 76 and 77. He backed a fourth, Proposition 75, but it was not something he had originated. Prop. 74 extended the time period before public school teachers could get tenure, from two years to five years. Prop. 76 offered a spending cap, albeit one with a variety of loopholes. Prop. 77 reformed the state's political districts to provide more competitive districts and make it easier to create change through the legislative process. Prop. 75 required public employee consent for political contributions.

In an interview with the *Los Angeles Times* editorial board, the governor gave a good explanation of the importance of Prop. 75: "As much as you should give a written permission if someone wants to take money out of your wallet, or out of your check, out of your bank, or anywhere else. So you should get... give written permission... Protect the workers, protect their paycheck."[234] Four other unrelated initiatives were on the statewide ballot (parental notification for abortion, two prescription drug matters and an electricity regulatory matter). Everything lost, and almost everything lost by significant margins.[235] The unions flexed their power and won. They were gloating afterward. And the governor, who seems to crave adulation more than anything else, fell on his sword and vowed to move on.

Although he has continued to say that the special election had some good ideas, the governor pulled one of the strangest political changeovers I've ever seen. He essentially abandoned his government-reform ideas. He switched to the other side. He appointed liberal Democrat Susan Kennedy—amazingly, a former functionary of recalled Gov. Gray Davis— as his chief of staff. As he headed into the 2006 statewide elections he refused to be seen with the Republican down-ticket candidates, including McClintock, who was running for lieutenant governor. He backed a large increase in the minimum wage, advocated a costly slate of environmental proposals, backed a liberal prescription drug program and refused to support an initiative that would have reined in eminent domain abuse.

And according to John Hagar, the special master appointed to oversee reform of the state's prison system, Schwarzenegger and his new inner circle cut some ugly deals with the prison guards union. "As Hagar sees it," reported the *Los Angeles Times*, "Schwarzenegger's bid for reelection has prompted his aides to improperly snuggle up to the prison guards union, a deep-pocketed powerhouse in California politics. To sweeten relations, Hagar asserts, Schwarzenegger is granting the union clout over key decisions and at least temporarily shelving his agenda of prison reform."[236]

What a massive victory for the state's public-employee unions. The governor again raised and then dropped the issue of pension reform in 2009, as the state once again faced record-breaking deficits. His plan was modest—to enroll new state employees in a defined-contribution plan. CFFR Vice President Marcia Fritz, writing in the *Los Angeles Times*, argues that the governor needed to address the pension issue once again because of the desperate fiscal situation of the state. She was rebutting a union official who argued that the average pension for a state worker is just over $24,000 a year: "The average new state retiree in 2008 received $120 per month for every year of service—$4,200 per month for a career (35-year) employee. The average new California Highway Patrol retiree last year received $247 per month for every year of service—$7,414 per month for a 30-year veteran. These pensions include survivor benefits and guaranteed cost-of-living increases as well."[237]

Older retirees complain that they don't receive such generous benefits, so these numbers must somehow be skewed. But the vast increases in benefits have come along in the last decade, and these new state retirees are practically killing the state. But after the political experiences of the governor, the lesson is learned. Anyone who takes on fundamental problems has to take on the state's muscular public-employee unions. The decks are stacked against anyone who tries, which means that California has little hope of ever getting its fiscal house in order.

## AG CANDIDATES GROVEL BEFORE UNIONS

In summer 2009, various Democratic candidates for attorney general came before the Police Officers Research Association of California (PORAC), a union lobbying organization, and made their cases for election support. According to one meeting attendee (who remains anonymous, given the obvious repercussions to his career), the organization had two basic questions for Assemblyman Ted Lieu, Assemblyman Alberto Torrico and Assemblyman Pedro Nava, each a candidate for the 2010 attorney general race. The first was no surprise and not particularly controversial: Do they support the death penalty for cop killers? The second: The PORAC officials wanted to know in no uncertain terms whether each candidate would, as attorney general, make sure the official summary for a state pension reform proposal would be slanted to destroy the chances of its passage.

The PORAC officials reminded the AG candidates that 90 percent of voters read nothing more than the ballot title and summary, and emphasized the importance of putting the kibosh on the measure by using the powers of the attorney general's office.[238]

My source was appalled, not just by the directness of the question, but by the eagerness by which the candidates—especially Torrico—answered it. Sure, they would do this. Torrico paraded his union roots and promised in essence to do anything the union leaders wanted him to do. As part of his information packet, Torrico handed out a *San Francisco Chronicle* article quoting him in a rebuttal to the proposed pension-reform measure by Gov. Schwarzenegger: Torrico called it "a windfall for Wall Street that would hurt the little guy." That's ironic language given Torrico's willingness to serve at the behest of some of the biggest, richest and most powerful big-guy organizations in the state.

Nava's campaign literature boasts of his wide array of union-backed bills. He's proud, for instance, of AB 376, sponsored by PORAC and an SEIU local chapter that allows airport law enforcement officials to receive the public safety pensions. He authored AB 325, sponsored by PORAC, which "creates the Peace Officer Recruitment and Retention Commission, which will make recommendations to the governor and the Legislature on what actions the state can take to address the shortage of peace officers...."

Don't expect Nava to explain one of the real reasons for police shortages—the "3 percent at 50" benefit that encouraged an exodus of officers out of departments given that long-term employees past age 50 would essentially be working for free if they stayed on the job. Most departments will acknowledge that the shortages began once these enhanced benefits were put in place. Nava also introduced a PORAC bill that would unseal juvenile sex crime records and another one that would keep juvenile sex crimes on the offenders' records past the age of 18.

Lieu handed out info that showed all the law-enforcement union bills that he introduced—expansion of the ability of police to confiscate firearms, a DNA-related measure, exemptions so that law enforcement officials do not have to comply with certain public records requirements, a bill to forbid motorists from using their cell phones during a vehicle stop by a police officer. Lieu also championed his efforts to expand benefits for union and government workers and included a column he wrote blasting the Orange County Board of Supervisors for challenging the retroactive portion of a pension increase in court. Lieu's column read like something written by a police union official:

"Going after the pensions of public safety personnel is not only incredibly short-sighted and destabilizing; it undermines the first priority of government, which is to protect our citizens. [S]ociety owes a special duty to public safety personnel. My grandfather was a police officer. He wore a uniform. He carried a gun. There were occasions when his life was put at great risk. Serving as a law enforcement officer or firefighter is not the same as working at, say, a store or a business."[239]

These are the types of emotional arguments union officials count on. And you know how completely sold out the Democratic officials are to the law enforcement agenda. It's not much different for Republicans, who also outdo themselves to show their commitment to law and order.

It's easy to get more benefits and to skew public-policy discussions when you own both parties in the Legislature.

## BUDGET DEBACLE

Let's consider the result of union dominance. The obvious one: there is no fixing the budget problem if serious spending cuts and structural reform in spending practices are off the table. ABC News' coverage in July 2009 of the state's budget crisis put it in stark terms: "Perhaps no state has a more daunting problem to overcome than California. Its massive deficit is larger than the entire budgets of several states. The state has almost a $27 billion gap to close before balancing its budget. The $53.7 billion figure adds in the massive gap that the state has already closed. There's very little fat to trim without residents feeling even more pain... The Golden State's problems are emblematic of the nation's. But whatever happens in California could actually have implications for all of us: the state accounts for 12 percent of the nation's gross domestic product and the largest share of retail sales of any state. The cash flow shortage is so bad that last week the state, which if counted as a country would have the eighth largest economy in the world, had to start issuing IOUs to make its bills. The IOUs, issued for the first time since 1992, are being given to vendors and residents who were owed tax refunds."[240]

The *Bee*'s Walters argued that Enron—or a Third World country awash in debt—might be the proper metaphor for California. The state, he explains, has "ongoing spending obligations that are nearly 50 percent higher than its ongoing revenues… and debts that would be daunting even were the economy to improve dramatically." A large part of the state's debt problems are directly tied to payments for government workers—"something in excess of $100 billion in unfunded liabilities for public employees' pensions and post-employment health care, roughly $50 billion for each."[241]

*Associated Press* pins the unfunded pension liability at $63 billion, "an amount equal to roughly two-thirds of all annual general fund spending."[242] *AP* puts the unfunded health-care liability at $118 billion thanks to a state benefit that costs taxpayers about $1,100 a month for each retiree. When Orange County scaled back its retiree health program and required a small contribution by retirees, you would have thought that the world was coming to an end.

But as detailed earlier with regard to the Schwarzenegger budget fights, it's apparent also that union control of the state derails all types of fiscally responsible reform. It also degrades public services and explains why California's infrastructure—once the shining example for the nation—is decrepit. You can't give away these types of pensions and have much left over for public works. Said Tom McClintock at a recent speech, "I look back a generation ago when California was spending far less than it is today, our taxes were far lower than they are today, and yet we had the finest highway system in the world, we had the finest public school system in the country, we were producing electricity and water so cheaply that many communities didn't bother to measure the stuff. And the only thing that has changed between those days and these days is public policy."[243] During the administration of Pat Brown—the father of Jerry Brown, the former and possibly next California governor—the state spent about 20 percent of its budget on infrastructure compared to about 3 percent today. It's clear that spending on unnecessary programs and absurdly generous compensation packages crowds out spending on things that benefit the public.[244]

Power corrupts and absolute power corrupts absolutely, which no doubt explains why California's public sector unions give no ground on anything. The *Sacramento Bee*'s Daniel Weintraub reported on Aug. 27, 2008 on a volunteer program run by the American River Parkway Foundation to clean up trash and debris around the riverfront greenbelt in suburban Sacramento communities. Thanks to union domination, legislators refused to exempt the group from requirements that it pay its volunteers wages and conform to other pay regulations. "This might sound like a bureaucratic mix-up," he wrote. "People want to volunteer their time, but the state says they must be paid, so they can't work at all. But this is no screw-up. It is the intended result of policies adopted by the Democrats who control the Legislature, lawmakers who are more concerned about union politics than the communities they are supposed to represent."[245]

The city of Los Angeles is in tough financial straits, also, but the L.A. Now blog reports that one of the city's largest unions, the Engineers and Architects Association, is threatening to sue the city to stop an early retirement plan that includes a 0.75 percent contribution from workers.

Rather than being ashamed of its ham-fisted techniques, California's coddled class of government workers is surly as ever. As the state struggled to make ends meet in August 2009, "Members of California's largest state employees union have voted to authorize a strike due to anger over Gov. Arnold Schwarzenegger's decision to furlough them three days a month," according to the *San Francisco Chronicle*.[246] This isn't just the result of out-of-touch union leaders: 74 percent of the union's voters gave the strike their OK. Their contract has a no-strike provision, but apparently it's only state officials and taxpayers who are required to live up to the terms of signed agreements. A strike authorization is, most likely, a hissy fit, designed to showcase anger and stir up Democratic allies. It's unlikely that the workers would actually go out on picket lines. SEIU's leaders sent out a pro-strike flyer to their members arguing, "We must increase our pressure on Gov. Schwarzenegger. We have to show him that state employees will do whatever it takes to stop the assault on public services, obtain a vote on our contract and protect our rights."[247]

I've argued that they should go out on strike—it might remind the public how dispensable these jobs really are. Certainly, many public employees do perform important tasks, but there are so many levels of administrative staff and bureaucracy, so many unnecessary bureaus and commissions, that it's unlikely a walkout would affect many people.

Bullying appears to be a way of life for California's government union members. The L.A. Now blog reported in May 2009 that "The union representing Los Angeles police officers is pressuring the owner of San Diego's main newspaper to change the paper's editorial stance on labor issues or to fire its editorial writers."[248] The *San Diego Union-Tribune* has done a fine job documenting the pension issue and has been the scourge of public employee unions. But then the newspaper was purchased by a private Beverly Hills equity firm, Platinum Equity. The firm "relies on a $30 million investment from the pension fund of Los Angeles police officers and firefighters, along with large sums form other public-employee pension systems around the state, to help fund its acquisitions of companies."

In August, the *Union-Tribune* announced large-scale layoffs and did indeed fire two of its editorial writers in its opinion section, although it was unclear whether the police union threat had anything to do with it.

The unions are encouraged to be belligerent by California Democrats. Senate President Pro Tem Darrell Steinberg sent out an astonishing letter to public school and community college districts throughout California on Aug. 4, 2009. He was angry that some of these districts were showing prudent financial management by holding on to their precious reserves in the midst of a deep recession—one that showed no firm signs of ending soon. "It has come to my attention that numerous school districts throughout California are showing reluctance to use reserve funds to help lessen program cuts and mitigate layoffs," he wrote. "During these extraordinarily troubling fiscal times, I urge you to consider tapping into this source of funds as circumstances allow."[249]

Steinberg explained that "school districts throughout California have begun receiving additional federal funds for special education and the education of poor children, as well as fiscal stabilization monies that are intended to offset budget reductions made at the state level. I urge you to use these as President Obama has said they are intended: to help prevent education job losses that would harm both our students and our economy."

There Steinberg reveals his true motives: to protect union jobs, not to protect taxpayers or the financial health of school districts. Some community college officials were appalled by the letter.

## RUINING CALIFORNIA

Perhaps California has reached critical mass—where the numbers of government employees and their power in political circles assure an ever-quicker descent into financial chaos and decline. The UnionLabelBlog.com reports that California has the third-highest number of state employees per capita, with 105 of them per 10,000 residents. When they combined state and local government employees, California tops the nation with 486 per 10,000. California also is second for the number of teachers per capita, at 188 employees for 10,000 residents.

"According to the U.S. Census Bureau, California public employees are the highest paid of those in all 50 states," wrote Jon Coupal, president of the Howard Jarvis Taxpayers Association. "The nonpartisan Legislative Analyst's Office has rated California the most generous in pension benefits for its employees... State employees actually grew in 2008 over the previous year."[250]

Although California voters rejected the tax-hiking May 19, 2009 initiatives supported by the governor and some of the major public-employee unions, "overburdened taxpayers are being asked by pro-union legislators to pay more for services through increased bridge tolls, park use fees, airport fees, parking meters and garages, increased auto registration, increased water fees and now, even a 'user charge' for services provided by fire and police is becoming standard practice," writes *Marin Republican Examiner* columnist Mark Hill.[251] He is right that many of the new fees and taxes are really there to backfill pension and salary costs for public employees.

*San Bruno Beacon* Editor and Publisher Bill Baker was even more blunt: "The greatest threat to the state of California and its citizens may be the destruction of the state of California's educational, public safety and physical infrastructure as money is diverted from these critical life support systems to pay for the outrageous, taxpayer supported California public employee union pensions."[252]

Ironically, when taxpayers and other critics complain about the lush pension and pay packages, the unions accuse the critics of endangering public safety and not caring about education, infrastructure and other services. But they are the ones who are being greedy and are putting their own comfort above the public services they claim to champion. I've watched time and again as unions willingly cut services or allow infrastructure needs to go unmet simply so they can boost their already generous pension packages. These officials often are among the least-public-spirited people I've ever met, and that includes a large number of police and fire officials who claim hero status—but seem mainly interested in their own paychecks.

Here is Baker again: "Public employee union pensions are destroying California. Your safety and the safety of your family are being compromised to support people who collect fat taxpayer supported retirement checks and benefit packages. The education of our children is being trashed so these pampered retirees can sit around and collect their fat taxpayer supported retirement checks and benefits. Government services are being reduced to pay for these rich, platinum plated retirement plans and benefits. This is welfare taken to the extreme."[253]

Reason Public Policy Institute sums up the problems in numbers: California has a $26.3 billion budget deficit as of July 2009, spends $3,554 per person per year, has hired more than 46,000 new workers in the past five years, has 8,205 government employees who have annual pensions above $100,000, pays for health benefits for 100 percent of its state retirees and has a $48.2 billion unfunded liability simply for state employee health benefits.[254]

And if you think the Legislature is about to do anything about any of these problems, consider this story from the August 18, 2009 *Orange County Register*: "At least 87 Assembly staff members received raises totaling more than $430,000 this year, even as the state faced a growing budget deficit that led to furloughs and pay cuts for many other government workers and steep reductions in core services."[255]

According to a *Sacramento Bee* blog, the state's government workers are retiring in droves in response to the furloughs and other problems, with local government retirements rising by 17 percent this year and state government retirements rising at a 13 percent faster pace than normal. Government unions want to use this to make us feel sorry for the tough times California's elite are having and creating fear that government jobs will go begging. In reality, government workers have the option to do what most private sector workers can't do—jump ship as times get tough and head out into the well-paid sunset. Many others will take early retirement and take other jobs within government. But here again we see the two-tier system in place: government workers have the freedom to opt out of the recession and live well, whereas private workers need to tough it out. This is most pronounced in California, given that the growth in early retirements, per the article.[256]

Californians are facing cuts in services, increases in taxes and higher debt. Businesses are leaving the state for many reasons, including the soaring tax burden caused by union dominance. In one typical instance, the developers of an environmentally friendly project to turn ocean water into drinking water—to help meet the state's demand for water—were told by state officials that they needed to implement a Project Labor Agreement—a union-only contract that drives up the cost of construction and virtually everything else. It's one thing after another in this union-controlled state.

And these union tactics that are destroying the state budget are being replayed time and again at the local California city level. In Irvine, which usually tops the national list for low-crime cities, police staged aggressive protests demanding higher pay in the summer of 2009. They showed up in force at City Council meetings wearing black T-shirts, threatened job actions and held a loud protest at a fundraising event put on by one of the council members. Irvine police have little serious crime-fighting to do, earn the second-highest pay levels in Orange County (an average pay and overtime package of $118,000 a year) and had a 32 percent pay increase since 2002. They demanded raises at a time when the city was freezing pay and spending and dipping into reserve funds to stay afloat. The Irvine Police Association demanded that the council use up the reserve funds to enrich its members. Usually, cities give in to these tactics but, as of this writing, the city's liberal Democratic majority actually said no—a rare instance in a state where government employees are used to getting their way. If more officials don't say no, then the future of the state is bleak.[257]

But don't laugh at California. This disaster is coming to a state near you.

CHAPTER SIX

# THE EDUCATION RACKET

*When school children start paying union dues, that's when I'll start representing the interests of school children.*
## —ALBERT SHANKER
Former President of the American Federation of Teachers

I live in a community comprised heavily of recent, wealthy immigrants from Asia, mostly China, Taiwan and Korea. I'm constantly impressed by the lengths to which these immigrant parents will go to assure that their kids are well prepared for the future. Our local strip malls are filled with Saturday schools that provide additional training and English-language education for K-12 students. At open houses and school informational events, traffic is clogged for blocks and parents fill every seat in the auditorium and classrooms to learn about the education programs. During one event for incoming middle school parents, a school administrator asked if anyone had any questions about the GATE (Gifted And Talented Education) program, and virtually every parent's hand went up—instantly. Many people have seen firsthand the emphasis parents put on their kids' education. Our school district boasts—and it really does *boast*—some of the highest test scores in the state of California. Whenever funding issues arise, school officials champion these academic successes—and high rates of attendance at college and at some of the nation's premier universities—as evidence of their successful use of resources. In the Walnut Valley Unified School District, where my children attend, 99 percent of the students pass the California High School exit exam on the first try (in 10<sup>th</sup> grade!), and the small number of students who fail typically are recent immigrants who have yet to master English. When the school district asks parents to contribute money to fund various extracurricular activities, the coffers overflow with funds. These are impressive results and seem to signal the success of the public-education system.

But whenever I think about my kids' schooling, and participate in local school events, I'm left wondering about the bizarre way we have chosen to educate our children. It seems clear to me that the main reason for the high level of educational attainment is a school district filled with affluent people who are committed to their kids' education. Obviously, in my community and others, parents are deeply committed to doing whatever it takes for educational success. Yet they never question the basic foundation of the public-school system. Parents might occasionally complain about some specific element of their school or some strange policy practice, but they never complain about a system that is so bureaucratic, inflexible, costly and seemingly designed for the pleasure of those who work there, rather than for the needs of the students who attend the schools.

When I bring up issues of teacher unionization or question why our country relies upon monopoly government-run schools rather than on competitive market-based schools, people look at me like I'm crazy. Sometimes conservatives will discuss problems with the foundations of the public-school system, but they typically want a school system that's geared around their values. Liberals revere the concept of public schools and often recoil at questions about teacher unionization, regarding any criticism of teachers unions as an attack on the noble profession of teaching or on teachers themselves.

I don't expect everyone to agree with my "separation of school and state" argument, but we should at least be willing to discuss the foundations of the education system. We should be willing to talk about the way schools are designed and run. We should be willing to talk about the union dominance of the school system and the way work rules seem designed to thwart educational reform. We should be willing to talk about the need for competition and other ideas that could improve the schools. After all, there are few "services" as important to most people as the education of their children, yet from my experience as a parent the whole way that such services are provided are off-limits from polite conversation. Yet we've all come to accept the stories about failed schools, especially those in the inner cities. The *Los Angeles Times* investigative series, discussed in Chapter 4, on the difficulty of firing abusive teachers should have resulted in dramatic reform, but it didn't. What does it say about a system where it takes years to get rid of teachers credibly accused of sexual harassment and drug use and where no one even tries to fire mere incompetents?

I like to use the example of automobile manufacturing. Thanks to fairly open markets, competition and free choice, Americans can drive fine automobiles such as Toyotas and BMWs. Even though the American car companies have struggled financially (in large part because of union demands), they still produce some good cars at competitive prices. In the marketplace, the consumer is king. Each year, cars come with more features as manufacturers try to lure buyers into selecting their models rather than the competitors' models. Imagine if the government provided cars and if we had no choice in what cars to buy. We would all be driving Trabants (what the East German government built) or Yugos. And we would wait months or even years for the right to buy one of these contraptions. They would cost more than a year's salary. We know this is how it worked in nations that let the government bureaucracies make consumer products.

Think about how much more important your child's education is to you than the automobile you drive. Yet, if we're honest with ourselves, we know that the education is provided based on a model more similar to the way the Trabant was built and distributed. One size fits all. Central planning. Government domination. Bureaucratic control. If a parent doesn't like how a school is educating his kid, he has to go, hat in hand, to the appropriate officials and plead with them to do something about it. There are many fine public-school teachers, but they are trapped in a system that refuses to weed out the not-so-fine ones and a system in which bureaucratic control is supreme and innovation is frowned upon. They work in a world where seniority trumps quality teaching, yet so many people can't understand why that system produces such consistently poor results. American parents accept this reality—and are happy enough about it that they put bumper stickers on their cars proclaiming pride in their local school.

Unions in particular have been adept at using broad concepts about community to gain deep, often emotional support for their school systems. Most of us—even this public-school critic—are basically satisfied with our own kids' schools, even if we understand that many schools are deeply troubled. Supporters of past failed school-choice initiatives in California, for instance, forgot that fact—that most parents might agree with them about troubles in education in general, but that they are generally satisfied with their own local school systems. This is reminiscent of the polls that show Americans utterly disgusted with Congress, even as they give their own member of Congress high marks. People jump through big hoops to assure that they live in good school districts, and they aren't about to mess with something that is costing them a lot and producing decent-enough results. I've always argued that people misunderstand how mediocre their schools really are, even if they are great in comparison to other school districts.

That's why it was great to see a new book and movie by Lance Izumi, Vicki Murray and Rachel Chaney called *Not as Good as You Think: Why the Middle Class Needs School Choice.* Produced by the San Francisco-based free-market think tank, the Pacific Research Institute, the book doesn't dwell on poor schools—everyone knows how bad they are. It looks at the impact of current public education and unionization on the schools that educate most Americans' children. One recurring theme of this book is the price we pay for allowing the public's servants to turn themselves into the public's masters. All the pension spikes and other financial enrichment are resulting in higher taxes and a crushing level of public debt. The current school system is, of course, a key cause of tax hikes and debt, but in this chapter we deal with a much bigger problem caused by public employee enrichment and union control: the degrading of public services. When a city grants overly generous pensions and then has to cut back on policing or library hours to make up the shortfall, the public suffers. But in the public-school system, union control has created an almost criminal level of mismanagement and abuse that has led to a far lower standard of achievement for the 90 percent of children who are educated in the government-operated public schools. The price is high, even for the middle class. There are real costs in dollars and quality in allowing government workers and their unions to call the shots in the bureaucracies they administer.

*Not as Good as You Think* points to research from authors Elizabeth Warren and Amelia Warren Tyagi arguing that middle class families are sinking under a growing level of debt—not because they are financing luxuries at a higher level than before, but because they are buying houses that are more than they can comfortably afford so they can get their kids in the right schools. Writes Izumi et al.: "Warren and Tyagi say that the major reason middle-class families are willing to shell out so much of their incomes on housing is that 'when a family buys a house, it buys much more than shelter from the rain'; more to the point, it 'buys a public-school system.' 'Talk with an average middle-class parent in any major metropolitan area,' they say, 'and she'll describe the time, money and effort she devoted to finding a slot in a decent school.'"[258]

That's absolutely true. When we moved to pricey Southern California in 1998 from a small city in Ohio and faced median home prices that were triple what we were accustomed to paying, we were anxious to find a single-family home with a yard and not be stuck in a condominium. There was a great older neighborhood in central Anaheim with a lovely house at a bargain price ($160,000 in 1998). But my wife and I started looking at school district information and realized that we would have to send our three children to private schools. Once we added up the tuition costs, we realized it would be far more economical to pay the price premium to live in one of the better districts. We stretched ourselves to buy the cheapest house we could find in a costly suburban neighborhood. In our previous homes in Maryland, Iowa and Ohio, we did not have school-age children, so we bought in nice neighborhoods that were in iffy school districts—and were able to enjoy lower prices. Clearly, people with kids pay for good schools and go to great lengths to research and identify the right schools. The PRI book suggests that all of us who do this are paying a high price, but not getting as much as we think for it in return.

I've always argued that these efforts and costs provide us with relatively safe schools with good enough reputations to help our kids get into better colleges, but that doesn't mean that, as a whole, the school systems and educational achievements haven't been declining year over year. There's a reason school officials on occasion change the test standards. There's a reason people seem less knowledgeable over time when it comes to basic geography and other subjects. My wife used to work at a museum that featured a collection of letters sent from Civil War soldiers to their families. She was always amazed by the high level of discourse and reference to classic literature, even among a group of largely uneducated farm kids.

I'm often amazed by the reverse—the low level of basic knowledge from people who have a rather high level of education and university training. And we're just talking here about the effects on the supposedly educated middle class.

The Izumi book points to the overall academic problem: "In 2006, only about four in 10 California students in grade two through 11 scored at or above the proficient level in English-language arts and math on the California Standards Test, the state's main standardized test and measure of academic achievement. On the 2005 National Assessment of Educational Progress, commonly referred to as 'The Nation's Report Card,' only two out of 10 California fourth graders scored at or above the proficient level in reading, and only three out of 10 California fourth graders scored at or above the proficient level in reading, and only three out of 10 scored at or above proficiency in math. Scores for California's eighth graders were either the same or worse." The book explains that 30 percent of California ninth graders never graduate from high school and that "More than half of the incoming California State University freshmen in 2006 required remedial instruction in math or English" —even though one must be in the top third of one's high school class to be admitted to the university system.

These problems are widespread throughout the nation's education system, but the problems among poor Americans are particular dire and troubling. Even some of the most liberal politicians and commentators recognize that the nation's inner-city schools are failing and leading to one generation after another of poverty and other social ills. In 2006, Los Angeles Mayor Antonio Villaraigosa gave a speech blasting the Los Angeles Unified School District's "culture of complacency" and referred to the district's dropout problem as "the new civil rights issue of our time."[259] Yet nothing ever really happens to fix things. Any reform idea— even the one outlined in Chapter 4, to make it easier to fire misbehaving teachers—runs into the wall of union opposition, and then the problems fester decade after decade, and more students' lives are destroyed. A couple of years ago, Villaraigosa and School Superintendent Roy Romer had a heated argument about whether the school dropout rate was 33 percent or 50 percent. The exact number matters to some degree, but it's like arguing about whether one is dying of brain cancer or lung cancer.

In reality, both men might be understating the problem. The Los Angeles *Daily News*, reporting on an *Education Week* study, found that "Just 44 percent of Los Angeles Unified students receive a high school diploma, making the 727,000-student district's graduation rate amount the lowest of large urban school districts..."[260] Some districts—Detroit, Baltimore, New York City, Milwaukee and Cleveland—had even lower graduation rates. The district—which can't even tabulate the number of employees it has working for it—questioned the study's data and insisted that the numbers aren't accurate because many students get GEDs. Yet officials' main concern was stopping efforts to break up the massive district into smaller, more accountable parts. Can you imagine what people would do if any product or service they bought in the open market had only a 44 percent success rate? Don't worry—your brakes will work four out of 10 times you apply them! That computer will operate nearly half the time you turn it on! That doctor has a 44 percent success rate on that surgery!

Yet to the unions and government bureaucrats who control LAUSD and other big urban districts, the real problem is the data. Then-Superintendent Roy Romer complained to the *Daily News* that these studies masked the district's educational gains. That's the bureaucratic mindset at work. Don't expect these government workers or union members to be too interested in gains if those gains mean breaking their stranglehold on the school system by allowing competition or other serious educational reforms.

I attended George Washington University in Washington, D.C., in the early 1980s. I remember local officials were admitting the horrific failure of the district's school system and calling for massive reforms. Yet looking at the D.C. media in 2009, we see the same arguments made, the same problems debated, and nothing ever seems to change. If you were unhappy with your grocery store, would you spend the next 20 years of your life trying to change or reform its management, or would you simply shop elsewhere? In the real world, people do the latter. In the world of government monopolies, there's nothing we can do other than fight with the management—or move someplace else.

In an April 20, 2009 Fox News column, Juan Williams criticized the Obama administration for dismantling the D.C. voucher program—the one ray of hope in an otherwise hopeless school district: "The cause of my upset is watching the key civil rights issue of this generation—improving big city public school education—get tossed overboard by political gamesmanship. If there is one goal that deserves to be held above day-to-day partisanship and pettiness of ordinary politics it is the effort to end the scandalous poor level of academic achievement and abysmally high drop-out rates for America's black and Hispanic students."[261]

Specifically, Williams—hardly a conservative, by the way—was fuming that Secretary of Education Arne Duncan stopped allowing any new students to enter the program, ostensibly because if it doesn't get funding when it expires in 2010, the students will have to go back to their old school. But as Williams noted, the transparent purpose is to assure that there are "no living, breathing students profiting from the program to give it a face and stand and defend it.... The political pressure will be coming exclusively from the teachers unions who oppose the vouchers, just as they oppose No Child Left Behind and charter schools and every other effort at reforming public schools that continue to fail the nation's most vulnerable young people, low-income blacks and Hispanics."[262]

Writing in the Sept. 7, 2008 *Washington Post*, Michael Casserly, executive director of the Council of the Great City Schools (described as a coalition of the nation's largest urban public school systems), was defending the school system against congressional meddling and against the creation of vouchers and charter schools. But even this man, who represents the districts themselves, called the D.C. district "hapless and ineffective": "Until recently, the school district has not been able to tell how many students it served or how many adults it employed. It sometimes couldn't pay people on time or in the right amounts. And it couldn't teach most of its children to an acceptable level."[263]

If that's what your friends say about you, you know you might be in trouble. The Casserly article, titled "Can't Anybody Here Run a School?" misses the obvious point. No one can, and they haven't been able to run one in Washington, D.C., for half a century. The mismanagement of the school system has destroyed, or stunted, many young lives. Yet school administrators and union officials don't get particularly angry at the state of the current schools, but at the charter schools, voucher programs and other attempts, however limited and imperfect, to fix things. That's what really gets union hackles raised.

This is from an outrageous "open letter" in 2006 to the D.C. schools superintendent from a union-backed faux community organization called "The Save Our Schools Coalition":

"The Save Our Schools Coalition and other public school advocates support your bold and timely call for a city-wide moratorium on new charter schools, and we urge you to strengthen the moratorium to include expansion campuses of existing charters as well. You are absolutely right that charter schools in D.C. have failed, overall, to deliver quality. Although the *Washington Post* editorial board, predictably, did not stand with you in supporting the moratorium, their reporters, most notably in a front-page story on August 22, got it right when they stated that charter schools were 'imposed' on D.C. by Congress and that their proliferation is draining resources, money, and enrollment from our traditional neighborhood public schools. Because of D.C.'s lack of democratic representation, Congress has made us a laboratory in an educational experiment that is not yielding the positive results its proponents had hoped for."[264]

Get it: the real problem in D.C. is not the public schools, but the charters. This gives you an idea of the shamelessness of the unions and those who oppose serious educational reform. The costs are high for union domination of all areas of government, but the costs in the world of education are incalculable. The PRI book shows that even middle-class people are paying more and suffering from lower standards because of it, but in the inner city—Los Angeles, D.C. and cities throughout the country—the future of the most vulnerable youth is at risk. This is a travesty, yet nothing is ever done about it.

In Baltimore, the city teachers union demanded that a successful inner-city charter school pay its teachers more money—even though the teachers there didn't want to be paid more. One teacher quoted in a National Public Radio news story explained that their additional "pay" comes from the thrill of watching poor, inner-city kids succeed. But the teachers union would have none of it, and it even drew a sharp rebuke from the liberal *Washington Post* in this editorial:

"Apparently not content with their part in stifling needed change in traditional schools, teachers unions are now setting their sights on undermining public charter schools. A case in point is the high-performing KIPP Ujima Village Academy in Baltimore. Union demands for higher teacher pay are causing the school to lay off staff members and curtail instruction. Urban education is short on success stories, so union leaders need to come to their senses and—equally urgent—Maryland lawmakers must change the law that gave rise to this perverse situation."[265]

It's crucial to recognize the reality of public schools—they mostly range from mediocre to dangerous—in order to pierce the control teachers unions have. They have been able to maintain their control by keeping people from focusing on how poorly they are educating the children.

## HOW PUBLIC SCHOOLS (DON'T) WORK

Let's go back to the Toyota vs. Trabant model. Toyotas are created in a largely free and competitive market. Consumers are awfully particular. They shop for the specific vehicle that fits their needs at a price they can afford. Some people like those weird little boxy Scions and other people like Ferraris. Some people prefer minivans, while other people wouldn't be caught in public driving one. This is obvious, but it's worth thinking about in some detail. Cars come with every sort of option and in an amazing array of styles and colors and with an endless choice of drivetrains and options. Government is involved in some ways (various environmental and labor regulations, etc.), but the government doesn't design and build the cars. Unions control many car-building factories, but if they impose too many work rules and conditions on the automakers, profitability suffers and the customer suffers and will choose other manufacturers. That harms the viability of the company. Think GM.

Now imagine if we bought our cars the way we "buy" public education. We would have one choice, and it would be made for us by government workers. The price would be high and we would have little recourse, no matter how often the car broke down along the freeway or no matter how dangerous it might be in a wreck. Americans wouldn't put up with it.

A Hoover Institution book, *Education and Capitalism*, captures the essence of the modern public school system: "The way government schooling is organized ensures there is little or no competition for students. Students are assigned to schools based on where their parents live, and transfers to schools outside a district typically are made only with the approval of administrators of both the sending and receiving schools. Because of their 'lock' on public funds, government schools face little effective competition from private schools. The result is a public school monopoly that limits parental choice, is insulated from competition, and is institutionally opposed to significant structural reform."[266]

The last portion—institutional opposition to reform—is a huge understatement. Essentially, the lunatics are running the asylum, and they appear to be running it for their own benefit. In my view, the key reason for all of the problems—the lack of competition, the inability to remove bad teachers, the one-size-fits-all curriculum, the excess costs, the politicization of the process, the resistance to even the most modest reforms—is the fact that unions control everything. In the school system, there are no consumers. Just as Albert Shanker said in his quotation, he'll start paying attention to kids when they start paying union dues. Shanker—who had some serious reform ideas, but also waged two illegal strikes in New York City and was instrumental in sparking public-school unionization around the country—ran a union that was less loathsome than the National Education Association, but the end result of union activism is not better education.

"Government schools in hundreds of cities, towns, and counties have been effectively taken over by unions, and children are increasingly exploited, thwarted, and stymied for the benefit of organized labor," wrote author James Bovard in the *Freeman*. "Government schools are increasingly run by the unions and for the unions... Teachers unions are increasingly dictating policy to the schools. The NEA has denounced back-to-basics programs as 'irrelevant and reactionary.' The union is the leading advocate of 'no-fault' teaching—whatever happens, don't blame the teacher. The *Chicago Tribune* concluded in 1988 that the Chicago Teachers Association has 'as much control over operations of the public schools as the Chicago Board of Education' and 'more control than is available to principals, parents, taxpayers and voters.' The *Tribune* noted that 'even curriculum matters, such as the program for teaching children to read, are written into the [union] contract, requiring the board to bring any proposed changes to the bargaining table.'"[267]

It has only gotten worse since Bovard wrote that in the 1990s. Bovard also pointed to a practice that I'm unfamiliar with, but has been common: school districts where teachers refuse to give letters of recommendation to students unless their parents write letters to legislators demanding higher teacher salaries. Talk about a thuggish union tactic, a form of blackmail that was legally permissible. That story peels away the facade of professionalism and high-mindedness by which the teachers unions typically hide. I'm sure these teachers are doing this for the benefit of "the children"!

## HOW UNIONS DISTORT THINGS

If you talk to private-sector managers in manufacturing industries, they will tell you that the union-level wages are not the main obstacle to building good products, but the union work rules. Many overseas manufacturers that open U.S. plants pay competitive union-level wages (although they tend to be more prudent regarding pension and health-care benefits) as long as they can avoid unionization. That's because unions grab control of crucial management decisions in their contracts, which often specify staffing levels, break times, overtime procedures and work rules. All these rules are designed to prop up employment levels, not to assure the efficiency of production.

I used to be a building and remodeling editor for a consumer magazine and used to be in trade shows. In those jobs, my colleagues and I would often oversee the design and construction of houses and studio sets. Sometimes the sets were built at places that employed union labor. Editors were always on a tight deadline and would typically show up on the site with photographers and various designers who were paid high daily rates for their services, so we needed to make efficient use of time. Construction almost always was behind schedule. Yet union workers couldn't care less about our particular deadline. They had work rules that governed how they worked and when they took breaks and when they left the job site. It was the classic tail-wags-the-dog scenario as the managers had to cajole and plead with the workers to finish the project correctly and on time. Many of these union guys seemed to relish the power they had and enjoyed jerking our editors' chain. They always found problems and always complained about things. That's because they had no stake in the project and were paid regardless of the success of the photo shoot. They couldn't get in trouble unless they did something egregious. By contrast, when we used open-shop labor, the laborers were extremely flexible and would work through breaks and late into the evening—anything to get the job done.

At a previous job, at an Air Force testing facility in Tennessee, our office needed to swap the locations of two computers in a small area. Union contracts governed things there. We needed to do a work order for the electricians, who would come and—no joke—unplug the computers from the outlets. Then we would need to do a work order for the moving people to come and move these PCs across the room. Then we needed the computer contractors (two of them, because each computer was different and governed by a different contract) to set them up. And then the electricians would need to be called again. The coordination involved would have taken a few days. Instead, we closed the doors after hours, looked up and down the hall to make sure no one was around, and did the switcheroo ourselves in about 30 minutes.

Now think of trying to make any meaningful reform or reorganization in that type of atmosphere. Now transfer that mindset to the classroom, and consider that once a teacher gets tenure there is virtually no firing that teacher. And consider that the administrators are not entrepreneurs who are trying to lure students to their schools, but bureaucrats who typically have the same mindset as those union workers they are supposed to manage. Even the most aggressive and innovative administrators, though, get crushed by reality.

Here's PRI again on the impact of collective bargaining in public schools:

"Because a collective bargaining contract requires the participation and approval of the union, it restricts flexibility of the school management in making decisions. Collective bargaining creates a shared-management relationship for the operation of the school. To the extent that discussion about an issue is included in the contract, it restricts the flexibility, discretion and power of school boards and administrators to make key decisions." And PRI sums it up: "Collective-bargaining agreements, therefore, create huge obstacles to placing the right teacher, with the right training, in the right place, at the right time."[268]

The Center for Union Facts does a great job detailing why, exactly, union contracts make it impossible to reform things: "One highly destructive feature of the typical teachers union contract is a system that forces principals to hire teachers who transfer from other schools within the district. Since these teachers frequently are transferring because of poor performance in their original schools, the practice is called 'the dance of the lemons' or 'passing the trash.'"[269]

Another name for it: "the turkey trot." Imagine running your business this way. You can't get rid of the worst performers, so you move them around to places where they can do the least harm or you ignore the situation and let them wreak havoc in the workplace. Think of the costs involved in this, and also in the degradation of the educational experience. Tenure was started to protect the best teachers from being at the mercy of craven administrators, who might punish them and replace them with, say, their friends and family members. But the result is that even the worst teachers cannot be removed and that union officials take a stand for virtually every fired teacher—no matter how worthy of firing that teacher may be. Unions don't have to go to bat for sexual abusers and thieves in their midst, but they do. They are geared to defend even the worst of their lot.

This has been going on for years and will almost certainly continue into the future. The teachers unions have so much power they can thwart even the most reasonable reforms. As Hoover Institution scholar Peter Schweitzer wrote in a 1999 article, "The process of getting rid of problem teachers, especially those with tenure, can be so arduous and expensive that many school districts don't even bother anymore. 'Getting rid of a problem teacher can make the O. J. trial look like a cakewalk,' says Mary Jo McGrath, an attorney in Santa Barbara, Calif., who helps administrators deal with bad teachers. 'For a principal, it can seem a lot easier to hang on to the deadwood. Teachers are more protected than any other class of employees, with all the procedural rights that can drag a civil case out for years.'"[270]

The Center for Union Facts explains that the transfer system is arduously long and makes it that much harder for principals to put the right teacher into the right vacancy. Teachers can't be hired until the senior teachers have their pick of the openings. This drives out applicants. Those who withdraw from these absurd hiring processes, according to a study referred to by CUF, have much higher grade-point averages than average teachers. Keep in mind also that education college curriculum is so bureaucratic and inane that graduates with education backgrounds tend to have lower GPAs than others. In other words, the union-dominated college curriculum weeds out many of the best students, and then the hiring practices at public schools weed out the good ones even further.

CUF explains that smart principals hide their vacancies after they identify the right person to fill the slot. Then they tell that teacher to sit tight. And then after the lemon dance or turkey trot is over, they discover the opening and pretend to sift through resumes. In other words, principals who care about the children and producing quality education have to game the system and break the rules. That means that the system is designed with the wrong priorities. CUF also argues that as a result of the seniority-based transfer policy, poor kids—who need the best-quality teachers and education—are "assigned to novice teachers almost twice as often as children in low-poverty schools." Yet the teachers union not only opposes the obvious solution—ending the seniority system—but even opposes "combat pay" proposals that would give bonuses to teachers who are willing to teach in the toughest schools. In the union-dominated public education world, pay increases are based on seniority—so those who hang around the longest time, regardless of their skills, are rewarded, whereas young, energetic and talented teachers are penalized. Again, think about your own business or line of work, and consider how it would function if these were the types of rules you had to follow.

The New Teacher Project's 2005 study, "Unintended Consequences: The Case for Reforming the Staffing Rules in Urban Teachers Union Contracts," conducted detailed research confirming the points that CUF made. Here are the study's conclusions:[271]

- "Urban schools are forced to hire large numbers of teachers they do not want and who may not be a good fit for the job and their school."

- "Poor performers are passed around from school to school instead of being terminated."

- "New teacher applicants, including the best, are lost to late hiring."

- "Novice teachers are treated as expendable regardless of their contribution to their school."

Concludes NTP: "Taken together, these four effects significantly impede the efforts of urban schools to staff their classrooms effectively and sustain meaningful school wide improvements... The damage, however, extends beyond individual schools; the overall operation of entire urban districts suffers. The transfer and excess processes require excessive centralization of hiring decisions. These staffing rules also hold every school hostage to staffing changes in others' schools and ensure that one school's gain is often another's loss—providing, we believe, at least a partial explanation for the persistent difficulty in taking pockets of excellence to scale in urban school systems."

The whole idea of charter schools is that these types of rules can be circumvented. That's one reason why unions despise such schools. Obviously, their very existence spotlights the way their work rules destroy education, and are harmful to efforts to improve inner-city school districts.

Given these job-protection rules and procedures, it's no wonder school systems have "rubber rooms" where the potentially dangerous teachers are sent and why they don't even try getting rid of the incompetent teachers. Never mind any attempt to help good teachers or to place the right kind of teacher in the right kind of classroom setting. The goal is not to provide good education for children, but to offer the maximum protection and convenience for union members. That's a disgrace, especially when we realize what's at stake—not just for individuals, but for the overall society.

Teachers unions go to great lengths not only to protect the bad apples, but to keep people from knowing who the bad apples are. The NTP study detailed the way administrators inflate the ratings of teachers in order to avoid union grievances and found that 99 percent of teachers received top rating in its study of 12 school districts encompassing four states. Why not? If you can't discipline, move or fire a bad teacher, why fight the union? It's easier just to give the teachers the high ranking and leave well enough alone.

The Manhattan Institute's *City Journal* argued that a revolutionary data system called Compstat, which helped New York City police track crime in the most troubled neighborhoods, could be an effective tool for tracking the performance of students within school systems. It could focus on teachers that do particularly good and bad jobs by using computerized systems to collate test data. "Currently, 21 states have data systems capable of matching teachers to students," wrote Marcus Winters.[272] "It seems like a no-brainer. After all, who's against having more information? The teachers unions, that's who. They're fighting hard against the adoption of these systems precisely because the information they reveal is so useful. The unions insist, against all evidence and logic, that no meaningful variation exists in teacher quality." Winters reported that the New York Legislature specifically banned the use of this type of data system for New York City schools and that California quickly followed with similar legislation. In a rare fit of good sense, the Obama administration has called on California to repeal the law or risk losing some federal funds.

## DATA ON UNION FAILURE

It seems obvious that any enterprise run with such counterproductive rules would fail to provide a quality product or service. Yet it always helps to have some data on the subject. The Marquette Warrior, an independent blog at Marquette University, points to peer-reviewed education research showing that union domination of public schools hurts school children. The blog quotes an abstract on the research from Terry Moe, a professor of Political Science at Stanford University:[273]

"Students of American politics rarely study public sector unions and their impacts on government. The literature sees bureaucratic power as rooted in expertise, but largely ignores the fact that bureaucrats often join unions to promote their own interests, and that the power of their unions may affect government and its performance. This article focuses on the public schools, which are among the most numerous government agencies in the country, and investigates whether collective bargaining by teachers—the key bureaucrats—affects the schools' capacity to educate children. Using California data, analysis shows that, in large school districts, restrictive labor contracts have a very negative impact on academic achievement, particularly for minority students. The evidence suggests, then, that public sector unions do indeed have important consequences for American public education.

"The unions use their power—their basic work-denial power, enhanced by their political power—to get restrictive rules written into collective bargaining contracts. And these restrictions ensure that the public schools are literally not organized to promote academic achievement...."

Research confirms the obvious: union work rules are designed to protect the jobs and salaries of teachers, and to make it more difficult for administrators to run the schools in a way that promotes quality learning. The unions, and their Democratic allies in particular, claim to speak for the poor, the downtrodden and the children, but they have created a system that is operated primarily for the teachers themselves, and educational progress suffers.

The problem rears its head at the university level also. "[W]hat if universities... turned into featherbedding, unionized factories that existed to protect their overpaid workers—who were impossible to fire?" asked LewRockwell's J.P. Zmirak, remarking on a new American Enterprise Institute paper about how unionization has degraded the university learning experience.[274]

## CRUSHING THE COMPETITION

The teachers unions clearly have taken the "let no flower bloom" approach to education reform, which isn't surprising given that the school system is run like those old Soviet systems. The only way unions can maintain their perks and power and keep the public from questioning such a dysfunctional educational system is by snuffing out the competition. And, of course, the main goal of the government bureaucrats who run the school districts is to keep the money flowing —hence their constant lobbying for school bonds and their push to keep kids in their schools, where they receive dollars based on ADA (average daily attendance) statistics. It's basically a money game, where the kids are used as props whenever teachers want higher pay or administrators want to avoid any belt-tightening.

One of the nastiest abuses of power by school officials took place in California in 2002 as the teachers union ideologue who was the state superintendent of public education, Delaine Eastin, tried essentially to outlaw homeschooling. The story is a bit complicated, but quite revealing about the totalitarian outlook prevalent among union officials and government school administrators. You'd think that they would have enough to worry about dealing with LAUSD and other school districts with 50 percent dropout rates, but—just as D.C. union supporters mainly are worried about the charter schools in their midst—so were California officials worried mainly about the tiny fraction of students who are taught at home by their parents.

California law is vague about homeschooling. The state has a compulsory education law that requires minors to be taught in public schools unless they attend private schools or are tutored by people with a teacher's certification. But the education code also exempts from that law "children who are being instructed in a private full-time day school by persons capable of teaching." Without a clear state legal standard, most school districts embraced what I've termed a "don't ask, don't tell" policy with a simple work around. Homeschooling parents would file affidavits with their county department of education and certify themselves as a private school. Over the years, a handful of districts harassed homeschoolers, but most were content with the affidavit system.

But when Eastin became superintendent, she was quite vocal about her opposition to homeschooling. Even though she—as head of government schooling for the state—lacked a teaching certificate herself, she insisted that homeschooling parents must have such a certificate to teach their kids at home. At the time, 13 percent of public school teachers lacked the certification (and it's highly questionable whether the certification has anything to do with being a good teacher), but that didn't stop Eastin from insisting that most homeschool students were truants. She sent a letter to local departments of education explaining her position that "homeschooling is not authorized in California, and children receiving homeschooling of this kind [without a credentialed teacher] are in violation of the state's truancy laws." She then changed the affidavit process—parents would have to send their applications to the state rather than to local counties. This naturally concerned parents. If the state had to approve their homeschool applications, and the state believed that their children were truants, then you see the problem.

Eastin's term ended, however, and the new superintendent, Jack O'Connell, was, despite being a liberal Democrat, uninterested in persecuting homeschoolers. He said homeschooling was a legitimate education choice and that ended the problem. I've always appreciated O'Connell for that act of sanity and decency. But then six years later, a state district court of appeal, ruling in a Child Protective Services-related case involving a homeschooling parent accused of physically and emotionally abusing his kids, declared that "parents do not have a constitutional right to homeschool their children." The court threatened parents that they could lose custody of their children if they persisted in teaching them at home. This rekindled the old battle—one that was eventually resolved after the court softened its opinion in response to outrage and after O'Connell and Gov. Arnold Schwarzenegger publicly declared that homeschooling is legal in California and that it was a settled question. Homeschoolers dodged a bullet.

After the ruling, however, the teachers unions began demanding a crackdown on homeschools, which is ironic given the few number of incidents of abuse in such schools compared to the widespread malpractice and abuse that has been reported on at LAUSD and other California public school systems. Had the unions had their way, they would have used the most heavy-handed tactics to shut down homeschooling, just as they have used such tactics to crack down on charter schools and to stop the burgeoning voucher movement.[275]

Public school unions are petrified of competition even though the government-run schools gain their money through taxation and hold enormous funding advantages over private schools, charters schools and homeschools. Ironically, the unions always blame a lack of money for any of the public schools' problems, yet they use their coercive power to stifle alternatives that are funded on shoestring budgets. Maybe it's just too embarrassing to watch homeschooled kids win spelling bees and soar academically when public school classrooms—which receive on average $11,000 or more per student per year—are often failing so miserably.

The LAUSD's effort to stop the creation of new charter schools was so flagrantly against the interests of the district's students that the *Los Angeles Times* editorial board blasted it in a July 31, 2009 editorial: "Teachers unions in California would be wise to listen as new challenges to their most cherished doctrines come from the very politicians they have counted on as allies. United Teachers Los Angeles is trying to kill a resolution under consideration by the Los Angeles Unified school board that would allow charter operators, community organizations and the union itself to submit proposals to run 50 new schools…. Non-district operators are less likely to accept contract rules that forbid merit pay or make it difficult to fire chronically underperforming teachers."

The good news, however, is that the school board did finally approve of the expanded charter plan—despite the opposition from the unions. As the *Los Angeles Times* reported on Aug. 29, 2009:

"The Los Angeles Board of Education voted today to open up 250 schools, including 50 new multimillion-dollar campuses, to outside charter operators and others. The move came after a nearly four-hour debate on a 6-1 vote, with board member Marguerite Poindexter LaMotte opposing…. Ultimately, it will be up to Supt. Ramon C. Cortines to select the winning bid for these campuses…. Cortines said he supported the proposal because 'for too long we have protected the status quo.' Labor unions were especially opposed to the plan, with teachers union head A.J. Duffy saying the district needs to be collaborative if it wants to reform schools."[276]

It's not a surprise that the unions were opposed to this, but it is good news that, when things get bad enough, it's possible to overrule the unions and advance some small reform plan. But think about how bad things have gotten in LAUSD. This success is unusual. Earlier this decade, the unions launched successful efforts to overturn voucher programs in Florida and Milwaukee—never mind the help those programs were providing to children.

## POLITICS TRUMPS EDUCATION

People often are shocked by the brazen politicization of the schools. Administrators and teachers, for instance, always are seeking out new ways to increase taxes and get parents to support bond measures (supported by tax increases) that enhance the local school budgets. Teachers unions are among the handful of most powerful interest groups in every state capitol. They are always pushing for larger budgets. At the local level, at times my kids come home with thinly veiled political letters from principals warning that if Measure X, Y or Z does not pass, then our kids will be suffering the results. Not long ago, the high school administrators urged kids to show up at a city council meeting to demand funds for a swimming pool. The letters and emails and robo-calls and mailers sent to our homes are transparently political—they represent the use of taxpayer resources to lobby for more tax dollars, even if they do follow the letter of the law and qualify as informational pieces because they don't have a "vote yes" tagline on them. Parents often complain also about some of the social engineering and political propaganda that passes for education curriculum these days. Sometimes activists get upset and try to lobby for specific reforms, but the bottom line is that public schools—being run by the government and funded by tax dollars—are purely political agencies. Because they are run by the government, the decisions made about them— ranging from funding levels to test requirements to history lessons—are made in a political environment, i.e., by administrators who answer to local elected bodies, which are subject to the whims of state officials.

Unions have learned most effectively to control all of those political bodies. So no wonder they get what they want and use terms such as "quality education" mainly as smokescreens to justify their budgets. Government schools are political by nature and the most aggressive political players will naturally control them. Libertarians like to talk about "concentrated benefits and dispersed costs." Those groups that gain the most from any governmental system have the incentive to organize to control those agencies. The costs of their benefits are dispersed among many people, so none of us has the same motivation to spend hours each week monitoring, say, school board meetings or reading curricula.

No wonder the vast majority of parents cannot stand up to the concentrated efforts of union organizers. Chester Finn, the former Reagan official who is now president of the Thomas B. Fordham Foundation, wrote in a *Washington Times* column that teachers unions have such enormous resources that they can thwart virtually any K-12 reform: "Combined [the American Federation of Teachers and the National Education Association] would comprise much the largest labor union in the land, and their millions of members pour hundreds of millions of dollars in dues into their national treasuries and those of their state and local affiliates. The actual figures are closely guarded but [author Peter] Brimelow estimates that the annual take totals a stupendous $1.25 billion."[277]

When a big political battle heats up, teachers unions typically place a surcharge on members' dues or they use their buildings as collateral to securitize low-interest loans against future dues to pay for big campaigns. In essence, they just write themselves whatever size check they need to fight the political battles at hand. Their opponents have to hustle for every dollar and typically are outspent 20 or 30 to one on every battle. Sometimes opponents win, but it's tough work and takes a convergence of events. One grandmother, named Eunice Cluck, spearheaded a campaign against an education parcel tax in Irvine with a $200 investment, and somehow stopped the combined forces of the unions and the business community (which often funds bond measures that pay for schools and infrastructure). The unions were so angry they complained that Eunice Cluck had violated campaign finance laws with her small amount of money taken from her own checkbook. But usually the big war chests from the unions roll over even decently funded opposition campaigns. And even when the good guys win one, they lose the long-term war. Often, activists battle a tax or bond proposal and actually win, especially in California where many such votes require a passage by a supermajority. But then the unions and their allies bide their time and come back the next election cycle. They almost always ultimately win after another election or two.

Here is Finn, again, writing on the sources of union influence (based on Brimelow's book, *The Worm in the Apple: How Teacher Unions are Destroying American Education*). He points to "the Teacher Trust's deep reserves of patience, relentlessness and discipline. Even when they lose a battle, they then end up winning the war because they outlast their opponents. A forceful governor like Tennessee's Lamar Alexander or Michigan's John Engler must eventually leave office. When he does, the union is still there, chewing away at unwanted reforms, putting caps and restrictions on charter-school laws, redirecting funds from voucher programs into class size reduction initiatives and emasculating 'alternative certification' by bringing teacher licensure under the aegis of an ostensibly independent (but, in reality, union- and ed-school-dominated) 'professional standards board.'"

This level of politicization is, according to the late Marshall Fritz, who headed the Alliance for the Separation of School and State, inherent in the nature of the government-run school system. He notes that schools were independent of the state from the 1620s to the 1840s and that the driving force for government control of education was the desire to promote "national unity." As a result, Fritz argues that schools put aside the bigger and most interesting questions about life—religion, philosophy, what he calls "the purpose question"—and focus instead on occupational success. Not that they've managed to do that particularly well, either. The answer is not to use the government to force schools to address these fundamental questions as some conservatives suggest, given that the current union-controlled environment will assure that such questions are answered in a stifled and insufficient way. The answer is a competitive system—where parents can send their kids to schools that are geared to the individual personalities of the students and the philosophical preferences of the parents. But union officials want to be sure that all Americans can choose only the education product they are offered at prices that cannot be negotiated.[278]

This national unity idea, in my view, is used by advocates of public schools to stifle complaints about the quality of education and to keep parents from focusing on problems within their school systems. During arguments over schooling, public school advocates often avoid arguments about educational quality and instead insist that public schools are necessary to inculcate a common culture. Liberals and conservatives alike will take that approach. One can almost hear the ghost of one of the most influential modern education philosophers, John Dewey, who, in his "My Pedagogic Creed," wrote, "I believe that the only true education comes through the stimulation of the child's powers by the demands of the social situations in which he finds himself. Through these demands he is stimulated to act as a member of a unity, to emerge from his original narrowness of action and feeling, and to conceive of himself from the standpoint of the welfare of the group to which he belongs. ...I believe that the school is primarily a social institution. Education being a social process, the school is simply that form of community life in which all those agencies are concentrated that will be most effective in bringing the child to share in the inherited resources of the race, and to use his own powers for social ends. I believe that education, therefore, is a process of living and not a preparation for future living."[279]

It's important to grasp the degree to which public school advocates embrace Dewey's reasoning and view the schools as institutions that mainly advocate the socialization of students into the prevailing wisdom of the day. They are, in a sense, centers for indoctrination, more than places for true learning. And those centers are dominated by unions, which assure that all the rules and regulations are written for the union's benefit. Given these parameters, it's unrealistic to expect that we are creating an educational system that will excel at educating students, let alone offer them a well-rounded education that enables them to address life's biggest questions.

Hence, American students placed 25th out of 30th in math literacy, according to a *Washington Examiner* column by Richard Berman. U.S. students, he noted, scored worse than students from impoverished Azerbaijan. American students scored 21st out of 30 developed countries in science literacy. Reading literacy scores were not tabulated, he wrote, due, ironically, to printing errors by American education officials. So even in the stated goals of preparing students for the work world, the current U.S. system is failing.[280]

Results remain poor despite constant increases in school funding in all states. The current system, Brimelow writes, is viewed "as a sort of religion or charitable endeavor rather than as an industry," which explains why more money always is considered better. "No consumer would boast about spending more on a purchase than was absolutely necessary. Why is education different?"[281]

Where does the money go?

To administration and bureaucracy, of course. One local school district was forcing kids into overcrowded trailers, yet was spending tens of millions of dollars building a Taj Mahal administration building on a bluff not far from the Pacific Ocean. In 1949-50, Brimelow wrote, schools employed 2.36 teachers for every administrator. In 2003, that number was 1.09 teachers for every administrator, and in six states the administrators outnumber the teachers. In Ohio, a report found that massive increases in public school spending over a decade (from the 1980s to the 1990s) resulted in most of the additional spending going to bureaucracy building. Does anyone believe this helps education? If a company raised prices and spent most of the additional money on offices and administrators, does anyone think that the consumer would be well served? Only in a school system insulated by tax funds and dominated by unions can this happen without any reform.

## NO REST FROM POLITICS

Even as California struggled with tough times and possible education cutbacks during the summer 2009 budget crisis, California Teacher Association officials were busy increasing dues and funding political initiatives—most of which have absolutely nothing to do with education.

CTA announced in summer 2009 a dues increase for its 340,000 members of about $22 a year and the NEA has announced an increase of $4 on top of the $1,000 in dues California teachers already pay to their unions annually, according to Los Angeles teacher Larry Sand, writing in the *San Diego Union-Tribune*. The increases are small amounts, but show how easy it is for the CTA and NEA to raise money to influence the political process. A teacher can get a $300 rebate if he goes through the cumbersome and often intimidating process of objecting to teacher union political causes, but there's no getting out of the bulk of the dues, which ostensibly are used for collective bargaining purposes. That figure, of course, includes paying the lavish salaries for CTA and NEA executives. The money, Sands adds, is deducted automatically from a teacher's paycheck. And he notes the degree to which the unions have funded measures such as universal health care, opposing California's Proposition 8 (which banned gay marriage), Planned Parenthood, District of Columbia statehood and other political causes that, regardless of what one thinks of them, have nothing to do with education.

In California, the CTA is an impediment not just to educational reform, but to any budgetary reform. Its war chest is so large that it must be reckoned with in almost every situation. A good example: the initiatives that Gov. Schwarzenegger and the state Legislature put on the ballot on May 19, 2009. These were bad measures, in my view, that would have increased taxes and put some insufficiently tight controls on spending to deal with a massive deficit. The unions were mixed on this one—they like tax increases, but some viewed the ever-so-modest spending reforms as too radical for their tastes.

In order to win the support of the powerful CTA for a spending cap and rainy day fund included in Proposition 1A, the governor and legislators put 1B on the ballot, which, according to the *Los Angeles Times*, "would send $9.3 billion to the state's school districts and community colleges in increments, starting in the 2011-12 fiscal year, to make up for earlier cutbacks in state funding."[282] The tactical move seemed clever, in that 1B would only go into effect if 1A passed. "Getting the backing of the California Teachers Assn. was a shrewd move by Schwarzenegger, who was unsuccessful in 2005 when he tried to pass several ballot measures that were unanimously opposed by the state's most powerful unions," according to a *Los Angeles Times* article. But the *Times*' editorial board was appalled at the obvious payoff to CTA to keep it on the side of the slate of initiatives. The ploy successfully split the state's most powerful unions, but voters—understandably angry at a state that can't stop spending and at the proposed extension of tax increases—wisely and resoundingly rejected most of the initiatives. The governor and Legislature came back with a better deal that doesn't raise taxes, although the deficit immediately started to rise. This was an instance of the CTA losing an election—but the creation of 1B speaks to its power and the fear that politicians have of crossing the union and its massive amounts of political cash.

Over the years, the CTA has racked up far more victories than losses. A *Los Angeles Times* article from Sept. 28, 2005 focuses on how the teachers union is knee-deep in that year's budget battles. It noted that the union had spent $21 million to stop a school voucher initiative, spent $9 million to get statewide approval of construction bonds worth $25 billion, gave a half-million bucks to Schwarzenegger's successful 2002 campaign to start after-school programs, and spent $10 million over five years to get local bond measures passed. "This year, none of the 14 bills that the union opposed made it out of the Legislature, except with changes that placated the group and its allies," Jordan Rau reported. Between 2000 and 2004, the CTA spent $47 million on ballot initiatives, $13.6 million on lobbying and $10 million on local and state candidates.[283]

The unions also fight against testing and any standardized measurement of student achievement. One newspaper article quoted teachers who complained that they had to spend most of their time teaching subject matter and had less time for those feel-good curricula. The CTA issued a position paper accusing the Obama administration of "repeating the past mistakes of NCLB [No Child Left Behind], including an over-reliance on test scores as an accurate measure of student achievement and support for interventions that do not have a track record of success, such as unregulated charter schools and compensation tied to test scores."[284]

What the union wants is a complex student assessment system—apparently one that only its members can understand. The goal of the CTA and teachers unions in general has always been to make it as difficult as possible to evaluate students and teachers. This way no one can be blamed and it won't even be possible to accurately pinpoint the failures. And, of course, virtually every position the CTA takes at some point ends up taking a slap at charter schools and any other educational idea that imposes any form of rigor or competition on the teaching process. These folks have a monopoly system, and virtually unlimited access to other people's money, yet their big fears remain objective analysis and competition.

Many people from across the political spectrum have mixed feelings on the current testing regimen. There's more to being educated than the mastery of tests, and my kids often complain about the endless teaching to tests that goes on these days. But the movement toward testing was a reaction to the days when school was often filled with puffery and where many schools failed to teach even the most basic standards. Here again the solution is a competitive system rather than legislative mandates, but the standards and tests at least provide some more objective measure of what schools are or aren't teaching. Testing at least assures that the kids are learning something, even if that something is determined by the legislature. This isn't just an American problem, by the way. The London *Telegraph* featured an April 2008 article by George Bridges decrying the way the country's National Union of Teachers had been striking—not just for higher pay, but to reduce the testing and educational standards, which they argued place "intolerable pressures on children." Actually, standards place intolerable pressures on teachers, many of whom fear that a strict testing regimen will spotlight their lack of teaching skills.

## LIBERAL HYPOCRISY

It's hard to understand how liberals—who claim to speak up for the hopes and aspirations of the poor and minorities—are willing to put up with the political dominance of unions, and teachers unions in particular, that clearly use their power to promote their group's specific financial interests. There's no doubt that union control of public schools has squelched reform proposals that would lead to a better life for students, especially for those in the inner cities.

*San Diego Union-Tribune* blogger Chris Reed asked liberals, in a May 14, 2009 post, why they think the concentration of Democratic power in public-sector unions is a good thing: "There is no evidence that this political power is being used to help the poor, the needy, the sick. Instead, the opposite is true. ... [P]ublic employees ... have by and large been spared because they have demanded cuts come elsewhere—which almost always translates into less help for the poor, the needy, the sick." In an August 10, 2009 post, Reed referred to a column by the *Los Angeles Times'* liberal columnist Steve Lopez that acknowledged that unions are an impediment to helping poor kids in Los Angeles. Lopez wrote, "[I]t's time for a change, and the spineless Democrats who dominate the state Legislature should quit counting all the cash piped into their pockets by the teacher lobby and start thinking about what's best for kids. Until they do we're stuck with the status quo: shameful dropout rates, middle-class parents abandoning public education and bitter wars between districts and teacher unions."[285]

Maybe there is some hope for reform as intellectually honest liberals such as Lopez recognize the truth about public choice theory: government workers, including teachers and their union representatives, use their power to advance their interests, not the interests of their charges. In public schools, as Reed notes, they use kids mainly as "props" to support their jobs programs.

Dana Goldstein, associate editor of the liberal *American Prospect*, wrote a fascinating 2008 column reporting on an event at the Democratic National Convention. Although Goldstein is defensive of teachers unions, she wrote about an unusual pre-convention event in Denver, by a group called Democrats for Education Reform: "The event, billed 'Ed Challenge for Change,' was sponsored by a coalition of foundations, nonprofits, and businesses supporting the charter-school movement, including Ed in '08, the advocacy group founded by Bill Gates and real-estate mogul Eli Broad. The evening provided a truly unusual spectacle at a convention: A megawatt group of Democrats, including Mayor Cory Booker of Newark, Mayor Adrian Fenty of Washington, D.C., and former Gov. Roy Romer of Colorado, bashed teachers unions for an hour. Amid the approving audience were Rep. James Clyburn of South Carolina, an icon of the civil-rights movement; Mayor Michael Nutter of Philadelphia, (in)famous as a high-profile African American Hillary Clinton endorser; and Mayor David Cicilline of Providence, the reformer of that once-Mob-ridden New England city."[286]

Even some Democrats realize that unions and dominance of the education system by a group of self-interested public employees is resulting in a disastrous educational system, especially for the nation's poor people. These are among the many real-world results of letting public servants become our masters.

## QUASHING VOLUNTEERISM

Just as California's state worker unions sued to stop volunteers from cleaning up trash around the American River near Sacramento, so have teachers unions flexed their muscle to stop volunteerism and philanthropy at public schools.

Reason Foundation's Lisa Snell, writing a column for the Heartland Institute, documented some of these shocking displays of political power for the sake of union members and at the expense of students:

"In October [2003], the Mayor of Detroit and Michigan Governor Jennifer Granholm turned away a $200 million gift offered to create 15 small charter high schools in Detroit. Philanthropist Robert Thompson wanted to build the small high schools; he would have charged just $1 a year in rent if the school operators maintained a 90 percent graduation rate.

"The governor decided to veto the charter school bill that included Thompson's proposal after Detroit teachers shut down the city's schools with a one-day walkout on September 25. More than 3,000 teachers held a demonstration at the state capitol. Despite the hundreds of students attending low-performing high schools in Detroit, the bottom line for the city's teacher union was that more charter schools would mean less money for the district."[287]

Snell also wrote about how the San Diego teachers union stopped parent volunteers from cleaning up an elementary school. She quoted the head of the union: "What happens when the district gets in better financial shape—why rehire the landscape crews when the work is being done free? If people really want to help, they should be writing their elected officials about the budget."

Snell explained that laws banning volunteer work at schools are common throughout the United States. We know what the priorities are of these unions: inflating their pay and benefits and protecting their jobs. They claim to be professionals—indeed, teachers had resisted unionization earlier in the century by pointing to their status as professional workers rather than Teamsters—but then engage in the kind of work stoppages and self-interested hardball politicking and picketing that are detrimental to students and the public.

The reason these preposterous restrictions get approved is that—as is the case with public unions at the City Hall and other levels—the unions control virtually every decision maker in the process. "And so what you have in many jurisdictions is, in effect, the union sitting on both sides of the bargaining table," said Stefan Gleason, vice president of the National Right to Work Foundation, in a 2002 speech. "The management is also the politician who is elected with union support. At that point, there's really no one representing the interests of the people. And as far as those independent-minded teachers who may not be in lock-step with the union hierarchy, they're not represented in that situation either. In fact, even the National School Boards Association and its state affiliates have been, to a great extent, co-opted into supporting this union monopoly model of running public schools, and they are not very helpful in getting school board members educated about what's happening or equipped to challenge it."[288]

When only one party is represented, then that party always gets its way.

## INCOMPETENCE AND WASTE

When government employees are in charge of things, and unions dominate the discussions, then tax dollars are frittered away on the most absurd projects and priorities. Individuals and private companies and private schools are incredibly careful with their money—if not, it can mean the difference between operating in the black or the red. Governments spend Other People's Money, so it's an entirely different story. After Santa Ana, Calif., voters passed a bond measure to fund school construction, the union-controlled school board immediately passed a Project Labor Agreement. PLAs require that bidders on construction and other projects not only pay union wages (every government bidder has to do that, whether union or open shop) but employ union labor. That drives up the cost of construction by around 25 percent because it cuts out a large chunk of the competition. Many companies do not want to become union companies for obvious reasons, and they are unable then to bid on projects even if they pay union wages. With fewer bidders, school districts (taxpayers) end up paying higher bid rates.

If you were taking bids for a home construction project you would want to get the most for your money. Instead, those entrusted with public dollars pass policies that assure that the public gets the least number of projects for the money. Typically, school districts—when they are convincing voters to vote for bond measures—will circulate a list of school projects that will be completed if the bond passes. Almost always, that list is quickly diminished and the districts complete only a portion of the promised projects. The districts always blame rising materials and labor costs, but one of the chief reasons is they give in to union demands for monopoly labor. As Santa Ana activist and blogger Art Pedroza writes, "[O]ver the years we have seen PLAs crop up even here in Orange County, and as expected they have been a negative return for public stakeholders. Nativo Lopez, a trustee on the Santa Ana Unified School Board, was recalled after he forced passage of a PLA. As is typically the case, a bond measure had been passed by voters to fund construction of new schools. Project costs soared under the PLA, which the board eventually cancelled. There is word now that a second bond measure may be presented to voters, in order to get the money to finish some of the planned projects that floundered under the PLA. Voters should insist that any future bond measures should be protected from a PLA yet to come."[289]

I quote here from a 2006 *Orange County Register* article regarding the Anaheim Union High School District's building program:

"Mismanagement of a $330 million construction program forced Anaheim Union officials Thursday to drop all but eight schools from a 22-campus improvement project. Costs for the eight schools ballooned from $177 million to $255 million because of rising prices, budgeting errors and a multitude of oversight failures at the high school district."[290]

The district couldn't even find a lot of the money and wanted to go right back to voters for another bond to backfill the money it blew from the past bond. This is not an aberration, but is completely typical.

The poster child for the mismanagement of building projects is the Belmont Learning Complex disaster in Los Angeles. Writes Susan Anderson in a May 2000 article in the *Nation* magazine:

"This site was to be the home of the Belmont Learning Complex, called the most expensive school in America, with its $200 million price tag. The development was originally conceived in 1985 by the Los Angeles Unified School District (LAUSD) as a middle school to alleviate the severe overcrowding in the area. The project ballooned into a planned thirty-five-acre, state-of-the-art, Internet-wired senior high campus, with a shopping mall to jump-start commercial development in the area, 120 affordable apartments to address the housing crunch, classrooms and innovative 'academies' for 5,000 students. More than ten years later, however, the Belmont development is mired in controversy over 'waste, fraud and abuse' (as one state assemblyman put it), lack of accountability and the public's discovery of what at least some in the school district already knew—that explosive methane gas, poisonous hydrogen sulfide, volatile organic compounds such as acetone, the carcinogen benzene and residual crude oil saturated the earth where the school was being built, on top of a former oilfield and industrial site."[291]

The school eventually opened 20 years and hundreds of millions of dollars later. As Peter Brimelow's book explains, the public school system reflects the problems in any socialistic system—political power dominates, resources are misallocated, bureaucracies become huge and unruly, decision-making gets made at the top and is imposed on everyone. No wonder the Belmont fiasco reads like something that came right out of communist Eastern Europe.

This is what happens when government bureaucrats, driven by political priorities and union demands, build things. Disasters happen in the private sector also, but in those cases private investors, rather than taxpayers, pay the freight. In those cases, consumers shop elsewhere. When LAUSD bungles something this terribly, student health and education is at stake. Taxpayers are at risk. Resources get diverted from more useful purposes. The price to pay for union dominance and bureaucratic monopoly control is much more than the bill for unfunded liabilities.

CHAPTER SEVEN

# HOW WE GOT HERE, WHERE WE'RE GOING

What many people nowadays consider an evil is not bureaucracy as such, but the expansion of the sphere in which bureaucratic management is applied. This expansion is the unavoidable consequence of the progressive restriction of the individual citizen's freedom, of the inherent trend of present-day economic and social policies toward the substitution of government control for private initiative. People blame bureaucracy, but what they really have in mind are the endeavors to make the state socialist and totalitarian.
—LUDWIG VON MISES, *Bureaucracy*

Few column topics elicit a more diametrically opposed reaction from readers than the subject of public employees. There are many people who view government officials as de facto heroes, as "first responders" and "educators" who perform vital tasks. Then there are those who view such officials as potential threats to our freedom and our tax dollars. I've always disliked bureaucracy in general, and get particularly frustrated being forced to jump through the often senseless rules and regulations enforced by oftentimes surly or uninterested workers. Anyone who has visited a Department of Motor Vehicles, or who has dealt with the court system, or a city building inspector, understands this latter perspective. Those who celebrate government workers tend to be the workers themselves or members of their families, although many average folks embrace that outlook when they think about police, firefighters and teachers. As this book has shown, people in those professions—and the unions that represent them—have been the most aggressive at exploiting such good will to expand their pay, benefits and special protections.

As Mises understood, bureaucracy is a cumbersome way to manage things, but it isn't necessarily evil. "America is an old democracy and the talk about the dangers of bureaucracy is a new phenomenon in this country," he wrote. "Only in recent years have people become aware of the menace of bureaucracy, and they consider bureaucracy not an instrument of democratic government but, on the contrary, the worst enemy of freedom and democracy. To these objections we must answer again that bureaucracy in itself is neither good nor bad. It is a method of management which can be applied in different spheres of human activity. There is a field, namely, the handling of the apparatus of government, in which bureaucratic methods are required by necessity."[292]

In other words, bureaucracy is simply a mechanism for running the government. Our society needs some of it, just as we need some government to handle, as the founders understood, some limited, clearly defined tasks mostly related to the protection of citizens' life, liberty and property. The problem starts when government expands beyond its legitimate tasks. That leads to the increased bureaucratization of areas of our life that should be left to private initiative. When government expands, the number of government workers expands, and the more that we all become subject to their dictates. That's the real problem—the expansion of government power and bureaucratic control beyond its proper sphere and into areas that should be handled in the private marketplace.

There are many reasons government grows. Writing during the Reagan era, as government grew even though the president was committed ostensibly to limiting government, Llewellyn Rockwell, president of the Ludwig von Mises Institute, pointed to the power of interest groups (many of which are government employee interest groups), the permanency of the government (the same people run things regardless of who wins elections), a media that supports big government, the use of crisis to keep people dependent on government, economic interventionism (the government has intervened so much that it continually needs to intervene) and the lack of education at the school and college level regarding free markets. It's not just the bureaucrats and their interest groups that explain the phenomenon, but it is a big part of the problem.

My argument in this chapter is simple: As government expands, our freedoms recede and bureaucratic control advances. Government—and the people who work for government—grab a greater share of power and intrude in areas that should be left up to individuals. Bigger government means more government employees. Those employees then become a permanent lobby for continual government growth. Public sector unionization is a fairly recent phenomenon and its expansion has led to the rapid plundering of the public treasury for the benefit of union members. The results of all this are less freedom, higher taxes, more public debt, more offensive police-state-style incidents and an overall lower standard of living. As Mises pointed out, bureaucracy isn't a problem as long as the bureaus are small and limited in their power and the bureaucrats aren't the ones calling the shots. Unfortunately, the opposite has taken place.

Government workers often say, "We pay taxes, also." Their suggestion is that they have a reason to want to keep the growth of government limited, also. But this is a case, again, of concentrated benefits and dispersed costs. As taxpayers, public employees do pay more taxes when taxes go up, just like everyone else. But they get such an intense benefit from the expansion of government that it's a great trade-off for them. This brings us back again to public choice theory, which was discussed in Chapter 1. It's the idea that government employees and elected officials are not noble doers of the public good, but regular human beings—good, bad and in between, just like everybody else—who seek to advance their personal interests. They seek to expand their departments (often for the best reasons, because they believe in what they are doing), enhance their power and increase their pay and benefits. Old civics-textbook theories of government that miss this level of natural self-interest miss some of the key reasons that decisions are made in the public sector. Yes, there's truth in the old theories, in which the public clamors for public services and elects officials to give those things to them, and those officials then empower the bureaucracy to implement the task at hand. But the permanent bureaucracy is constantly pushing its own prerogatives. Sure, you need some of this... but the beast keeps getting bigger and more powerful.

"Public choice models of bureaucracy imply that these same government employees may be partly responsible for the size and scope of governance within those territories," wrote Roger Congleton for the Center for Study of Public Choice at George Mason University in Fairfax, Va. "Such a possibility is neglected in pure electoral models which implicitly regard government agents to be faithful public servants of the pivotal voter or, equivalently, to be so constrained by political institutions that only policies advancing the pivotal voter's interests can be adopted."[293]

He further explains the theory that, "…bureaucrats have a personal stake in the size of their agency's budget and discretion over that budget that leads them to lobby for and secure larger budgets than would be optimal for the median voter. … As an agency's budget increases, every public spirited bureaucrat expects to be able to do a better job of advancing the agency's policy agendas and fulfilling its responsibilities. As an agency's budget increases, every bureaucrat must also realize that personal opportunities for advancement and perks tend to improve. Moreover, insofar as monitoring individual performance becomes more difficult as agencies increase in size, increased budgets tend to be associated with greater discretion. As discretion increases, the ability of bureaucrats to use bureau resources to satisfy their own preferences for policy, travel or leisure increases. In sum, bureaucrats have many reasons to prefer larger to smaller budgets, other things being equal, and larger budgets imply larger governments."

Congleton uses economic theory and economic models to explain what seems pretty obvious to this observer of politics: the bureaucracy is its own special interest that advocates for its members. There's a reason that the most influential political lobbies in the country include teachers unions, municipal employee unions, the League of Cities, the police and firefighter unions, prison guards and other government lobbies. The government growth and government worker connection perhaps is a chicken-and-egg kind of thing. I'm not sure which came first. But there's no question that, by any standard or measure, government has grown, the number of its employees has grown and their pay and benefits have grown. So has the government's tax take, the amount of public debt and its regulatory control over our lives. Let's take a look at that growth.

## GROWTH IN GOVERNMENT

There are many ways to evaluate the growth in government and many reasons for it (many of which have to do with the preferences of voters rather than the activities of government employees), but as government gets bigger, public servants have more power over us and more opportunity to tap into the treasury. My personal favorite way to evaluate government growth is the Tax Freedom Day analysis by the Tax Foundation. The group figures out the total average tax payments of Americans and then reports how many days of the year we work purely for the government. Tax Freedom Day is the first day of the year that we work for ourselves rather than for the bureaucrats. The earlier the day of the year, the less we pay in taxes, the later the day, the more we pay in taxes.

According to its April 2009 report, Tax Freedom Day for 2009 was April 13. That means that the average American works 3-½ months of the year just to pay the tax man. The foundation reports that the 2009 day is two weeks earlier than in 2008 because "the recession has reduced tax collections even faster than it has reduced income." But it offers this sobering thought: "Nevertheless, in 2009, Americans will pay more in taxes than they will spend on food, clothing and housing combined."[294]

For a quick comparison, the Tax Foundation looks at Tax Freedom Day and all taxes as a percentage of income going back to 1900. In that year, Tax Freedom Day was January 22 and the average American paid 5.9 percent of his income in taxation. Since then, Tax Freedom Day has gotten progressively later and the total tax take has gotten progressively higher, with a few tiny aberrations here and there. In the 1940s, Tax Freedom Day moved into March, with about 20-plus percent of income going to the tax man. The worst was 2000, when Tax Freedom Day came on May 3 and taxes hit 33.6 percent of income. This year, taxes consume 28.2 percent of income, and they appear likely to go up again given the political situation in Washington, D.C. and the state capitols. On a state-by-state basis, Alaska has the lowest taxes, with Tax Freedom Day coming on March 23. Connecticut has the highest taxes with Tax Freedom Day coming on April 30. Tax Freedom Day comes in California on April 20. That's a long time to work for the government.

This analysis is great because it describes the growth of government in terms that mean something to the average person—the percentage that it takes from our earnings. But Tax Freedom Day also misses the enormous amount of debt and the huge unfunded liabilities caused by government spending. Those are real costs that will eventually need to be paid. A liberal physician acquaintance is an advocate for the Medicare system. He explained that it costs less to administer than private systems. I asked him to reconcile that point with the trillions of dollars in unfunded liabilities—something he refused to do. This is like running up the credit card and not counting the debt, but looking only at the monthly minimum payment and declaring that it's such a good deal!

Let's look at the debt numbers. Deficits and debts represent government spending and control, even if the money is largely borrowed. Large debts do cost taxpayers money in the here and now, as interest rates go up and debt service consumes larger portions of government budgets and crowds out other things. Government borrowing also inflates the price of money, and other prices, for consumers. Eventually, the debt must be paid or defaulted upon. This is real spending, with real costs and it will cause real problems for future generations of Americans. The U.S. Debt Clock Web site pins the national debt at more than $11.7 trillion or $38,138 per citizen. That's almost 100 percent of the U.S. Gross Domestic Product. People who downplay the growth in government spending often compare the gross debt to the percentage of the GDP, with the thinking that the nation can handle more debt as it becomes wealthier. But debt as a portion of GDP has grown from about 52 percent in 1940 to 33.3 percent in 1980 to almost 100 percent today. That's not a good trend line, no matter how one justifies it.[295]

As of August 2009, U.S. spending topped $2.6 trillion annually, or more than $8,400 per person. That's just the federal government. The federal budget deficit topped $1.2 trillion—a figure that not long ago would have been a debt rather than deficit number. During the last four years of the Bush administration, the national debt basically doubled from around $5.8 trillion, thanks not just to the Iraq War but to a massive expansion in domestic spending. The Obama administration is trying to outdo the Bush administration with its stimulus spending and New Deal-style spending programs. The national debt increased more than $1 trillion in the first seven months of Barack Obama's presidency. The debt clock Web site also points to the nation's unfunded liabilities—the debt load to pay for all those pension and health-care promises. The amount is just under $59 trillion—or almost $192,000 per citizen. That figure only counts Medicare, Social Security and the prescription drug benefit. Local and state government pension plans and other unfunded liabilities add to that. The national debt clock in New York City ran out of digits in 2008.

To provide a calm idea of the impact of all this debt spending, this is from a 2008 speech by Richard Fisher, CEO of the Federal Reserve of Dallas:[296]

"Let's say you and I…and every U.S. citizen who is alive today decided to fully address this unfunded liability through lump-sum payments from our own pocketbooks, so that all of us and all future generations could be secure in the knowledge that we and they would receive promised benefits in perpetuity. How much would we have to pay if we split the tab? Again, the math is painful. With a total population of 304 million, from infants to the elderly, the per-person payment to the federal treasury would come to $330,000. This comes to $1.3 million per family of four—over 25 times the average household's income.

"Clearly, once-and-for-all contributions would be an unbearable burden. Alternatively, we could address the entitlement shortfall through policy changes that would affect ourselves and future generations. For example, a permanent 68 percent increase in federal income tax revenue—from individual and corporate taxpayers—would suffice to fully fund our entitlement programs. Or we could instead divert 68 percent of current income-tax revenues from their intended uses to the entitlement system, which would accomplish the same thing.

"Suppose we decided to tackle the issue solely on the spending side. It turns out that total discretionary spending in the federal budget, if maintained at its current share of GDP in perpetuity, is 3 percent larger than the entitlement shortfall. So all we would have to do to fully fund our nation's entitlement programs would be to cut discretionary spending by 97 percent. …I hope that gives you some idea of just how large the problem is. And just to drive an important point home, these spending cuts or tax increases would need to be made immediately and maintained in perpetuity to solve the entitlement deficit problem. Discretionary spending would have to be reduced by 97 percent not only for our generation, but for our children and their children and every generation of children to come. And similarly on the taxation side, income tax revenue would have to rise 68 percent and remain that high forever. Remember, though, I said tax *revenue*, not tax *rates*. Who knows how much individual and corporate tax rates would have to change to increase revenue by 68 percent?"

Taxes are up, debt spending is up and the number of government workers is growing rapidly—we already learned from past chapters that their pay and benefit levels are skyrocketing also. At all levels, state and local government employment grew by 13 percent across the United States from 1994 to 2004. The number of judicial and legal employees increased by 28 percent. The number of public safety workers increased by 21 percent. The number of teachers increased by 22 percent. The invaluable *Grandfather Economic Report*, by Michael Hodges, uses the Bureau of Labor Statistics to chart growth in state and local government employees since 1946.[297] That number has increased from 3.3 million employees to 19.8 million employees—a 492 percent increase as the country's population increased by 115 percent. Since 1999, the number of state and local government employees has increased by 13 percent compared to a growth of 9 percent in the population, he reported. Looked at another way, the United States had 2.3 state and local government employees per 100 citizens in 1946 and has 6.5 state and local government employees per 100 citizens now. In 1947, he wrote, 78 percent of the national income went to the private sector, 16 percent to the federal sector and 6 percent to the state and local government sector. Now, 54 percent of the economy is private, 28 percent goes to the feds and 18 percent goes to state and local governments.

"While state and local governments employ over 20 million people already, the federal government has become the largest single employer in the country with almost three million employees (not including contractors and military personnel)," wrote Alex Newman in the *New American*. "For comparison, after the New Deal from 1933 to 1939 there were about 700,000."[298]

I fear that the nation has reached critical mass—the number of government employees at every level has gotten so high that it is politically impossible to roll back the bureaucracy and rein in the costs. It's disturbing that the federal government is the nation's largest employer. For a real shocker, consider this article from the free-market Mackinac Center in Michigan: "Michigan has crossed an employment Rubicon of sorts. The BLS shows that 2006 was the first full year that total government employment in Michigan exceeded the number of manufacturing employees (this BLS data set goes back to 1956 and also is seasonally adjusted). Michiganians working for the automobile and other manufacturing industries are now outnumbered by government workers supported by taxpayers."[299]

A 2006 study "On the Size and Growth of Government" by the *Federal Reserve Bank of St. Louis Review* took a careful look at the issue, but concluded, "The size of the U.S. federal government, as well as state and local governments, increased dramatically during the 20th century." In every category—per capita expenditures, federal expenditures as a percent of GDP, local and state government expenditures, etc.—the government not only grew, but grew dramatically. It pointed to one theory arguing that "government bureaucrats maximize the size of their agencies' budgets in accordance with their own preferences and are able to do so because of the unique monopoly position of the bureaucrat."[300] The Federal Reserve Bank doesn't argue that this explains the whole reason for massive government growth but concludes that it remains a realistic partial explanation.

Government has grown in all ways and all levels. But even these obvious areas of growth—in the workforce, in annual spending, in taxation, in debt, in unfunded liabilities—only tell a portion of the story. Actually, the federal workforce had declined somewhat after the end of the Cold War, but as the Brookings Institution's Paul Light explains in his "Fact Sheet on the New True Size of Government," there was a massive growth in "off-budget" jobs—contract and grant jobs. These are considered private jobs, but they are not. They are government-funded jobs that conduct essentially government tasks. Writes Light: "According to new estimates generated on behalf of the Brookings Institution's Center for Public Service, federal contracts and grants generated just over 8 million jobs in 2002, up from just under 7 million in 1999, and 7.5 million in 1990. When these 'off-budget' jobs created by contracts and grants jobs are added to the 'on-budget' headcount composed of civil service, uniformed military personnel, and postal service jobs, the 'true size' of the federal workforce stood at 12.1 million in October, 2002 up from 11 million in October 1999."[301]

And even tallying those "off-budget" jobs does not tell the whole story of a quickly growing federal Leviathan. The government's regulatory growth has been phenomenal, and this speaks directly to the growth of government power and to expanded powers of local, state and federal bureaucrats. Back to the *Grandfather Economic Report*, which concludes that "complying with government regulations consumes $1.4 trillion" or 14.9 percent of the economy. That equals about $4,600 a person, he wrote, added to the already high $13,568 per person spent by government at all levels. This regulatory burden exacts real costs on the economy and on individual freedom. As the report points out, "Even if government should hold at current ratios, but continue to accelerate unfunded regulatory mandates to the productive private sector, then the effective government, non-productive share of the economy will continue to increase at the expense of the private sector. It would be naïve to believe regulatory costs will decline per capita (and as a percent of the economy) as long as total government size and spending remain large. As an example, the *State & Local Government Report* shows such employees growing in numbers faster than the general population. A rising quantity of government employees does not normally result in fewer regulations, of less detail—quite the contrary."[302]

It's a disturbing picture that portends poorly for the future.

## FROM CIVIL SERVICE TO UNIONIZATION

Government workers rarely have a clue about how employment matters are handled in the private sector. Whenever anyone questions the fairness of unionization for government workers, these workers complain that they could otherwise get fired for any reason without union protections. Welcome to the real world. Government workers should try things outside the government world where that's largely how things work. You produce and make your boss happy or you lose your job. Even if you do a good job, you are still dependent on the overall success of the enterprise and the economy. It's bizarre that government workers think that they should be exempt from the same rules that apply to everybody else. But their claims about the necessity of unions to protect them are wrong given that they are part of the civil service system, which provides vast protections for government workers, regardless of whether or not they have union representation.

The U.S. Office of Personnel Management, which is the agency that manages the federal civil service workforce, produced an interesting book (a hagiography, but that's to be expected) about the history of the federal civil service called *Biography of an Ideal*. In the early federal administrations, there were few major controversies regarding the government workforce. For starters, there weren't that many government jobs and they were mostly clerical in nature and the amount of government money in those days "was not temptingly high." Furthermore, the first presidents were the founders of the nation who were motivated, to a large degree, by high-minded ideals. They weren't about to get into office as a means to enrich themselves and their families, although the book points to some job-related controversies. But as time went on and idealism faded, the nation entered into the era of the spoils system, where winning office was viewed as a means to enrich one's political allies, friends and family members. On the East Coast that tradition continues to this day. It is indeed a revolting and low-minded spectacle, something the OPM book refers to as a "plague of locusts."[303]

*Biography of an Ideal* quotes from an 1870 civil service reform activist named George William Curtis:

"Every four years, the whole machinery of the Government is pulled to pieces. The country presents a most ridiculous, revolting, and disheartening spectacle. The business of the nation and the legislation of Congress are subordinated to the distribution of plunder among eager partisans. Presidents, secretaries [of departments], senators, representatives are dogged, hunted, besieged, besought, denounced, and they become mere office brokers. The country seethes with intrigue and corruption. Economy, patriotism, honesty, honor, seem to have become words of no meaning."

The goal of civil service reform was to professionalize the growing federal workforce, eliminate the spoils system and create an orderly merit-based system to run the nation's bureaucracies. According to the book, civil service reform was an issue that had modest support from voters, the president and Congress, but not much of significance—beyond a few regulatory changes—was likely to take place after the 1880 election of James A. Garfield as president. But then Garfield was assassinated by Charles Guiteau, described as an eccentric man who believed he had a claim to a federal patronage job. The book quotes from an 1881 *Harper's* editorial:

"But for the practice which we have tolerated in this country for half a century, and which has become constantly more threatening and perilous, Guiteau would not have felt that working for the party gave him a claim to reward, or a right to demand such a reward as his due and to feel wronged if he did not get it. This dire calamity is part of the penalty we pay for permitting a practice for which as a public benefit not a solitary word can be urged, and which, while stimulating the deadliest passions, degrades our politics and corrupts our national character. The spoils system is a vast public evil."

The OPM publication offers, obviously, a celebration of the events that created OPM and the federal bureaucracy that it oversees. It doesn't deal with the massive flaws in the civil service system. But few people question the wisdom of moving away from the crass spoils system. Still, a system designed to choose government workers based on merit and protect them from political payback has evolved into one that rewards workers based on seniority and makes it nearly impossible to fire or correct them or even to move them around in a more efficient manner. The civil service system creates vast protections for government workers, and such a system has spread from the federal level down through every government bureau and agency.

OPM highlights the principles of the merit system. Basically, recruitment should be from qualified individuals and from across the widest spectrum of society, all employees and applicants should be treated fairly, pay should be based on excellence in performance, employees should maintain high levels of integrity, and—most significantly—employees should be "protected against arbitrary action, personal favoritism or coercion for partisan political purposes" and "prohibited from using their official authority or influence for the purpose of interfering with or affecting the result of an election or a nomination for election." Employees are also given whistleblower protections, so they are free to disclose information if they believe government officials are breaking the law, abusing authority or engaging in a gross waste of funds.

That's the history and the theory. Again, it's not an altogether unreasonable system given the alternative. But the reality is that civil service workers are afforded an absurd level of protection. As *Slate* magazine's Brendan Koerner wrote in a 2002 article about Democratic insistence that Department of Homeland Security workers be granted full civil service protections, "Even in the most egregious cases, dismissing a career appointee can be a drawn-out process. Since civil servants are considered to 'own' their jobs, they are entitled to due process before their property can be seized. Axed employees are entitled to in-person hearings, a right guaranteed by President John F. Kennedy in 1962. If that fails, the employee can appeal to the independent Merit Systems Protection Board, created by President Nixon in 1974. ... Hearings and appeals are not limited to terminations but can concern demotions, reprimands and performance appraisals, too."

That was the first time in years that the federal government has had serious policy discussions about the nature of civil service protections. To its credit, the George W. Bush administration tried to reform the national personnel system with regard to the creation of the then-new Department of Homeland Security. He called for the replacement of 2,000 pages of personnel rules with a broad standard that allowed flexibility in employment. "In all likelihood, Bush kicked off the most far-reaching reform of the federal civil service in more than a century by declaring that with its current personnel system, the government can't win the war on terrorism," wrote Brian Friel in *Government Executive* magazine. That's a reasonable concern given what we've seen in this book about the inflexibility of government work rules, about the impossibility of firing bad workers and about a workforce that, quite frankly, doesn't have to hustle or go the extra mile given the incentives and job security. This certainly impedes the ability of the government to react to terrorism threats. (But Eugene McCarthy's cynical quotation is apt: "The only thing that saves us from bureaucracy is inefficiency. An efficient bureaucracy is the greatest threat to liberty.")[304]

Friel is a defender of the current system, but he goes into great detail about the mind-numbingly complex rules that govern the pay scales and performance evaluations of civil servants. He also makes it clear that federal managers play games with the system to get around the rules. Federal managers, for instance, are supposed to follow the "rule of three"—hiring from among the top-three qualified candidates. There are many ways to interpret that demand and managers can easily rig the criteria to assure that the preferred candidate is selected, Friel notes. The civil service system has so many restrictions on pay that it's impossible to reward good workers—that's apparently by design as a way to avoid "favoritism." My wife has worked in the federal government and the system virtually drives out the most talented people, who simply can't stand the way seniority is rewarded at the expense of skill. Bottom line: civil service offers protection against firing. Friel tells a joke that sums it up: "Have you heard the one about the drunk Border Patrol agent? Obviously, he walks into a bar. But then he goes to work and, still intoxicated, lets a terrorist into the country. The punch line is he doesn't get fired, at least not for 30 days. Or maybe it's 540 days, depending on who's telling the story."[305]

One of the costs of a system that puts the prerogatives of the worker above the needs of the employer and taxpayer is that it becomes much more difficult for the agencies to perform even those tasks that are important and legitimate. News reports following the 9/11 attacks explained that the FBI had been provided mounds of evidence from the French government about Osama bin Laden before the attacks, but the agency never got around to translating the documents from French into English. That's bureaucracy and civil service in action—and there's a potentially high price to pay for it even though no freedom-loving person would want a bureaucracy that's too well run or efficient.

I like how one Atlantic City blogger explained civil service in response to an article involving some abusive city employee: "Civil service ensures that a city government employee can work for a few years, earn civil service protection, and then relax their work effort to the slow monotony of government bureaucracy."[306] The city of Seattle Web site has posted a civil service overview sheet that explains to employees their many protections. It details the appeals process for any termination, suspension or demotion. And then at the end it points out that union members can choose to use the union's grievance process and that "Union membership does not preclude an employee from utilizing the Civil Service Commission."[307]

So we've created a system with some of the most amazing worker protections ever developed ... and then we add union representation and protections on top of that system. We can't be surprised if this creates a government sector immune from change and bureaucracy filled with people who don't have to work particularly hard given that they know they can't be fired. There are real costs to the taxpayer and the public for these kinds of systems.

But whatever one's view of the civil service system, why exactly is there any need to have public-sector unions that offer protections on top of it?

## SOLIDARITY FOREVER!

Unionization has a long history in the United States, even though, as Morgan Reynolds explained in an article for the Ludwig von Mises Institute, in colonial times "the unions were far from respectable; in fact, they had a well-earned reputation for being antisocial, even criminal. ... Private property, freedom of contract, competition and freedom of movement across occupations (slavery and indentured servitude aside) were celebrated concepts, while government-granted monopolies and cartels were not popular at the founding of the American Republic." But soon enough, he explained, printers and shoemakers began to organize in Philadelphia and New York. Unionization always was based on coercion and the threats of violence, of course. Yet Reynolds depicts the union movement as fairly small until World War I. From then on, private unionization grew—aided and abetted by various laws that gave unions special rights and privileges. These included the Railway Labor Act of 1926 (allowing government involvement in labor strikes, per Reynolds), the Davis-Bacon Act of 1931 (setting wage levels), the Norris-LaGuardia Act of 1932 (giving unions vast protections against prosecution and liability), the National Labor Relations Act of 1935 (encouraging unionization) and on and on. Unions continued to gain a privileged political and legal position in America, despite the ultimate harm they would do to industry. Eventually, union numbers fell precipitously. Here is Reynolds again: "Union density in the private sector now is not much higher than it was in the early 1900s despite massive federal intervention on behalf of unionism since World War I. The wage-boosting success of private-sector unions has gone hand in hand with their decline in membership (nothing fails like success), as the silent, steady forces of the competitive marketplace continually undermine government-sanctioned labor cartels."[308]

In other words, because private-sector unions imposed counterproductive work rules and imposed above-market wages on employers, they sowed the seeds of their own destruction. Despite governmental efforts to maintain labor cartels, protect unions against prosecution for violent acts and give them a leg up in negotiations, they ultimately have diminished in importance as the marketplace has become more free and open. We can debate the merits of private unionization, but there is no debating that the modern American labor union movement has become increasingly a public-sector movement—one that gained steam only since the early 1960s when public-sector associations and unions gained collective-bargaining rights. Writes Reynolds again, "Public-sector unions are on pace to claim an absolute majority of union members in a traditionally private-sector-dominated labor movement within a few years. Government jobs constitute the 'healthy' part of organized labor where external competition provides little or no discipline against union inefficiency, costs and privilege."

In the private sector, there is at least the competitive pressure to rein in the worst union abuses. Ultimately, unionized private companies must make a profit, even if the biggest union-hobbled entities such as General Motors were able to muddle along with mediocre-quality products and losses for decades. In the public sector, there is nothing to countervail against union demands. Hence, the enormous unfunded liabilities and the massive growth in government as management more often represent the interests of the unions—than of the taxpayers.

Reynolds points to President John F. Kennedy's 1962 executive order promoting federal unionization and the follow-up within union-friendly states of similar legislation allowing unionization within civil service organizations. Government control of the nation's education system began after the Civil War, according to John Hood, in an article for the *Freeman*. We went from a system of mostly private education to one where 57 percent of students were educated in public schools after the Civil War to the current situation in which more than 90 percent of school-aged children attend schools run by the government. Regarding the unionization of teachers, however, that also came about in the 1960s. Writes Terry Moe for *Education Next: A Journal of Opinion and Research*:

"Until the early 1960s, only a tiny percentage of teachers were unionized. The American Federation of Teachers (AFT) was the only teacher union to speak of, and it organized no more than 5 percent of the nation's teachers clustered in a few urban areas. The leading force in public education was the National Education Association (NEA). It attracted about half of the nation's teachers, but it functioned as a professional association and was controlled by school administrators."[309] Moe points to 1961 as the watershed year, when "the AFT won a representation election in New York City. This victory set off an aggressive AFT campaign to organize teachers in other cities, forcing the NEA to compete as a union or risk losing its constituency." Since then the vast majority of American teachers has become unionized and the NEA has long ceased functioning as a professional organization.

In 1968, California local government bureaucrats were granted collective-bargaining rights under the Meyers-Milias-Brown Act. A key provision: "Except as otherwise provided by the Legislature, public employees shall have the right to form, join, and participate in the activities of employee organizations of their own choosing for the purpose of representation on all matters of employer-employee relations." The act details the rights of public unions in great depth, something that still gives local city officials—or the few of them not closely allied with unions—difficulties in standing up for public disclosure and taxpayer protection. In a short period, then, government unionization has expanded.

Ironically, despite the reductions in unionization nationwide over the past five decades, U.S. unionization rates increased in 2008, according to the UCLA Institute for Research on Labor and Employment. The reason: increases in unionization in California, mainly in the government sector. The pro-union institute celebrates this, but this signals increasing trouble for the nation.

Writes Charles Baird, director of the Smith Center for Private Enterprise Studies at California State University, East Bay: "Since 1983 the percent of government workers who are unionized has fluctuated between 36% and 39%. In 2004 it was 36.4%. The percent of union workers employed by government has increased steadily to 47.1% in 2004. In contrast, only 16.1% of all civilian workers are government employees. The main reason for this success is that government sector unions and employers sit on the same side of the bargaining table. Both are eager to obtain and spend other people's (taxpayers') money. Agency heads want bigger budgets and bigger staffs. Union heads want more dues money and are happy to help agency heads expand their budgets, and their staffs. Agency heads know that politicians cater to the interests of organized interests at the expense of the public interest, so they are delighted to promote unions in their workplaces. Politicians, too, are delighted to play the game in exchange for organized financial and in-kind electoral support. Only taxpayers and government employees forced to pay for unwanted union representation lose."[310]

Yet despite the already rigged game on behalf of government employees, there is no end to the legislation being promoted to give public-sector unions even more "rights" and privileges. Just one example at the federal level: The House of Representatives was considering the Public Safety Employer-Employee Cooperation Act of 2009. According to attorneys writing for *Western City* magazine, the act would "require all state and local governments to collectively bargain with public safety officers, which includes any employee of a public safety agency who is a police officer, firefighter or emergency medical services personnel..."[311] The bill would give unions even more collective bargaining power than they already have in California, according to the analysis. This is just a simple example of the relentless efforts in Congress and state legislatures to expand the powers of government employee unions. There are few interest groups that have the muscle to stand up to this, even though not every bill ultimately becomes law.

## DISTORTING SOCIETY

Public sector unionization has been here for only a relatively short time and—because there are no real checks and balances—it is growing like kudzu and devouring every public budget it gets near. This truly is a problem for the nation's future. Here are the fruits of public-sector unionization and the growth of the civil-service-protected government bureaucracy.

### A CORRUPTED POLITICAL CULTURE

OPM's history of the civil service system focused on the corrosive nature of the old spoils system. It was so corrosive that it undermined the democratic system and even led to the assassination of a president. Well, the current system is corrosive of democracy as well. The current system is a spoils system, albeit one that is highly regimented and arguably more corrosive than the old system. In the old way, the people enriching themselves at the public's expense would be tossed out of their jobs when the new political leaders took over. In the current system, the government elite cannot be fired, their benefits are vested and there is virtually nothing that can be done to reduce their power or privilege. Their interest groups and unions virtually run state capitols. Increased media coverage of the pension situation is leading to widespread anger among Americans who will retire with a tiny percentage of the amount enjoyed by public employees. Most Americans will have few of the health benefits and none of the cost-of-living increases enjoyed by government retirees. The government retirees will be retired at much earlier ages, usually in their 50s, while the rest of Americans will work late into life. This is highly corrosive and is a corrupting influence in public life.

"Public employee unions contribute heavily to political campaigns," writes University of Buffalo Professor Michael Rozeff, writing for LewRockwell.com.[312] "They affect legislation and crucially influence who is elected. They then sit down and bargain over wages and benefits with the same units of government they have so busily bought and paid for. Breathing in the stench, the taxpayers afterwards suffocate under the tax bills. Unions hand in hand with politicians, lobbyists cheek by jowl with statute-sellers—these faces fill the portrait of that ugly and immoral creature we name democracy. A government with the powers ours today has cannot help but fertilize fetid monstrosities assembled by their creators to devour taxpayers."

## DEPENDENCY ON GOVERNMENT

A growing bureaucracy becomes a lobby for more government. The more government we get, the more government workers we get. And the more government workers we get, the stronger the lobby they have for even bigger government. This cycle of government expansion also relates to government bureaucracy and dependency. The more government programs we have, the more people who will sign on to them and the more government workers who will administer them. That creates a lobby for even more programs and bigger program budgets and more people ultimately become dependent on government. "The shift from personal autonomy to dependence on government is perhaps the defining characteristic of modern American politics," wrote Charlotte Twight in her 2002 book, *Dependent on D.C.: The Rise of Federal Control over the Lives of Ordinary Americans*. "In the span of barely one lifetime, a nation grounded in ideals of individual liberty has been transformed into one in which federal decisions control even such personal matters as what health care we can buy—a nation so bound up in detailed laws and regulations that no one can know what all the rules are, let alone comply with them."

## MORE BUREAUCRACY

All those rules described above add up to the bureaucratization of our lives. The classical liberal ideal was simple—individuals have a God-given right to make their own choices, live their own lives, start their own businesses and enjoy the fruits of their success (and suffer the consequences of their failure). In a bureaucratic society, the functionaries make the decisions. We go, tail between our legs, to DMV-like agencies and ask permission to do things. In a free society, we have no right to harm others—protecting against such harm or intrusion is the proper role of government. But in our highly bureaucratic society, we must jump through myriad hoops that exist simply because they exist. It doesn't matter if the rules make sense or not. Again, we need some bureaucracy—a small number of officials running a small number of departments—but not a society entangled by it at every level. This is a great quotation from Honore de Balzac: "Bureaucracy is a giant mechanism operated by pygmies." Bureaucracy doesn't promote entrepreneurship or greatness. It crushes the soul and places obstacles in the way of success. Bureaucracies are massive machines that sap the life out of the public and the people who work for it. This is not a model for a healthy society. Yet the power of the bureaucracy and of the organized people who work for it assures its self-perpetuation and the comfort of those who work within it.

Most people know about "Parkinson's Law": "Work expands to fit the time available for its completion." We all know how that works from our personal experience and from watching others work. As a journalist, I know how dependent I am on tight deadlines to get my work done. If I have a day to write an article, it will take a day. If I have a week, it will take me a week. That's Parkinson's Law. But most people don't know much about Cyril Northcote Parkinson, the British naval historian and author who wrote humorous essays and books about bureaucracy. His "law" was coined in the mid-1950s.

Parkinson described how bureaucrats behaved. He gave an example of "a civil servant called A who finds himself overworked. Whether this overwork is real or imaginary is immaterial; but we should observe, in passing, that A's sensation (or illusion) might easily result from his own decreasing energy—a normal symptom of middle-age. For this real or imagined overwork there are, broadly speaking, three possible remedies: (1) He may resign. (2) He may ask to halve the work with a colleague called B. (3) He may demand the assistance of two subordinates, to be called C and D. There is probably no instance in civil service history of A choosing any but the third alternative."[313]

Here's Parkinson on a real-world result of the above attitude: "What we have to note is that the 2,000 Admiralty officials of 1914 had become the 3,569 of 1928; and that this growth was unrelated to any possible increase in their work. The Navy during that period had diminished, in point of fact, by a third in men and two-thirds in ships. Nor, from 1922 onwards, was its strength even expected to increase, for its total of ships (unlike its total of officials) was limited by the Washington Naval Agreement of that year. Yet in these circumstances we had a 78.45 per cent increase in Admiralty officials over a period of fourteen years; an average increase of 5.6 per cent a year on the earlier total."

The result of bureaucratization: a constant push for more government, irrespective of any reason for it.

## LESS FREEDOM AND PERSONAL INITIATIVE

People who push for government "solutions" to problems forget the essence of government. I'll quote George Washington again: "Government is not reason, it is not eloquence, it is force; like fire, a troublesome servant and a fearful master. Never for a moment should it be left to irresponsible action." Government officials are members of the force-based community. That's because—no matter how decent or kind any particular official may be—government actions always and ultimately are backed by the threat of force. If you do not go to the DMV and get your license you can be forced not to drive. If you do not pay your taxes, you will end up in jail, perhaps after a long legal battle. If you do not listen to the command of your local police officer, he can arrest you. If your business does not comply with an EPA regulation—even if that regulation is convoluted and those who wrote it and enforce it don't really understand it—you could face stiff penalties, lose your business and end up in jail. If you do not comply with the demands of Child Protective Services, you will lose your family. If you build a house without the proper permit, you will be forced to knock it down. If you resist any of this long enough you will be forcibly restrained. That's government. I'd hate to think of what life would be like if government were big enough to enforce all of its rules or had enough officials to enforce them all. Many contractors, for instance, have experienced the heavy-handedness of the nation's Americans With Disabilities Act, by which various sets of enforcement officials (local and federal) can mandate costly renovations if, say, a drive-through is a fraction too low or a doorway a fraction too narrow.

The more laws we have, the less free we are to make our own decisions. The more officials we have, the more people we will have who are backed by the power of the state who can force us to conform to massive numbers of rules, laws and regulations that legislators keep voting for. The more decisions are made in government bureaus, the less room there will be for private initiative. The more money the government spends, the less money that will be available for private businesses and initiatives. The larger the portion of the economy dominated by government, the smaller the portion dominated by individuals. That means we are becoming less free—shockingly less free and quickly, too.

Let's not forget the words of Mencken: "It [the State] has taken on a vast mass of new duties and responsibilities; it has spread out its powers until they penetrate to every act of the citizen, however secret; it has begun to throw around its operations the high dignity and impeccability of a State religion; its agents become a separate and superior caste, with authority to bind and loose, and their thumbs in every pot. But it still remains, as it was in the beginning, the common enemy of all well-disposed, industrious and decent men."

Mencken wrote that in 1926. Imagine what he would say if we told him about "3 percent at 50."

### HIGHER TAXES

As the Tax Freedom Day analysis earlier in this chapter shows, Americans work more days each year to pay their total tax bill. There are many hidden taxes also—taxes on manufacturing, for instance, that increase the cost of products and are generally not included in these analyses. One caveat—the tax bill is not evenly divided. The burden falls heavily on the most productive members of society. "IRS data shows that in 2004, the richest 50% of the taxpayers paid 96.7% of all income taxes," writes Craig Steiner. "From 1986 to 2004, the share paid by the richest half increased from 93.5% to 96.7%, and the share paid by the richest 1% increased from 25.75% to 36.89%. At the same time, the amount paid by the poorer half decreased from 6.5% in 1986 to 3.3% in 2004. While the poor's contribution was cut in half, the richest Americans saw their contribution increase by nearly 50%. When you get past the propaganda, for the last two decades the rich have been paying *more and more* while the poor have been paying *less and less.*"[314]

This has created a perverse incentive. As columnist George Will wrote, "Partly because of changes endorsed by presidents from Ronald Reagan to Barack Obama, approximately 60 percent of taxpayers now pay either no income tax (43 percent) or less than 5 percent of their income."[315] That imbalance, he said at a 2009 Claremont Institute dinner in Santa Monica, results in this reality: a permanent majority of Americans who will always lobby for bigger government, because it effectively costs them nothing.

This means even more bureaucracy and higher taxes, but the most productive members of society are the ones who will be paying the bulk of them.

## MORE POLICE-STATE TACTICS

Chapter 4 discussed some of the common abuses by government agents and police authorities. As unions representing government employees get even more powerful and the numbers of such laws and law-enforcers get more numerous, we will witness more abuses. There will be more SWAT-style raids and more deadly shootings by police officers. We will find more jail abuses and no solution to dreadful prison conditions. More average people will experience these things. Law enforcement will become less helpful and more militaristic. Check out Will Grigg's ProLiberate blog and Radley Balko's the Agitator for continuing examples as government agents adopt an us–vs.–them mentality, rather than the community policing model more appropriate for a free society.

## ENORMOUS DEBT AND UNFUNDED LIABILITIES

As detailed earlier, the situation will lead to unsustainable debt levels and an unsustainable level of unfunded liabilities. This will burden future generations—actually, it already is intolerably burdening them —and will constrict economic opportunities.

## A LOWER STANDARD OF LIVING

The dominance of unions and government employees has, of course, enriched the class of those employees, but it is leading to fewer economic opportunities, higher taxes, costlier money and other problems for everyone else. It is, in short, leading to a lower cost of living for those of us who must help sustain the platinum-plated pensions and pay levels for government workers. It's very simple, but as Matthew Falconer put it in an *Orlando Sentinel* blog: "In simple terms, high levels of local government spending put downward pressure on the wages of private sector employees. When real estate taxes on your place of business triple (like they did in the past six years) your employer cannot raise his prices because his competition does not have those expenses. Your pay is lower as a result. On the expense side, everything you buy is affected by government spending. From apartment rent, clothes, and food, they all are adversely affected by high levels of government spending. It increases your cost of living."[316]

## A TWO-TIERED SOCIETY OF RULERS AND RULED

Finally, we get to a psychological result. Our society has always celebrated equality before the law. One foundation of a free society is that the rulers have to live by the same laws as the ruled. Newt Gingrich's "Contract with America" in the mid-1990s included a sensible populist reform—forcing the members of Congress and their staffs to live by the laws they pass. There's something anger-inducing about the lawmakers harrumphing about something the American people are doing and passing restrictions on it, but then exempting themselves from the very standards they are imposing. Well, as this book has documented, government employees have many special privileges—special bills of rights, protections from firing, special license plates that allow them violate certain traffic laws, professional courtesy for members of law enforcement, civil service protections and other things that regular Americans can only dream about. On top of that, these employees have inordinate sway over the political process, something they use to constantly ratchet up their pay and benefits. Federal workers earn double the average pay of other Americans and government employees have retirement and retiree health-care plans that are many times more generous than what other Americans have. They are a special class. We have created a two-tier society, of the haves and have-nots. The haves are powerful Americans who work for government and the have-nots are everyone else. This is not a healthy situation in a free society.

## Chapter Eight

# CONCLUSION:
# IT'S TIME FOR MORE THAN OUTRAGE

Every normal man must be tempted at times to spit on his hands,
hoist the black flag, and begin to slit throats.
– H.L. Mencken

The problems detailed in this book are deep ones. There's no quick fix to deal with multi-trillions of dollars in unfunded liabilities, or to control the burgeoning national debt, or to rein in the growth of government. There's no magical solution that will bring government pay and benefit levels in line with the private sector or will force government agents to abide by the same laws that the rest of us must live by. It took a long time to create the current mess, and it's going to take a long time to fix the problems outlined here. But Americans do need to start by recognizing that the current situation is unsustainable. We need to break down these problems into more digestible pieces and consider a variety of solutions ranging from small policy tweaks to paradigm shifts.

First, let's break down the problem. Simply put, the public's servants have become the public's masters. The people who work for the government and are supposed to serve the overall public have become a privileged elite that has exploited their political power for vast financial gains and special protections and privileges. Because of its political power, this interest group has rigged the game so there are few meaningful checks on its demands. This has manifested itself in higher pay and far higher pension and benefit levels than those received by the vast majority of Americans working in the private sector. This power has protected government employees—even incompetent and abusive ones—from being fired, except after long processes and only for the most grievous offenses. This situation has eroded public services, made it impossible to reform even the poorest performing agencies and school systems and resulted in higher taxes, less freedom and unsustainable levels of debt spending that will be borne by future generations. It has also created a two-tier system whereby the rulers are treated better than the ruled. These problems are getting worse, especially with a tough economy.

There are the big, overarching problems—an overly large and costly government, powerful unions and the resulting encroachment of the government sector in areas of life that used to be defined by private initiative. These big problems in particular can only be solved when the public begins to value its freedoms more dearly and relearn the lessons from our founding fathers. Americans need to remember that the bigger government gets, the more it intrudes into our personal lives. Americans need a reawakening. They need a renewed understanding that our republican form of government—with its checks and balances and limits on governmental authority—was designed so that government at all levels would be minimal, and would stick to the tasks of protecting everyone's God-given rights to life, liberty and property. The founders advocated a system of negative rights—areas in which the government promised not to intrude, such as the right to free speech and worship—rather than a system of positive rights, where the government promises certain goods (health care, education, etc.). Negative rights are basically rights to be left alone, whereas positive rights come at someone else's expense. If the government promises you free health care, then someone must be forced to provide that care or to pay for it. Not until these founding ideas become fashionable again will Americans rein in the level of government growth, debt spending and interest-group domination that's at the heart of the problem. It's no easy task to figure out a blueprint to fix those problems, and indeed the current situation—where union school teachers and government curricula teach kids what they need to know—makes it even harder to figure out a way to revive these vital lessons that were crucial to the nation's founding. This is a subject for another book.

For the purposes of this essay, it's important to focus on two types of solutions. There are technical solutions and political/legal ones. Those distinctions are vital. We can easily figure out ways to reform the pension and pay situation—solutions that will reduce the problems without any major upheavals or much pain and suffering. But the problem is implementation. The political realities, especially in union-dominated states such as California, make it tough to implement even the most modest technical reforms. Legal obstacles also weigh down serious reform attempts. For instance, because the courts have ruled that pension increases granted by elected bodies are vested benefits that must be paid no matter what, policymakers cannot simply go back and change past agreements. That's a legal hurdle. This chapter will detail some of the policy approaches that will reform the system and then we'll look at some of the political and legal approaches that might help get some of these ideas implemented. It's a long battle, but it's time for us to engage in it.

## PENSION AND PAY REFORM

California Foundation for Fiscal Responsibility President Marcia Fritz came up with some simple technical pension-related reforms that she says would save the state of California $5 billion a year and more than $500 billion over 30 years. None of the reforms amounts to gutting pensions, as public employee unions claim whenever any reasonable reform is proposed.[317]

For starters, she says the state should do one of the following: "Temporarily suspend earning of service years for pension benefits or require employees to pay employer pension costs." Either of these ideas would save the state $3 billion annually. Regarding the first proposal, Fritz argues that the state government is busy granting early retirements to push people out of the workforce now and save some immediate costs, even though this adds enormous costs down the line. A temporary suspension would allow the employees to keep working and save the government retirement contribution. As a result, public employees would simply have to work a little longer before retiring—they already "retire" years before most people can retire in the private sector. Requiring the employee to make a higher pension contribution is only fair and it would save a bundle.

Her second idea is to get rid of those noxious "airtime" credits that allow employees to "purchase risk-free annuities for five service years to tack onto their 'years worked' formula. Because of a flaw in the government code the price is a bargain compared to what would be paid for a similar annuity in the private sector." Fritz notes that "airtime" offers no benefit to taxpayers or the public agency. The core of any reform ought to be policies that benefit taxpayers and the employer/agency, not what benefits the union and its members.[318]

She also calls for a reduction in the compensated time off (sick days, holidays, vacation days) given that government employees earn so many more of these days off than private employees, for the tightening of domestic-partner labor laws for benefit coverage, and also for the standardization of disability processing. She calls for the auditing of current disability recipients. Currently, the disability rules are inconsistent and lax, which allows for, say, a majority of CHP officers to retire on disability and then go on and take other stressful policing jobs at age 50.

Fritz champions the most significant reform idea I've heard: creating a second retirement tier for new employees. These new tiers should be defined-*contribution* plans, or far more modest defined-*benefit* plans. And the retirement ages should be more reasonable, such as 65 for general employees or 55 for public-safety employees. This system is necessary and it takes nothing from existing employees, who would continue to receive their overly generous defined-benefit plans. New employees would understand that their retirement plan is different and lower than the existing plan. It's always fair to revise benefits for new employees who would clearly understand the terms of the deal when they decided to take the job. They could take the deal or leave it—just like anyone can do in the private sector.[319]

It's always surprising to learn that many public agencies not only pay the employer contribution for pensions, but also pay the employee contribution, which means that many government workers—police and fire in particular—pay absolutely nothing for their generous retirement packages. Fritz wisely believes that every government employee should pay something for their plan. She also would end those bizarre pension-spiking schemes detailed earlier in this book (reciprocity, which allows employees to switch to higher-paying jobs for their last years of work to spike pensions and other scams). She would also require public employees to pay a portion of their health benefits and pay a tax on cost-of-living adjustments. And, finally, she would ban those absurd retroactive increases that are little more than gifts of public funds to union members.

These are good ideas. There are plenty of other ones from other sources also. States should ban those DROP programs, eliminate pensions for people who are convicted of work-related crimes, stop double-dipping and insist that if workers are so disabled they can receive a disability retirement, then they should not be allowed to work in any government job again. There should be no terminal pay for city employees. Pensions should never be allowed to top a final year's pay. Pensions should no longer be based (as in California) on the highest earning year, but should instead average the earnings over several years. There should be no pension benefit for volunteer service. Retirement ages on all government pension programs should be higher. The government needs more aggressive fraud divisions to deal with those government employees who game the system by making fraudulent disability claims. Conflict of interest laws should be used to assure that union officials do not dominate retirement panels. All cities and counties should adopt requirements such as those in San Francisco and Orange County that require public votes on any pension-enhancement plan. Public employees should not be allowed to receive a retirement from one public employee pension system, then work at another government job and collect another pension from a different public employee retirement system. Sick days should be limited, holidays reduced. Retiree health care should not be pooled with that for current workers, which ends up as another large subsidy for government retirees.

These are responsible, moderate reforms, not radical ideas. Here's another from the *Los Angeles Times* editorial board, which has a decidedly left-of-center outlook: "Let workers and others argue over whether defined-benefit plans for state employees are overly generous or unnecessarily stingy; the immediate problem is that, at their current levels, they are not fiscally responsible. The governor's plan to roll back benefits for new employees to more rational pre-1999 levels is a reasonable starting point for reform. Without at least this modest change, obligations to retirees will eat up all the discretionary money for the human services and other programs that Californians want to keep."[320]

A number of changes are needed at the public-employee pension funds, which are, after all, union-controlled investment pools. Those who run them try their darnedest to hide reality from policy makers. New rules are needed to force the funds to adopt the type of disclosure requirements used in the private sector—a sort of GASB 45 full-disclosure rule for pension benefits. GASB 45, of course, dealt only with other-than-pension benefits. State governments need to consider new rules limiting the ability of the pension funds to embrace overly aggressive smoothing procedures and other tricks to under-fund their pensions.

Certainly, we need to stop the bleeding— i.e., stop the promotion of additional state and federal rules that make it even easier for unions to gain power. The Employee Free Choice Act, known as "card check," would end secret union elections and therefore encourage union intimidation of those who would prefer not to join their organizations. It would also insert government arbitration into union disputes, thus allowing unions to more easily get their way if they hold out for a few months. Although geared more toward private unions, this is the type of union favoritism that is causing havoc nationwide.

States should also embrace civil-service reform. In 2003, Colorado had attempted such a thing. As the *Colorado Springs Gazette* argued in an Oct. 10, 2003 editorial, "Picking up the recommendations of the Governor's Commission on Civil Service Reform, which included former Democratic Gov. Dick Lamm, [Gov. Bill] Owens hopes to get a measure on the ballot in 2004 to remove archaic and inflexible personnel policies enshrined in Colorado's constitution, which make improving state government efficiency all but impossible. The changes would increase the number of positions that could be hired without going through the state's laborious and lethargic personnel system, enhance the ability to contract out state jobs that could more cheaply and effectively be done by the private sector, streamline the hiring and firing process and make it easier to discipline or fire lousy state employees."[321]

One of the allies of the current government-employee plundering is secrecy. States have open-government laws, but the government officials are adept at circumventing the spirit of them and keeping their deals away from serious scrutiny. You recall how the city of Fullerton conspired with unions to ram through a massive retroactive pension increase for city employees. You read how public officials conceal topics on public agendas and use closed session in ways that are not appropriate. The California Newspaper Publishers Association had proposed legislation that required more forthright explanations about agenda items. Although it failed, these are the types of reforms that are needed. One local council member argued to me that contract negotiations with labor unions should be done in open session, in full view of the public. That really is a great idea, and it would provide some pro-taxpayer balance in a system where both sides of the table stand to benefit from the deal. Pension and salary information should be public records, despite efforts by some cities and counties to fight the release of this information.

Regarding contracts, municipalities should refuse to enter into those "evergreen" contracts that require raises if the next contract is not approved. Those deals give future councils limited bargaining authority. The unions know that if they can't strong-arm the council into granting a bigger raise, they will still get some raise. This means the unions rarely are forced to grant significant concessions, even in tough economic situations. It should be illegal for cities to tie their employees' level of compensation to other cities—such as when police unions gain contracts guaranteeing that they will be the fourth-highest paid in the county. These contracts take budget control away from local cities, as they are dependent on the decisions of all the cities around them. If a second city decides to further enrich the cops, then the first city has to find the money to increase police salaries.

Many work rules in union contracts should not be part of contract negotiations, but rather should remain legitimate management decisions. City managers and council members, for instance, should decide the right staffing levels. Unions always want higher staffing levels, but management should decide based on public policy, not union feather-bedding.

## SCHOOL REFORM

The public school reform issue is, again, another topic worthy of an entire book. But a key to that reform is breaking the power of teachers unions so that school officials are able to make the sorts of management changes needed to improve school performance. Within the current public-school model, we need changes to the tenure law so that abusive teachers—and incompetent ones, also—can be quickly removed from the payroll. I'd argue that tenure should be eliminated completely. Again, this isn't some radical idea. The following news report is from the April 10, 2009, Newark

(N.J.) *Star-Ledger*: "Advocates and educators statewide have been calling for a reform to teacher tenure rules for some time. Clifford B. Janey, who took over the troubled Newark school system last year, is among them. He said last month tenure has become a big obstacle in getting rid of bad and ineffective teachers in his district. And while grumbling about teacher tenure is nothing new, Janey has outlined a plan to replace the antiquated system. He seeks to put in place a program where a team from Seton Hall University would evaluate Newark teachers and identify their strengths and weaknesses."[322] At the minimum, it should take several years before a teacher is granted tenure.

Furthermore, principals need the latitude to hire and place teachers based on merit, not just seniority. Schools should be forced to disclose if a teacher has a troubled history before transferring that teacher to another school. Merit pay—based on performance—and combat pay—additional bonuses for those teachers willing to work in the toughest schools— should be adopted. New rules are needed to reduce the ability of school administrators and teachers to send out taxpayer-funded mailers that advocate for political measures even if the mailers technically meet the current "informational" standard. Districts should eliminate union rules that ban parents from volunteering on many projects. Districts should not be allowed to enter into Project Labor Agreements that squander bond proceeds.

Any one of these relatively minor reforms will generate enormous opposition from the unions and even from most school administrators. It's unlikely that enough of these reforms could be approved to change the entire system of perverse incentives. After all, the school systems operate in many ways like Eastern European Soviet-era bureaucracies, which is not surprising given that school systems function under the same monopolistic, government-controlled rules that animated those non-market-oriented nations. No one would have supposed that a reform here or there could have turned those systems into free, competitive and entrepreneurial ones, however worthy each reform might be.

The more useful task would be to create some competitive pressure on the current top-down government monopolies. That's the idea behind school vouchers, charter school programs and the old tuition tax-credit idea that would give parents a tax break to send their kids to a private school of their choice. The best idea (advocated by the late Marshall Fritz and others)—the complete separation of school and state—sounds radical, but there's no reason it shouldn't be part of the discussion. When I've raised the issue to public school educators, I reminded them that in a private system, good teachers would still be in great demand, and they might even get better pay and benefits based on performance. Every public school teacher complains about school bureaucracy or misplaced resources. Not every private school would be a good one (just like not every private business of any sort is good), but competitive pressures would force the bad schools out of business and help focus resources on the student and their parents—on customers, rather than on politicians and union representatives. Teachers would have greater choices in working environments. But regardless of how far down the private path one wants to go, there's little doubt that competition is a desperately needed cure for much of what ails the current monopoly school systems.

And homeschooling is another important option—not just for conservative and religious people, but for many others, as well. Pacific Research Institute's Lance Izumi argued in the *New York Times*: "This summer, I attended a large gathering of liberal/progressive home-schoolers. When I asked parents why they decided to home-school their children, I got many different answers. Some said that they were worried about the violence and bullying in their public schools. Others said that they disliked the standardization of many public schools and the testing and other curriculum requirements that they felt hindered their children's learning. Unlike Mr. Obama's narrow measure of choice, these people chose home-schooling for the equity reason that it was their right and it was in the best interests of their individual child."[323]

In some of the nation's most troubled school districts, these competitive ideas are being tried simply because the status quo is so dysfunctional. Charter schools are still government schools, but they at least circumvent the worst bureaucratic restrictions and offer a fresh alternative for many parents. Vouchers sometimes scare suburban parents, because they allow inner-city kids to choose "their" schools, and vouchers end up being another form of government subsidy. Nevertheless, they offer an even broader quasi-private alternative that would result in something of a competitive education market. From a practical standpoint, charters and homeschooling have advanced while the voucher movement remains mired in endless political battles. It's a tougher reform to achieve given natural opposition from the teachers unions.

## PRIVATIZATION

Competition is king. We know that. No consumer wants to buy products from a monopoly provider. There's a reason your regulated utility provides such spotty service. We all like to shop around for everything we buy. Why should governmental services be any different?

More than 70 percent of the nation's fire departments are volunteer departments. There's no evidence they provide less-quality service than the costly governmental alternatives. Yet firefighter unions and their legislative allies impose artificial impediments on these volunteers as a way to cut down on the competition. For instance, they always impose more training requirements—many of these are dubious and serve as a cartel to make it tougher for volunteers (working at other jobs to pay the bills) to compete with government workers who are paid for their training time. Unions have crushed private paramedic services also. Police services cannot easily be privatized, although major private companies are able to rely on private guard services rather than public police services. Often, the public agencies require that people who hold public events hire off-duty cops at inflated overtime rates—those types of cartels also need to be stopped.

Privatization generally is a good thing, but one needs to be careful, especially in the law-enforcement realm. It is dangerous to marry a private profit motive with public power. With the red-light cameras that are becoming a disturbing fixture of public life, we've seen that private operators have shortened the yellow lights as a way to increase red-light tickets. The private company and the agency sometimes split the revenues. This subverts justice for a profit motive. Former House Majority Leader Dick Armey produced a report questioning whether the shortened times are intentional:

"But why have so many people become wanton red light runners all of a sudden? The answer seems to be that changes made to accommodate camera enforcement have produced yellow light times that, in many cases, are shortened to the point that they are inadequate. And when people come upon an intersection with inadequate yellow time, they are faced with the choice either of stopping abruptly on yellow (risking a rear end accident) or accelerating. The options for those confronting such circumstances are limited and unsafe. But each time a driver faces this dilemma, government increases its odds for hitting the jackpot."[324]

Every privatization effort needs to be examined to see if it reduces government control or whether it simply is being used to more efficiently gin up government revenue. The goal should be to shift power from the authorities to individuals and to save costs by reducing government expenses, not to shift them to motorists or taxpayers.

One interesting and laudatory privatization experiment takes place in Sandy Springs, Ga., a suburban Atlanta community that uses almost all private workers except in the area of public safety. As *Reason* magazine explained: "What makes Sandy Springs interesting is that instead of creating a new municipal bureaucracy, the city opted to contract out nearly all government services. City leaders started with a blank slate, enabling them to ask fundamental questions about what role government should play. Every 'traditional' service or function was required to prove its worthiness and proper role and place within government, and officials had to decide whether to 'make' or 'buy' public services. Ultimately they decided to 'buy' most services from the private sector, signing a contract with CH2M-Hill, an international firm that oversees and manages the day-to-day operations of the city. The $32 million contract was just above half what the city traditionally was charged in taxes by Fulton County. That will save the new city's citizens millions of dollars a year."[325]

Sandy Springs residents receive better quality services than before at a much lower price and they don't have to deal with bloated bureaucracies, overpaid government workers and local government unions dominating the political process. This is the kind of real-world reform that more cities need to consider and that could actually reduce the size of government and the power of government workers and their uncooperative unions. Private is always better than privatized—real private is done with private dollars, whereas privatized refers to the creation of taxpayer-funded services by private firms. Nevertheless, privatization usually is better than government command and control. In Orange County, quasi-private toll agencies built top-quality freeways when it became apparent that the lumbering state and local transportation bureaucracies were too busy with their social engineering plans (pushing suburbanites out of cars and into transit) to build the roads needed to meet the demands of a growing population.

## UNION REFORMS

Public unions should be outlawed. There is absolutely no public good served by it, especially in a world of civil service protections. In fact, such unionization is a relatively recent phenomenon. We need to roll back the clock here. Legislatures should impose tighter restrictions on union political contributions. States should also pass paycheck protection measures that allow union members to withhold dues payments that are used for political purposes. As the Heritage Foundation's James Sherk explains, "Paycheck protection legislation has a clear negative effect on public sector union contributions to candidates for state legislative offices. These laws reduce union campaign donations by approximately 50 percent."[326] Sherk argues that many unions have found loopholes that allow them to circumvent some of these restrictions, but it still helps. Union power is what leads to these absurd benefit levels and work rules, so reducing union power is essential in order to reform any of these government systems.

Paycheck protection is crucial because without it government unions can forcibly take as much money as they need from members to maintain their grip on the political system. During the Proposition 226 battle in California in 1998, unions launched a brazenly dishonest campaign—but they had so much money that their distortions went unchallenged. Unions spent $30 million (versus $3 million spent by supporters) to stop Prop. 226. As the Heritage Foundation wrote at the time, "On June 2, 1998, California voters will be asked to decide whether union workers who are required to pay dues as a condition of employment should have those dues used without their permission for political purposes. Ten years ago, the Supreme Court ruled in *Communications Workers* v. *Beck* that such workers may not be required to pay dues beyond those necessary for collective bargaining purposes. Still, not only are many union members unaware of the *Beck* decision, but—as firsthand congressional testimony has demonstrated—those who do try to prevent any of their dues from being used to support political purposes that violate their beliefs frequently are stonewalled or intimidated by their unions."

Unions argued that Prop. 226 would result in the death of police officers. They surmised that the permission form would include officer addresses and that those addresses would be available to the public as public records. Then, they argued, criminals would look up the information and go to officers' homes and kill them. But there are so many layers of protection for police officer addresses and personal information, that this was nothing more than a blatant lie meant to scare voters. Making this argument, unions targeted phone calls to Republican women.

Unions also argued that non-profit organizations would lose donations because the initiative limited money that could be taken out of a paycheck for organizations that are political. They argued that non-profits—although not legally allowed to be involved in politics—conduct some minimal level of political activity. This was another stretch of an argument designed to scare voters. But some non-profits sent out letters during the campaign opposing Prop. 226 for that very reason. Prop. 226 supporters simply did not have the money to respond to these charges. Exit polls found that voters overwhelmingly supported the concept of paycheck protection, even as a majority of them voted against that particular initiative. If anything, the campaign against it proved the need for it.

In state government or school systems, changes in the collective bargaining process are the key to achieving other change. As Stan Greer wrote in a FrontPageMag.com article, "The real obstacle to the successful implementation of merit pay isn't teachers or federal employees, it is the monopoly-bargaining system imposed on public education and federal employment by politicians acting at the behest of union officials. Discussions about teacher merit pay in California, Rhode Island, Minnesota and the 31 other states that have laws authorizing and promoting monopoly bargaining in public schools will be fruitless unless their basic labor-relations policies change. To have a chance of succeeding, merit-pay proposals must abolish monopoly bargaining or, at the very least, sharply restrict its scope."

Maybe it's pie in the sky, but former *Reason* magazine editor Virginia Postrel's idea from a May 1998 article, "A new vision for America's workers," is a good one: "American unions face a choice. On it depends their future. They can continue to pursue their current course, taking their old-fashioned ideology to the only workplaces where it still applies—the monopoly shops owned and operated by government. Or they can reinvent unions as organizations that primarily serve workers rather than fight management. … Rather than commit suicide this way, unions can adopt an entrepreneurial vision. Instead of treating workers as indistinguishable factory drones, they can offer them skills that will command both respect and high wages. That means getting into the training business—a business companies often neglect for fear of investing in workers who will then move on to other jobs. As umbrella organizations supported by dues, unions wouldn't face that disincentive."[327]

Although Postrel's ideas are designed to help private-sector unions, there's some chance for cultural change within government unions. In the mid-2000s, a new California Department of Motor Vehicles chief managed to noticeably improve customer service and reduce wait times at that notoriously bureaucratic and customer-unfriendly agency. It took effort, but the right leadership can effect real change. Quite a few government workers agree with this harsh assessment of their unions and their pay and benefit scales. One local union boss, Nick Berardino of the Orange County Employees Association, is usually an adversary on these issues, but he has constructively negotiated cost-savings agreements on retiree health care (moving retirees out of the general pool) and has even agreed to a voluntary second-tier retirement system. Other local unions—especially the sheriffs' deputies union, where the bullying union boss once publicly threatened to release prisoners in the neighborhood of a rival union leader—have resisted even the most modest reforms. There is some hope, however slim, on this score.

## LAW ENFORCEMENT REFORM

Here again, privatization could help. Private prisons have a better record of producing humane conditions mainly because it's too costly and politically problematic for private prison companies to have to deal with abuse issues. Private firms face lawsuits, whereas abusive jailers in the public system gain union protections and enjoy sovereign immunity. Prison guards unions have, for transparent reasons, highlighted examples where private prisons have been troubled, but, as former *Village Voice* writer Nat Hentoff once explained, the private system is generally more conducive to respecting civil liberties than less-accountable public systems—despite a few examples of bad private prison situations.

Jon Coupal, president of the Howard Jarvis Taxpayers Association, called for privatization in the context of California's absurdly expensive costs to incarcerate prisoners—$45,000 a year compared to $27,000 a year for the highest of the other 10 most populous states. The cost of living is high in California, but this is outrageous! Coupal refers to former Indianapolis Mayor Stephen Goldsmith's Yellow Pages test: "If a service could be found in the Yellow Pages, he favored government buying or hiring it rather than producing it." Yet in California, any privatization effort gets blowback, such as when the state engineers' union fought against efforts by the state to contract with private highway engineers.

The key to more sensible policing is cultural change. Organizations need to embrace what one local council member refers to as "constitutional policing"—a culture that understands that its core mission is to protect individual constitutional rights. Right now, police agencies cannot change their cultures without running into the union-backed culture that defends the code of silence, that protects the most abusive officers and that battles any management reform. It's similar to the teachers union situation, where it's virtually impossible to get rid of a bad actor.

Overall, we need more oversight of police records and behavior. In California, legislators need to overturn the *Copley* decision so that the public can learn about abusive officers and so that civilian oversight panels can function effectively. We need more sunshine—so that police investigations of deadly shootings, for instance, are open for public view. Independent review offices are a good idea, as are state bans on professional courtesy. It should not be legal for police officers to give a pass to drunken drivers or traffic scofflaws simply because the scofflaws work for a law enforcement agency.

In reality, police and prison reform faces a tough road. In my experience, both major political parties support the unions, although for different reasons. When we in Orange County were battling a corrupt sheriff and horrendous jail abuse, local liberals sided with law enforcement—as they put union solidarity above civil libertarian concerns. Limited government conservatives seem to embrace unlimited government when it comes to their friends in the law-enforcement community.

## TAX AND BUDGET REFORM

Americans need to get behind serious budgetary reforms that force the government to live within its means. Many of the pension and pay excesses are the result of governments that are perfectly comfortable overspending given that there are no real checks on that process. Californians had passed the Gann limit in 1979, which limits state spending growth to the growth in population and inflation. It was gutted by another initiative voters passed in 1990. But every state and the federal government needs a true hard-and-fast spending cap

## POLITICAL AND LEGAL SOLUTIONS

The ideas listed above comprise only a partial list of solutions. The crucial issue is implementation. How do we get any of these ideas through legislatures that are often dominated by government unions? In states with the initiative process, how do we overcome the enormous financial advantages that unions have as they can so easily raise money for political purposes?

An older engineer made an appointment to see me at the newspaper and share his solutions for a re-use project for Marine Corps Air Station El Toro. The project was called the Great Park—which turned into a giant boondoggle. I dubbed it the Great Pork. The engineer was sure his ideas would be warmly welcomed. We went over them and, indeed, he offered a plausible technical solution to the reuse of the 4,700 acres of vacant land. But it didn't make any difference.

The decade-long battle at El Toro was not about technical solutions to a land-use problem, but about politics. There were politicians who favored building an international airport on the site and the vast majority of local voters who wanted anything but an airport. After years of competing voter initiatives and ugly political wrangling and protests, the political compromise had been struck and that meant the entitlement of a "Great Park" that would be built based on a rather fanciful financing scheme. My engineer visitor was angry that the editorial board wouldn't champion what he viewed as a clearly superior design idea. He just couldn't get my point: Even if his idea were the best thing ever designed, it wouldn't matter because the political wheels had turned and the compromises had been made and the battles had been fought. It was over, even before the first shovel of dirt was turned. That story offers a sobering reminder that the reform ideas I listed earlier in this chapter, no matter how good they may be, are only as useful as the political realities that might allow for their implementation.

One practical (although long-shot) idea, formulated by Orange County Supervisor John Moorlach and supported by the majority of the other supervisors, is to challenge the retroactive portion of a pension increase that a previous board had granted to the deputies union. Although an Orange County lawsuit, this idea could set a precedent that saves tens of billions of dollars throughout California. In 2001, in the height of the up market and as municipalities statewide were increasing pension formulas for police unions, the Orange County Board of Supervisors voted 5-0 (all Republicans) to give the deputies' union a retroactive pension increase from 2.7 percent at 55 to 3 percent at 50. This was a large boost and it was made for past service. There is no reason for retroactivity. As Girard Miller of *Governing* magazine explains, "[T]he practice of awarding pension benefits on a retroactive basis is the devil's doing. Retroactive pension increases neither attract nor retain employees. They serve no purpose except to buy favor with incumbent union members in order to get a contract signed — at the expense of future taxpayers who don't even know what hit them."[328]

In 2008, the new board of supervisors decided to challenge only the retroactive portion of that benefit increase. As the *Register* reported, Supervisor Moorlach argued that "when the Board of Supervisors approved the new formula, and applied it retroactively, it violated three provisions of the California Constitution: Debt limitations on local governments; The ban on gifts of public funds; The barring of extra compensation for work already performed."[329]

The board lost the first legal round, as expected, but voted 4-1 in

August 2009 to challenge the ruling. The deputies complain about the $2 million the board is spending on legal fees, but a successful challenge could save many billions of dollars. It is ironic that a union that has never seen a public dollar it hasn't wanted to spend on its members had suddenly gotten concerned about wasteful tax expenditures when it came to that lawsuit. The challenge was ongoing as this book goes to press, but this type of aggressive strategy is just what's needed to start chipping away at this enormous and nearly insurmountable problem.

County voters also passed an initiative to require a countywide vote for any pension increases. It's too late to reverse the damage done the past decade. But it's an important reform once the economy picks up and the unions get back to their business of demanding more. The county also reformed the retiree medical system, thus reducing the county's unfunded liability from $1.4 billion to $598 million.[330] Costs for these benefits were skyrocketing. Thanks to a previous benefit deal, retirees were kept in the same pool with current retirees. That meant they got to pay lower rates, given that retirees are older and generally have more health problems than younger workers. If they were in their own pool, costs would be much higher. The county negotiated a deal to split the pool, which ended up costing retirees a few hundred dollars extra a month. In return, the county agreed to increase its contribution to the trust fund. It was a reasonable deal, and is a model for other government agencies struggling with health-care liabilities. The county retirees sued the county (of course), but lost. Those health-pooling benefits were never vested, which meant that the county had every right to renegotiate them. The Orange County situation is worth discussing because in this county the new political leadership is deeply committed to pension reform. Without such commitment, which means a willingness to directly confront the unions, it is nearly impossible to enact meaningful reform. There's got to be the will to find a way out of the morass. Moorlach took them on directly in his supervisor election and won with nearly 70 percent of the vote.

In California and other Western states with liberal initiative requirements, the best hope lies in direct democracy. Gov. Schwarzenegger has proposed pension reform, then rescinded his proposal in the face of union opposition, then proposed it again during the thick of the 2009 budget crisis. The public cannot count on their political leaders having sufficient spine to stick with such important reforms. But as of August 2009 taxpayer activists in California were circulating a petition that would place on the ballot an initiative that would call for "Renegotiation of Public Employee Pension Contracts." It "allows vested pension benefits to be reduced for existing and prospective public sector retirees."

No wonder the left-wing blogs are apoplectic and public employees are strong-arming attorney general candidates into pledging to rig the ballot language. As a rule of thumb, if the unions aren't apoplectic, then the reform has little chance of creating meaningful change. Well, this one has them screaming. And other activists are talking about reviving a statewide paycheck protection initiative after the failure of Proposition 75 in 2005. I've watched many good initiative ideas qualify for the ballot, however, and then die on the vine as supporters lack funds in the election to stand up to union misinformation. Perhaps the time is ripe for real change and for the serious funding of a union reform campaign.

Education reform will need the same statewide initiative approach in California and elsewhere. The recall election also is a useful option. Currently, political activists are mounting a serious recall campaign against a Republican Assembly member who defied his campaign promises and voted for a tax increase. Unless the politicians know there will be a price to be paid for such actions, they will continue to sell out taxpayers. My theory is that legislators face great pain if they defy the unions, so they go with the path of least resistance. So our side needs to inflict just as much pain on those legislators who support the unions—regardless of the electoral price to be paid. Who cares if the Republican loses and an even worse Democrat takes his place? Anyone who sides with unions over taxpayers must pay a political price, period.

Ultimately, it's time to start a new political movement. We've seen the TEA parties get going largely through genuine grassroots outpourings— even though establishment Republicans have tried to co-opt these events and Democrats have tried to demonize the participants. We've seen angry Americans show up at health-care town hall meetings to express their displeasure at the Obama administration's attempts to give government more control over this vital industry. It's time for the grassroots—and not just conservatives or libertarians, but everyone who is concerned about the misuse of resources and abuse of power to benefit a special group of powerful Americans—to get agitated and to decry the plundering of America. The nation can't afford the price, and the result—if left unchecked—is the creation of society that is a pale imitation of the free one that the founders envisioned. We may not want to hoist the black flag and follow Mencken's tongue-in-cheek advice, but the time for anger and action is now.

## CalPERS Life Expectancy Data

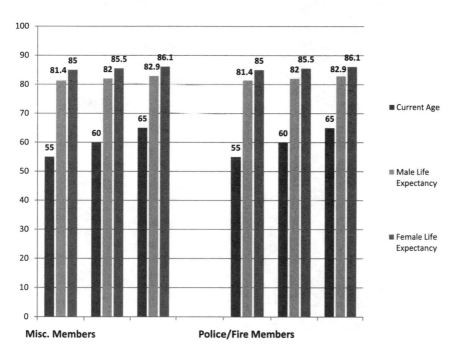

**Misc. Members**    **Police/Fire Members**

- Current Age
- Male Life Expectancy
- Female Life Expectancy

Source: CalPERS, September 2009

# Comparison of Total Compensation Per Hour

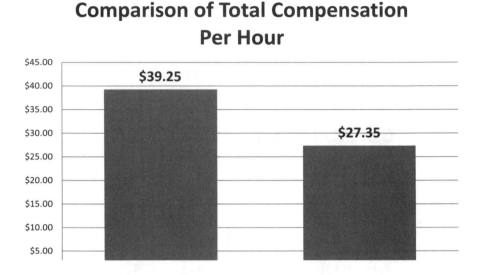

| | |
|---|---|
| $39.25 | $27.35 |

# Comparison of Earned Benefits Per Hour

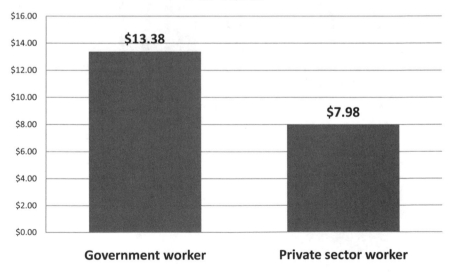

| Government worker | Private sector worker |
|---|---|
| $13.38 | $7.98 |

Source: USA Today, "Benefits widen public, private workers' pay gap," 4/10/09
http://www.usatoday.com/money/workplace/2009-04-09-compensation_N.htm

# Comparison: Fatal occupational injuries by occupation

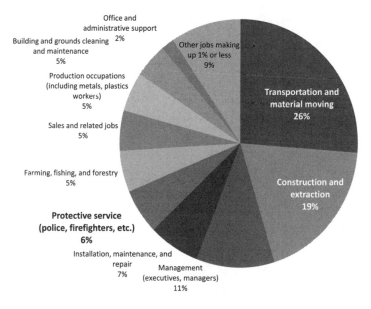

Source: Bureau of Labor Statistics, 2008 (http://www.bls.gov/news.release/cfoi.htm)

# Per Capita Pension Deficit by State

Source: Standard & Poor's Ratings Direct, Feb. 23, 2009
http://www.nasra.org/resources/S&P0903.pdf

| STATE | Funded Ratio % | Per capita unfunded liability |
|---|---|---|
| Alabama | 79.3 | 2,228 |
| Alaska | 74.3 | 5,845 |
| Arizona | 79.7 | 1,808 |
| Arkansas | 86.6 | 1,317 |
| California | 87.9 | 2,879 |
| Colorado | 75.1 | 2,765 |
| Connecticut | 62.6 | 7,971 |
| Delaware | 103.7 | 1,871 |
| Florida | 105.6 | 635 |
| Georgia | 94.4 | 1,278 |
| Hawaii | 67.5 | 7,563 |
| Idaho | 104.9 | (126) |
| Illinois | 61.4 | 4,419 |
| Indiana | 66.2 | 2,152 |
| Iowa | 90.2 | 792 |
| Kansas | 70.8 | 3,117 |
| Kentucky | 70.3 | 4,014 |
| Louisiana | 69.8 | 3,130 |
| Maine | 79.7 | 2,354 |
| Maryland | 80.2 | 2,724 |
| Massachusetts | 75.7 | 6,256 |
| Michigan | 88.2 | 1,411 |
| Minnesota | 81.1 | 2,289 |
| Mississippi | 73.7 | 3,766 |
| Missouri | 84.1 | 1,485 |
| Montana | 85.6 | 1,412 |
| Nebraska | 90.6 | 428 |
| Nevada | 77.2 | 3,954 |
| New Hampshire | 67 | 2,245 |
| New Jersey | 76 | 6,341 |
| New Mexico | 82 | 3,772 |
| New York | 101.5 | 2,139 |
| North Carolina | 106.9 | 370 |
| North Dakota | 85.2 | 1,315 |
| Ohio | 88 | 2,599 |
| Oklahoma | 59.5 | 3,195 |
| Oregon | 112.2 | (442) |
| Pennsylvania | 89.5 | 1,594 |
| Rhode Island | 56.2 | 6,106 |
| South Carolina | 69.7 | 2,918 |
| South Dakota | 97.1 | 414 |
| Tennessee | 95.1 | 463 |
| Texas | 90.3 | 966 |
| Utah | 100.3 | 568 |
| Vermont | 91.6 | 1,162 |
| Virginia | 82.3 | 2,001 |
| Washington | 73.3 | 2,914 |
| West Virginia | 68.8 | 2,690 |
| Wisconsin | 99.6 | 1,747 |

# States Ranked by Per Capita Unfunded Liability

Source: Standard & Poor's Ratings Direct, Feb. 23, 2009
http://www.nasra.org/resources/S&P0903.pdf

| STATE | Funded Ratio % | Per capita unfunded liability |
|---|---|---|
| Connecticut | 62.6 | 7,971 |
| Hawaii | 67.5 | 7,563 |
| New Jersey | 76 | 6,341 |
| Massachusetts | 75.7 | 6,256 |
| Rhode Island | 56.2 | 6,106 |
| Alaska | 74.3 | 5,845 |
| Illinois | 61.4 | 4,419 |
| Kentucky | 70.3 | 4,014 |
| Nevada | 77.2 | 3,954 |
| New Mexico | 82 | 3,772 |
| Mississippi | 73.7 | 3,766 |
| Oklahoma | 59.5 | 3,195 |
| Louisiana | 69.8 | 3,130 |
| Kansas | 70.8 | 3,117 |
| South Carolina | 69.7 | 2,918 |
| Washington | 73.3 | 2,914 |
| California | 87.9 | 2,879 |
| Colorado | 75.1 | 2,765 |
| Maryland | 80.2 | 2,724 |
| West Virginia | 68.8 | 2,690 |
| Ohio | 88 | 2,599 |
| Maine | 79.7 | 2,354 |
| Minnesota | 81.1 | 2,289 |
| New Hampshire | 67 | 2,245 |
| Alabama | 79.3 | 2,228 |
| Indiana | 66.2 | 2,152 |
| New York | 101.5 | 2,139 |
| Virginia | 82.3 | 2,001 |
| Delaware | 103.7 | 1,871 |
| Arizona | 79.7 | 1,808 |
| Wisconsin | 99.6 | 1,747 |
| Pennsylvania | 89.5 | 1,594 |
| Missouri | 84.1 | 1,485 |
| Montana | 85.6 | 1,412 |
| Michigan | 88.2 | 1,411 |
| Arkansas | 86.6 | 1,317 |
| North Dakota | 85.2 | 1,315 |
| Georgia | 94.4 | 1,278 |
| Vermont | 91.6 | 1,162 |
| Texas | 90.3 | 966 |
| Iowa | 90.2 | 792 |
| Wyoming | 94 | 691 |
| Florida | 105.6 | 635 |
| Utah | 100.3 | 568 |
| Tennessee | 95.1 | 463 |
| Nebraska | 90.6 | 428 |
| South Dakota | 97.1 | 414 |
| North Carolina | 106.9 | 370 |
| Idaho | 104.9 | (126) |

# RESOURCES TO HELP YOU FIGHT FOR REFORM

The accomplice to the crime of corruption
is frequently our own indifference.
**—Bess Myerson**

The following organizations and Web sites offer information about public employee unions, labor statistics and public employee pensions.

**These groups and Web sites are focused mainly on union or pension issues:**

**The Citizen Power Campaign**
www.unplugthepoliticalmachine.org
A grassroots effort to stop the corrupt political machine, made up of Public Employee Unions and the Sacramento politicians they control, which is bankrupting California.

**Public Masters**
www.publicmaster.org
This Web site was established as part of this book project.

**The California Foundation for Fiscal Responsibility**
http://californiapensionreform.com
CFFR is run by Libertarian activist Jack Dean, CPA Marcia Fritz and former California Assemblyman Keith Richman. The site is filled with good information, including a database of the $100,000 Pension Club that allows you to search for California retirees who earn pensions of more than $100K.

**Calpensions**
http://calpensions.com
Former San Diego Union-Tribune Capitol reporter Ed Mendell writes this informative blog about California pension issues.

**Pension Tsunami**
www.pensiontsunami.com
Jack Dean runs this site, which links to many pension-related articles found in newspapers, magazines and blogs throughout the country. You'll save hours of research by regularly checking this site.

### The Center for Union Facts
www.unionfacts.com
This is an entertaining site run by a conservative union watchdog organization. It deals with private and public unions.

### The National Right to Work Legal Defense Foundation
www.nrtw.org
8001 Braddock Road
Springfield, VA 22160
This is a national organization opposing compulsory unionization.

**These organizations deal with the union and pension issues among many other issues:**

### The Acton Institute
www.acton.org
161 Ottawa NW
Grand Rapids, MI 49503
A national free-market think tank that provides a Christian perspective on labor and other issues.

### America's Finest Blog
http://weblog.signonsandiego.com/weblogs/afb/
San Diego Union-Tribune blogger and editorial writer Chris Reed does a great job covering these public-employee issues.

### Ballotpedia
http://www.ballotpedia.com/wiki/index.php/Main_Page
An invaluable source of national election and initiative information.

### The Buckeye Institute
www.buckeyeinstitute.org
88 E. Broad St., Ste. 1120
Columbus, OH 43215
An Ohio free-market think tank.

### The Bureau of Labor Statistics
www.bls.gov
2 Massachusetts Avenue, NE
Washington, DC 20212-0001
This is *the* source for federal statistical data regarding the nation's work force.

**The Cascade Policy Institute**
www.cascadepolicy.org
4850 SW Scholls Ferry Road
Suite #103
Portland, OR 97225
An Oregon free-market think tank.

**The Cato Institute**
www.cato.org
1000 Massachusetts Ave., NW
Washington, DC 2001
A national libertarian think tank.

**The Center for the Study of Public Choice**
http://www.gmu.edu/centers/publicchoice/
MSN 1D3-Carow Hall
George Mason University
4400 University Drive
Fairfax , VA 22030-4444
Scholarly research on public choice theory.

**The Evergreen Freedom Foundation**
www.effwa.org
P.O. Box 552
Olympia, WA 98507
A Washington free-market think tank.

**The Foundation for Economic Education**
www.fee.org
30 S. Broadway
Irvington-on-Hudson, NY 10533
A national libertarian think tank and publisher of the *Freeman* magazine.

**The Goldwater Institute**
www.goldwaterinstitute.org
500 E. Coronado Rd.
Phoenix, AZ 85004
An Arizona free-market think tank.

*Governing* **magazine**
http://www.governing.com/
This magazine is about government and for government officials, but it has dealt
seriously with pension issues. Pay particular attention to columnist Girard Miller.

**The Grassroot Institute of Hawaii**
www.grassrootinstitute.org
www.hawaiireporter.com
1413 South King St., Ste. 1163
Honolulu, HI 96814
A Hawaii free-market think tank.

**The Heritage Foundation**
www.heritage.org
214 Massachusetts Ave. NE
Washington, DC 2002
A national conservative think tank.

**The Hoover Institution**
www.hoover.org
Stanford University
Stanford, CA 94305-6010
A national free-market think tank.

**The Howard Jarvis Taxpayers Association**
www.hjta.org
921 11th Street, Suite 1201
Sacramento, CA 95814
These keepers of California's tax-revolt flame offer solid information on all tax
matters and on the pension crisis.

**The Independent Institute**
www.independent.org
100 Swan Way
Oakland, CA 94621-1428
A national libertarian think tank.

**The Independence Institute**
www.i2i.org/main/page.php?page_id=1
13952 Denver West Pkwy.,
Suite 400
Golden, CO 80401
A Colorado free-market think tank.

**The John Locke Foundation**
www.johnlocke.org
200 W. Morgan St.
Raleigh, NC 27601
A North Carolina free-market think tank.

**The Ludwig von Mises Institute**
www.mises.org
www.LewRockwell.com
518 W. Magnolia Ave.
Auburn, AL 36832-4528
A national think tank that specializes in the Austrian school of economics.

**The Mackinac Center for Public Policy**
www.mackinac.org
140 West Main Street
P.O. Box 568
Midland, MI 48640
A Michigan free-market think tank.

**The Manhattan Institute**
www.manhattaninstitute.com
112 W 31st St # 2
New York, NY 10001
A New York City conservative think tank that specializes in urban issues.

**The Pacific Research Institute**
www.pacificresearch.org
One Embarcadero Center, Ste. 350
San Francisco, CA 94111
A California free-market think tank.

**The Reason Foundation**
http://reason.org/
3415 S. Sepulveda Blvd., Suite 400
Los Angeles, CA 90034
A national libertarian think tank and publisher of *Reason* magazine.

# ENDNOTES

## —CHAPTER ONE—

1—Jennifer Muir, "Special license plates shield officials from traffic tickets," *Orange County Register*, April 4, 2008.

2—Steven Greenhut, "Out of the way, peasants," *Orange County Register*, April 20, 2008.

3—Jennifer Muir and Brian Joseph, "O.C. legislator works to stop abuse of license plates," *Orange County Register*, April 7, 2008.

4— Tami Abdollah, "U.S. probes Orange County's jail system," *Los Angeles Times*, August 14, 2009.

5—"Public Safety Officers Procedural Bill of Rights Act," Peace Officers Research Association of California (PORAC) Web site, http://www.porac.org/POBOR.html (accessed September 13, 2009).

6—"Assembly Bill 2819," California Legislature Web site, http://info.sen.ca.gov/pub/07-08/bill/asm/ab_2801-2850/ab_2819_cfa_20080428_102323_asm_comm.html (accessed September 13, 2009).

7—Editorial, "Legislation would give immunity to firefighters," *Orange County Register*, April 30, 2008.

8—Jason Method, "Across the nation, federal employees making top dollar," *Asbury Park Press*, June 24, 2007.

9—David Cho, "Growing Deficits Threaten Pensions: Accounting Tactics Conceal a Crisis For Public Workers," *Washington Post*, May 11, 2008.

10—Carolyn Jones, "Vallejo's fire union partied on city's dime," *San Francisco Chronicle*, March 12, 2008.

11—Steven Greenhut, "Government Workers Are America's New Elite," *Freeman*, July 2008. Entire article reprinted with permission by The *Freeman*, Foundation for Economic Education.

12—"The CalPERS $100,000 Pension Club," California Foundation for Fiscal Responsibility Web site, http://www.californiapensionreform.com/calpers/ (accessed September 13, 2009).

13—Editorial, "$100K Pension Club is Growing," *Sacramento Bee*, May 6, 2009.

14—Ibid.

15—Chris Rizo, "Calif. judge orders release of public pension data," *Lega Newsline*, July 4, 2009.

16—Evan Hessel, "Welcome to Paradise," *Forbes*, February 26, 2007.

17—Jeff Ackerman, "How did government workers become the aristocracy?", *Grass Valley Union*, June 23, 2009.

18—D.A. Gougherty, "Did Former Elk Grove City Manager John Danielson Game City, Public For Huge Financial Gain?," ElkGroveNewsNet, March 16, 2009.

19—Rich Connell, "Amid cost cutting, L.A. city pensions continue to soar," *Los Angeles Times*, August 9, 2009.

20—James A. Odato, "6-figure club for school retirees," *Albany Times-Union*, June 1, 2008.

21—Chuck Bennett, "Library Retirees' Serious Ca-sssh," *New York Post*, February 23, 2009.

22—Wayne Allyn Root, *The Conscience of a Libertarian: Empowering the Citizen Revolution with God, Guns, Gambling & Tax Cuts*, (Hoboken, New Jersey: John Wiley & Sons, Inc., 2009), 144.

23—Kari Larson, "Top 12 Most Dangerous Jobs," *Associated Content*, May 13, 2009.

24—Andrew McIntosh, "Awareness campaign or lobbying campaign for peace officers?", The State Worker blog/*Sacramento Bee*, August 24, 2009.

25—William Shughart II, "Public Choice," *The Concise Encyclopedia of Economics/ The Library of Economics and Liberty*, http://www.econlib.org/library/Enc/PublicChoice. html (accessed September 13, 2009).

26—Geoffrey Brennan and James M. Buchanan, *The Collected Works of James M. Buchanan Volume 10: The Reason of Rules—Constitutional Political Economy*, (Indianapolis: Liberty Fund, 2000), xv.

27—Tami Abdollah, "Orange County's planning department in 'critical condition'", *Los Angeles Times*, July 23, 2009.

28—Murray Rothbard, "Bureaucracy and the Civil Service in the United States," http://mises.org/story/2181 (accessed September 13, 2009).

29—Adam Sage, "EDF strikers cut power to French homes," *Times of London*, April 23, 2009.

30—Steve Malanga, "Unions vs. Taxpayers: Organized labor has become by far the most powerful political force in government," *Wall Street Journal*, May 14, 2009.

31—Ibid.

—CHAPTER TWO—

32—Editorial, "Lack of money didn't toughen firefight," *Orange County Register*, October 31, 2007.

33—Steven Greenhut, "A family fire drill," *Orange County Register*, November 22, 2008.

34—Fire Protection report, Reason Foundation, http://www.privatization.org/database/policyissues/fire_local.html (accessed September 13, 2009).

35—Peter Greenberg, "Why They Serve," *Parade Magazine*, July 5, 2009.

36—Amanda Janis, "Retirement benefit costs continue to grow," *Reporter*, No date.

37—Steven Greenhut, "CalPERS' risky schemes hit the wall," Orange Punch blog, December 19, 2008.

38—Michael Corkery, Craig Karmin, Rhonda L. Rundle and Joann S. Lublin, "Risky, Ill-Timed Land Deals Hit Calpers," *Wall Street Journal*, December 17, 2008.

39—Rob Feckner, "Another View: CalPERS' long-term investment strategy helps weather the market," *Sacramento Bee*, November 9, 2008.

40—John Moorlach, "Investment losses at CalPERS," *Orange County Register*, December 22, 2008.

41—Daniel Borenstein, "Guide to bad pension policy," *Oakland Tribune*, May 2, 2009.

42—Ibid.

43—Stephane Fitch, "Gilt-Edged Pensions," *Forbes*, January 22, 2009.

44—Troy Anderson, "Public Payroll Soars," *Los Angeles Daily News*, March 22, 2004.

45—Dennis Cauchon, "Pension gap divides public and private workers," *USA Today*, February 21, 2007.

46—Thomas J. Aveni, "Shift Work and Officer Survival," The Police Policies Studies Council, http://www.theppsc.org/Staff_Views/Aveni/Shift-Survival.htm (accessed September 13, 2009).

47—Memo to members of the Oregon Public Employees Retirement System board, from Paul Cleary, executive director, "Actuarial Equivalency Factors Update," November 17, 2006, http://oregonpers.info/library/Download.aspx?docid=488 (accessed September 13, 2009).

48—Ron Seeling and David Lamoureux, "Pension Myth Busters," Preparing for Tomorrow/CalPERS Educational Forum 2008. Sent to me by CalPERS actuarial office.

49—Steven Greenhut, "Cops don't die early after all," *Orange County Register*, September 8, 2009.

50—Jeremy Margolis, Gene Martin and Richard Raub, "Police Officer Retirement: The Beginning of a Long Life," National Criminal Justice Reference Service, U.S. Department of Justice, http://www.ncjrs.gov/pdffiles1/pr/109485.pdf (accessed September 13, 2009).

51—John Moorlach, "2002 OC Retroactive Pension Spike Appears Unconstitutional," FlashReport.org, July 21, 2007.

52—Lou Correa, comments to author, September 2009.

53—Bob Taylor, "Pension Crisis Swamps Cities and Counties," *Cal-Tax Special Report/Cal-Tax Digest*, April 2003.

54—Ibid.

55—Norberto Santana Jr., "Questions rise over how county OKs labor pacts under Brown Act," *Orange County Register*, August 8, 2006.

56—Ibid.

57—Chris Prevatt, "Shawn Nelson is no hero," TheLiberalOC, August 17, 2008 http://www.theliberaloc.com/2008/08/17/shawn-nelson-is-no-hero/ (accessed September 13, 2009).

58—Editorial, "Pension spiking behind closed doors," *Orange County Register*, August 13, 2008.

59—Chris Norby, "None Too Soon For Pension Plan Airing," *Norby Notes* (also published on Red County), September 7, 2008.

60—Reed Royalty, "Orange County Taxpayers Association takes Costa Mesa to task for boosting firefighters' pensions," California Pension Reform Web site http://www.californiapensionreform.com/?p=299 (accessed September 13, 2009).

61—Teri Sforza, "Water district plans to boost pension plans," *Orange County Register*, September 1, 2009.

62—Liz Pulliam Weston, "Tap into America's best pension plans," Money Central/MSN, http://moneycentral.msn.com/content/Retirementandwills/Retireinstyle/P95335.asp?Printer (accessed September 13, 2009).

63—Garrison Keilor, "A Prairie Home Companion," http://prairiehome.publicradio.org/about/podcast/ (accessed September 13, 2009).

64—Jon Ortiz and Phillip Reese, "California's state work force grew despite budget woes and cut promises," *Sacramento Bee*, March 16, 2009.

65—Floyd Norris, "Job Growth Where Bush Didn't Want It," *New York Times*, February 9, 2008.

66—Declan McCullagh, It's A Good Time to Work For Uncle Sam," CBS News blog EconWatch, May 12, 2009.

67—Ibid.

68—Dennis Cauchon, "Benefits widen public, private workers' pay gap," *USA Today*, April 10, 2009.

69—Editorial, "Myths do not excuse pension reform. OUR VIEW: Local government needs to scale back benefits," *North County Times* (Escondido, Calif.), February 13, 2009.

70—San Francisco Grand Jury, "Pensions Beyond Our Ability to Pay," http://www. sfgov.org/site/uploadedfiles/courts/divisions/Civil_Grand_Jury/Pension_Beyond_ Our_Ability_To_Pay_Final.pdf (accessed September 13, 2009), July 16, 2009.

71—Chris Edwards, "Federal Pay Continues Rapid Ascent," Cato@Liberty blog, August 24, 2009, http://www.cato-at-liberty.org/2009/08/24/federal-pay-continues-rapid-ascent/ (accessed September 13, 2009).

72—Stephen Janis, "Double trouble: Some city workers double salaries with OT during fiscal crisis," *Investigative Voice*, August 7, 2009.

73—Brian Balfour and Michael LaFaive, "What Price Government?", Mackinac Center for Public Policy, February 6, 2007.

74—Frank Geary, "Salaries Questioned: Pay for government workers in Nevada are straining budgets," *Las Vegas Review-Journal*, May 10, 2009.

75—Ibid.

76—Ibid.

77—John Hill and Dorothy Korber, "CHP urges pension probe: Disability retirements may involve abuse or fraud, a report concludes," *Sacramento Bee*, December 1, 2004.

78—Ibid.

79—Steven Greenhut, "Fullerton mayor's intimidation tactics," *Orange County Register*, October 17, 2004.

80—Brent Begin, "Proposal may curb overtime abuse," *San Francisco Examiner*, August 5, 2008.

81—Norberto Santana Jr. and Natalya Shulyakovskaya, "Overtime policies push 100 sheriff's officers over $150,000," *Orange County Register*, June 13, 2008.

82—Ibid.

83—Ibid.

84—Jack Anderson, comments to author, 2009.

85—Norberto Santana Jr. and Natalya Shulyakovskaya, "Overtime policies push 100 sheriff's officers over $150,000," *Orange County Register*, June 13, 2008.

86—Susan Schulman, "Firefighters piling up big overtime, bigger pensions," *Buffalo News*, March 15, 2009, http://blogs.buffalonews.com/inside_the_news/2009/03/firefighters-piling-up-big-overtime-bigger-pensions.html (accessed September 13, 2009).

87—San Francisco Grand Jury, "Pensions Beyond Our Ability to Pay," http://www.sfgov.org/site/uploadedfiles/courts/divisions/Civil_Grand_Jury/Pension_Beyond_Our_Ability_To_Pay_Final.pdf (accessed September 13, 2009), July 16, 2009.

88—John Hill and Dorothy Corber, "How law fattens state pensions," *Sacramento Bee*, December 19, 2004.

89—Helen Gao, "Benefits for ex-city employees examined in San Diego: Some on payroll after last workday," *San Diego Union-Tribune*, June 18, 2009.

90—Billy Parker, "Mafia Cops Will Still Collect Pensions," Gothamist, March 7, 2009.

91—Lou Minatti, "Obscene government pensions: It's not just California," louminatti.blogspot.com, May 31, 2009.

92—David Zahniser and Maeve Reston, "City Council OKs early retirement deal despite opposition," L.A. Now, June 26, 2009.

93—Phil Willon, "Small Town, Big Scandal," *Los Angeles Times*, October 17, 1999.

94—Alan Tu, "In Philadelphia, it's DROP, in other places it's called a 'sham retirement,'" WHYY It's Our City blog, June 15, 2009.

95—Helen Gao, "City sees victory in DROP lawsuit," *San Diego Union-Tribune*, June 11, 2009.

96—Girard Miller, "Time to Drop DROPs: Alice-in-Wonderland math can't work for Deferred Retirement Option Plans," *Governing* magazine, June 4, 2009.

97—Employee Benefits Legal Resource Site, Calhoun Law Group, Bethesda, Md., http://benefitsattorney.com/modules.php?name=Content&pa=showpage&pid=20 (accessed September 13, 2009).

98—Hillary Chabot, "Compromise reached on pension perks bill," *Boston Herald*, June 10, 2009.

99—Sean P. Murphy, "Ex-state senator Brennan says he'll forgo pension benefits," *Boston Globe*, April 3, 2009.

100—Maria Cramer, "Injured officers stay on payroll for years," *Boston Globe*, March 21, 2009.

101—Stephen Janis, "Blank Check: Suit reveals millions in city pension giveaways," *Investigative Voice*, March 5, 2009.

102—Staff Report, "Pensions for retirees to increase 2 to 4 percent," *Marin Independent Journal*, March 14, 2009.

103—Office of the Governor, Iowa, Press Release, "Governor Culver Signs Increased Health Benefits for Fire Fighters and Police," May 8, 2009.

104—Dan Ring, "Romney appointee boosted pension," *Republican* (Springfield, Mass.), April 11, 2009.

105—Laura Bischoff, "Ex-lawmakers use contacts to boost careers," *Journal News* (Hamilton, Ohio), May 3, 2009.

106—Susan Schulman, "Government double-dippers collect pensions while on the job," *Buffalo News*, May 30, 2009.

107—George Passantino and Adam B. Summers, "The Gathering Pension Storm: How Government Pension Plans are Breaking the Bank and Strategies for Reform" (Study 335, Reason Public Policy Institute 2005), 35.

108—Teri Sforza, "Golden Parachutes for Public Retirees Will Sink Us All, Experts Say," *Orange County Register*, August 28, 2009.

109—Marcia Fritz, e-mail to author, September 2009.

110—Frank Mickadeit, "King of the platinum parachute," *Orange County Register*, October 14, 2009.


—CHAPTER THREE—

111—Danny Hakim, "Pension Costs for Local Governments May Triple," *New York Times*, July 7, 2009.

112—Ibid.

113—Wikipedia, "Washington Monument Syndrome," http://en.wikipedia.org/wiki/Washington_Monument_Syndrome (accessed September 19, 2009)

114—Brian Westley and Brent Zongker, "National Mall sinks into disrepair while funds go elsewhere," *Boston Globe*, July 26, 2009.

115—Ibid.

116—Stanley Allison and Seema Mehta, "Huntington Beach May Impose Fees to Fix Sewers," *Los Angeles Times*, April 1, 2001.

117—Ed Mendell, "San Francisco pensions: conservative trendsetter," *Calpensions*, February 27, 2009, http://calpensions.com/2009/02/27/san-francisco-pensions-conservative-trendsetter/ (accessed September 19, 2009).

118—2008-2009 San Francisco Civil Grand Jury, "Pensions, Beyond Our Ability to Pay," July 16, 2009, http://www.sfgov.org/site/uploadedfiles/courts/divisions/Civil_Grand_Jury/Pension_Beyond_Our_Ability_To_Pay_Final.pdf (accessed September 19, 2009).

119—Ibid., 3.

120—Ibid., 3.

121—Ibid., 3.

122—Ibid., 3.

123—Tami Abdollah, "O.C. sheriff targets top brass with deep cuts," *Los Angeles Times*, July 28, 2009.

124—Editorial, "Ghost of Christmas past haunts sheriff," *Orange County Register*, August 3, 2009.

125—Nanette Byrnes with Christopher Palmeri, "Sinkhole!", *Business Week*, June 13, 2005.

126—Dan McDonald, "GM retirees, workers worry about health care benefits, pensions," *Metro West Daily News*, June 2, 2009.

127—Marian Callahan and Scott Kraus, "Pension costs could spike school taxes in 2012," *Morning Call* (Allentown, Pa.), July 12, 2009.

128—Dennis Cauchon, "Public workers' pensions swelling," *USA Today*, January 16, 2006.

129—David Kocieniewski, "Government microcharges closing budget gaps, but what's next?", *New York Times* (as printed in *Deseret News*), August 29, 2009.

130—Robin Prunty and David G. Hitchcock, "Market Declines Will Shake Up U.S. Pension Funding Stability," (Standard & Poor's RatingsDirect), February 26, 2009, 5.

131—Michael Corkery, Craig Karmin, Rhonda Rundle and Joann Lublin, "Risky, Ill-Timed Deals Hit Calpers," *Wall Street Journal*, December 17, 2008.

132—Ibid.

133—Mark D. Hill, "Stunning $128 billion in losses since 2007 for California pensions—all taxpayer guaranteed," *Marin Republican Examiner*, July 22, 2009.

134—Bloomberg News Staff, "State's debt-laden budget prompts Moody's to put it on watch list," *Daily Herald* (suburban Chicago, Ill.), July 16, 2009.

135—E.J. McMahon, "NY's pension peril," *New York Post*, June 1, 2009.

136—Staff, "Unsatisfactory state," *Economist*, July 9, 2009.

137—Tim Hoover, "Colorado PERA benefits in peril," *Denver Post*, July 14, 2009.

138—Bob Lewis, "Market collapse may boost public retirement costs," *Daily Press* (Newport News, Va.), July 13, 2009.

139—Sam Allis, "Running on empty: With big ideas without support, New Bedford's mayor trudges on," *Boston Globe*, July 12, 2009.

140—Joe Weisenthal, "The Pension Problem Isn't Going Away," *Business Insider*, April 9, 2009.

141—Ed Mendell, "From CalPensions: CalPERS actuary says pension costs are not sustainable," *Capitol Weekly*, August 12, 2009.

142—Daniel Borenstein, "CalPERS chief actuary silenced for telling truth," *Contra Costa Times*, September 6, 2009 [On September 10, 2009, the newspaper printed this correction: "This column was wrong about CalPERS actuary being silenced." Borenstein did not correct the substance of the column, but explained that Seeling was not silenced.]

143—Staff, "Public employees ready to sue state over pensions," Fosters.com, July 17, 2009.

144—Jon Coupal, "A Big Win for Taxpayers," *Metropolitan News-Enterprise*, October 29, 2003.

145—George Passantino and Adam B. Summers, "The Gathering Pension Storm: How Government Pension Plans are Breaking the Bank and Strategies for Reform" (Study 335, Reason Public Policy Institute 2005), 33.

146—James Kelleher, "Promising more, saving less: the roots of San Diego's pension crisis," *Orange County Register*, April 26, 2005.

147—George Passantino and Adam B. Summers, "The Gathering Pension Storm: How Government Pension Plans are Breaking the Bank and Strategies for Reform" (Study 335, Reason Public Policy Institute 2005), 37.

148—Daniel Strumpf, "San Diego's pension scandal for dummies," *CityBeat*, June 15, 2005.

149—Ibid.

150—Ibid.

151—George Passantino and Adam B. Summers, "The Gathering Pension Storm: How Government Pension Plans are Breaking the Bank and Strategies for Reform" (Study 335, Reason Public Policy Institute 2005), 37.

152—Ibid., 38.

153—Steve Francis, "The City of San Diego's 'Financial Katrina'," *San Diego News Network*, July 9, 2009.

154—Editorial, "No subterfuge: Pension board must not jigger the numbers," *San Diego Union-Tribune*, July 17, 2009.

155—Carl DeMaio, "Still not living within our means," *San Diego Union-Tribune*, July 23, 2009.

156—Scott Lewis, "Amazing Admission: It's Either This or Bankruptcy," *Voice of San Diego*, September 19, 2009.

157—Ibid.

158—Andrew G. Biggs, "Public Pensions Cook the Books," *Wall Street Journal*, July 6, 2009.

159—Wikipedia, "GASB 45," http://en.wikipedia.org/wiki/GASB_45 (accessed September 19, 2009).

160—David Zion and Amit Varshney, "You Dropped a Bomb on Me, GASB," (Credit Suisse Equity Report, March 22 2007).

161—Peter Cohan, "Is CalPERS suing ratings agencies to mask its own negligence?", *Daily Finance*, July 15, 2009.

162—Kristen Johnson, "Governments Face Prospect of Tripled Pension Costs," *Post-Journal* (N.Y.), July 12, 2009.

163—Editorial, "Our view on retirement benefits: Public-employee pensions put cities, states in tight squeeze," *USA Today*, July 13, 2009.

164—Editorial, "The Albany-Trenton-Sacramento Disease: How three liberal states got into deep trouble with 'progressive' ideas," *Wall Street Journal*, June 26, 2009.

165—No byline, "White House Vows to Defend Democrats on Health Reform, Will 'Punch Back Twice as Hard'," FoxNews.com, August 7, 2009.

166—Tom McClintock, speech to the Competitive Enterprise Institute, July 10, 2009, http://www.tommcclintock.com/blog/californias-morality-play-in-three-acts (accessed September 19, 2009).

167—Steve Chapman, "States in a fiscal hole they dug for themselves," *Chicago Tribune*, July 30, 2009.

## —CHAPTER FOUR—

168—Andrew Cotlov, "Animal Farm—George Orwell," Culturazzi, May 25, 2009, http://culturazzi.org/review/literature/animal-farm-george-orwell (accessed September 19, 2009).

169—Steven Greenhut, "Out of the way, peasants," *Orange County Register*, April 20, 2008.

170—Samuel Gregg, "Why Risk Matters," Acton Institute

Commentary, March 7, 2007.

171—Ibid.

172—Wayne Allyn Root, *The Conscience of a Libertarian: Empowering the Citizen Revolution with God, Guns, Gambling & Tax Cuts,* (Hoboken, New Jersey: John Wiley & Sons, Inc., 2009), 135.

173—Stephen Barr, "Job Security Lures Young and Old to Government Work," *Washington Post*, February 20, 2007.

174—Liz Wolgemuth, "7 Jobs for Job Security in a Recession," *U.S. News & World Report*, August 2, 2009.

175—Jason Song, "Firing tenured teachers can be a costly and tortuous task," *Los Angeles Times*, May 3, 2009.

176—"Before the Commission on Professional Competence, Board of Education of the Los Angeles Unified School District, State of California," (OAH No. L2007010087 http://www.latimes.com/news/local/la-me-teachers-landing-html,0,1258194.htmlstory (accessed September 19, 2009).

177—Jason Song, "Firing tenured teachers can be a costly and tortuous task," *Los Angeles Times*, May 3, 2009.

178—Jason Song, "L.A. Unified pays teachers not to teach," *Los Angeles Times*, May 6, 2009.

179—Jason Song, "Judge rules L.A. Unified can fire special ed teacher paid to stay out of schools," L.A. Now, July 13, 2009.

180—Jason Song, "Accused of sexual abuse, but back in the classroom," *Los Angeles Times*, May 10, 2009.

181—Editorial, "Paying for bad teachers," *Los Angeles Times*, June 15, 2009.

182—Nick Schou, "OC Sheriff's officials call deputy in Jail Murder Probe 'Lazy' and a 'Bully'," *OCWeekly*, April 7, 2008.

183—Joseph McNamara, "50 Shots," *Wall Street Journal*, November 29, 2006.

184—Lora Le Sage, Zach Christman, Peggy Cassidy and BJ Lutz, "Fat, Drunk and Stupid Is No Way to Go Through Life, Son," NBCChicago.com, June 26, 2009.

185—J.D. Tuccille, "Chicago cop recorded beating bartender gets probation," *Civil Liberties Examiner*, June 24, 2009.

186—Carol Marin, "City must end shameful history of bad cops now," *Chicago Tribune*, March 28, 2007.

187—Carlos Miller, "Miami police officer was most likely drunk when she crashed the squad car," Carlosmiller.com, May 7, 2009.

188—Ryan Orr, "Former deputy sues sheriff's department for damages," *Victor Valley Daily Press*, June 13, 2008.

189—Steven Greenhut, "Breaking the code of silence," *Orange County Register*, May 15, 2009.

190—Tony Rackauckas, "From the 2007 Special Criminal Grand Jury Inquiry into the Death of John Derek Chamberlain," (Investigative Report, April 2008) http://orangecountyda.com/docs/chamberlain_report.pdf (accessed September 19, 2009).

191—Ibid.

192—No byline, "The Brotherhood," Abuseofpower.info, http://www.abuseofpower.info/Culture_Brotherhood.htm (accessed September 19, 2009).

193—Tony Barboza, "Ketchup-theft trial is latest forum for Steve Rocco," *Los Angeles Times*, April 15, 2009.

194—No byline, "Professional Courtesy," NJLawman.com, July 2004, http://www.njlawman.com/Feature%20Pieces/Professional%20Courtesy.htm (accessed September 19, 2009).

195—Ibid.

196—Jim Baxter, "The Privileged Many: 'Professional Courtesy' Exposed," National Motorists Association, April 10, 2008.

197—"Public Safety Officers Procedural Bill of Rights Act," Government Code Sections 3300-3312, Peace Officers Research Association of California Web site, www.porac.org/POBOR.html (accessed September 19, 2009).

198—Alan Suderman, "Montgomery attorney: Police officers get light punishments thanks to union," *Washington Examiner*, May 7, 2009.

199—William March and Ray Reyes, "Law enforcement bill passes despite opposition of sheriffs, chiefs," *Tampa Tribune*, April 29, 2009.

200—"Frequently Asked Questions about Copley Press and SB 1019," ACLU of Northern California, http://www.aclunc.org/issues/criminal_justice/police_practices/frequently_asked_questions_about_copley_press_and_sb_1019.shtml (accessed September 19, 2009).

201—Steven Greenhut, "Cop lobby flexes its muscle," *Orange County Register*, July 1, 2007.

202—Jarret B. Wollstein, "Revoking the Government's License To Kill: The Case For Abolishing Sovereign Immunity Laws," International Society for Individual Liberty, July 1997.

203—James Bovard, "Government's License to Inflict Injustice," *Freedom Daily*/The Future of Freedom Foundation, March 2003.

204—Denisse Salazar, Eric Carpenter, Jon Cassidy and Doug Irvine, "Police chief: Officer fatally shot innocent man," *Orange County Register*, October 28, 2008.

205—Tony Perry, "San Diego sheriff seeks probe in use of pepper spray at political event," L.A. Now, June 29, 2009.

206—William Grigg, "Taser-Thugs Ruin a Baptismal Party," *LewRockwell.com*, August 4, 2009.

207—R. Scott Moxley, "Training Day: Police admit they planted a gun at Huntington Beach crime scene," *OCWeekly*, November 9, 2006.

208—Steven Greenhut, "Secrecy shrouds cops' rough justice," *Orange County Register*, December 17, 2006.

209—Steven Greenhut, "Militarization of American Police," *Freeman*, March 2008.

210—No byline, "Feature: Can Medical Marijuana Cost You Your Kid? In California, It Can," *Drug War Chronicle*, November 2, 2007.

211—Steven Greenhut, "Child abuse by the government," *Orange County Register*, February 17, 2008.

212—Esemeralda Bermudez, "On the prowl for water-use scofflaws," *Los Angeles Times*, August 16, 2009.

213—Steven Greenhut, "Jim Silva wins big-government award," Orange Punch blog, March 13, 2009.


—CHAPTER FIVE—

214—Tom McClintock, speech to Competitive Enterprise Institute, Washington, D.C., July 10, 2009.

215—Off-the-record GOP source in conversation to author, September 2009.

216—Dan Walters, "Public worker unions are seeking more clout," *Sacramento Bee*, July 8, 2009.

217—Chris Reed, "Finally, an explicit acknowledgment of union control of Legislature," America's Finest Blog, July 8, 2009.

218—Jim Lobe, "Unions Cheer Defeat of Prop 226," *Albion Monitor*, June 26, 1998.

219—Ruth Milkman and Daisy Rooks, "California Union Membership: A Turn-of-the-Century Portrait," University of California Institue for Labor Employment 2003.

220—Ibid.

221—Ibid.

222—Evan Halper, "SEIU may be linked to ultimatum on withholding stimulus funds," *Los Angeles Times*, May 11, 2009.

223—Warner Todd Huston, "Obama Gives Union Veto Power on State Funds," Red State, May 12, 2009.

224—Joe Guzzardi, "View From Lodi, CA: President...Davis?," V-Dare, March 22. 2002.

225—Evelyn Nieves, "California's Governor Plays Tough on Crime," *New York Times*, May 23, 2000.

226—Ibid.

227—Dan Walters, "Governor must get tough with union for prison guards," *Oakland Tribune*, January 22, 2004.

228—Ibid.

229—Geoffrey Segal, "Cashing In on Gov. Davis' Prison Contract," Reason Foundation, July 24, 2002.

230—Van Jones, "Prison Industry Has a Lock on Davis," AlterNet, July 16, 2003.

231—No byline, "Judge Rejects State's Request To End Prison Health Receivership," *California Healthline*, March 25, 2009.

232—Robert Salladay, "Lockyer Is Accused of Stacking Deck Against Initiatives," *Los Angeles Times*, August 1, 2005.

233—Steven Greenhut, "Nurse Ratchet," *Orange County Register*, April 24, 2005.

234—Arnold Schwarzenegger, "Transcript: Gov. Schwarzenegger and the 2005 Special Election," *Los Angeles Times*, No date.

235—No byline, "All Four of Schwarzenegger's Ballot Initiatives Fail," FoxNews.com, November 9, 2005.

236—Jennifer Warren, "Prison Guards' Clout Called 'Disturbing'," *Los Angeles Times*, June 22, 2006.

237—Marcia Fritz, "Sobering questions on pensions," *Los Angeles Times*, August 10, 2009.

238—Off-the-record source who attended meeting, comments to author, September 2009.

239—Ted Lieu, "Political Attacks on Pensions Are Short-Sighted," Assemblymember's Message, May 2009.

240—Scott Mayerowitz and Nathalie Tadena, "Budget Nightmare: 10 Most Broke States," ABCNews.com, July 7 2009.

241—Dan Walters, "California has amassed a mountain of debt," *Sacramento Bee*, August 12, 2009.

242—Judy Lin, "Pensions draw scrutiny amid state budget crisis," *San Mateo Daily Journal*, August 1, 2009.

243—Rand Green, "U.S. Rep. Tom McClintock Speaks Out on the Disastrous Effects of Poor Public Policy on the California Economy," *Perspicacity Press*, March 10, 2009.

244—Joel Kotkin, "Sundown for California," *The American: The Journal of the American Enterprise Institute*, November 12, 2008.

245—Dan Weintraub, "California lawmakers to volunteers: Drop dead," *Sacramento Bee*, August 27, 2008.

246—Heather Knight, "SEIU votes to authorize strike over furloughs," *San Francisco Chronicle*, August 2, 2009.

247—Yvonne Walker, M. Cora Okumura, Jim Hard and Kathleen Collins, "Strike Authorization Summary: Your Local 1000 Officers and Council Recommend a 'Yes' Vote," flyer given to Local 1000 SEIU membership, No date.

248—Joel Rubin, "L.A. police union wants San Diego newspaper writers fired," L.A. Now, May 21, 2009.

249—Darrell Steinberg, "Re: South Orange County Community College District Unrestricted Reserves," letter, August 4, 2009.

250—Jon Coupal, "Exposing union dominance in Sacramento," *Los Angeles Times*, June 29, 2009.

251—Mark Hill, "California public employee union retirees—the new bourgeois?," *Marin Republican Examiner*, July 20, 2009.

252—Bill Baker, "The Enemy Within: California Public Employee Union Pensions Devouring Tax Dollars & Moving Us Toward Bankruptcy," *San Bruno Beacon*, July 21, 2009.

253—Ibid.

254—Adam Summers, "California Budget Deal Is a Bad Band-Aid," Reason Public Policy Institute, July 29, 2009.

255—Staff, "Raises for state staff questioned," *Orange County Register*, August 18, 2009.

256—Jon Ortiz, "More public workers retiring early," State Worker blog, August 23, 2009.

257—Steven Greenhut, "Guess who told police union 'no'," *Orange County Register*, August 23, 2009.

## —CHAPTER SIX—

258— Lance T. Izumi, Vicki E. Murray, Rachel S. Chaney with Ruben Peterson and Rosemarie Fusano, *Not As Good As You Think: Why The Middle Class Needs School Choice*, (San Francisco, Calif.: Pacific Research Institute, 2007), 3.

259—Shannon Holmes, "Los Angeles Mayor Villaraigosa Calls High School Dropout Rate the New Civil Rights Issue," *U.S. Mayor Newspaper*, March 20, 2006.

260—Naush Boghossian, "LAUSD's Graduation Rate: 44%; District 6th Worst Among U.S. Cities, New Study Finds," Los Angeles *Daily News*, June 21, 2006.

261—Juan Williams, "Obama's Outrageous Sin Against Our Kids," FoxNews.com, April 22, 2009.

262—Ibid.

263—Michael Casserly, "Can't Anybody Here Run a School?", *Washington Post*, September 7, 2008.

264—Various organizations, "Open Letter to DC Public Schools Superintendent Clifford Janey From the Save Our Schools Coalition and Public School Advocates," September 5, 2006, www.saveourschoolscoalition.org (accessed September 20, 2009).

265—Editorial, "Undermining a Success Story: Maryland law lets a teachers union jeopardize a high-achieving charter school," *Washington Post*, August 15, 2009.

266—Joseph Bast and Herbert Walbert, *Education and Capitalism: How Overcoming Our Fear of Markets and Economics Can Improve America's Schools*, (Palo Alto, Calif.: Hoover Institution Press, 2003), 4.

267—James Bovard, "Teachers Unions: Are the Schools Run for Them?", *Freeman*, July 1996.

268—Lance T. Izumi, Vicki E. Murray, Rachel S. Chaney with Ruben Peterson and Rosemarie Fusano, *Not As Good As You Think: Why The Middle Class Needs School Choice*, (San Francisco, Calif.: Pacific Research Institute, 2007), 109.

269—No byline, "The Union Contract: Bargaining Away Quality, Wrapping Schools in Red Tape," Center for Union Facts, 2008.

270—Peter Schweitzer, "Dance of the Lemons," *Hoover Digest*, 1999, No. 1.

271—Jessica Levin, Jennifer Mulhern and Joan Schunck, *Unintended Consequences: The Case for Reforming the Staffing Rules in Urban Teachers Union Contracts*, Executive Summary, The New Teacher Project, 2005.

272—Marcus A. Winters, "Compstat for Teachers," *City Journal*, July 14, 2009.

273—John McAdams, "New Education Research: Unions Hurt Children," Marquette Warrior, March 5, 2009.

274—J.P. Zmirak, "The Ugly Secret Why Tuition Costs a Fortune," LewRockwell. com, September 2, 2009.

275—Steven Greenhut, "Court Holds California's Homeschoolers in Suspense," *Freeman*, May 2008.

276—Howard Blume and Jason Song, "Vote could open 250 L.A. schools to outside operators," *Los Angeles Times*, August 25, 2009.

277—Chester Finn, "Schools Choked," *Washington Times*, February 2, 2003.

278—Marshall Fritz, "How government control—even local—has ruined public education and what you can do about it," Alliance for the Separation of School & State, October 15, 2002.

279—John Dewey, "My pedagogic creed," *The School Journal*, Volume LIV, Number 3, January 16, 1897, 77-80.

280—Richard Berman, "Teachers' unions are ruining our kids schools," *Washington Examiner*, March 16, 2008.

281—Mary Walsh, "How Teacher Unions Have Ruined Our Public Schools: The Rotting of America's Educational System," *Human Events*, February 3, 2003.

282—Seema Mehta, "Proposition 1B would provide $9.3 billion for California schools," *Los Angeles Times*, April 22, 2009.

283—Jordan Rau, "Powerful Teachers Union Is in the Thick of Ballot Battles," *Los Angeles Times*, September 28, 2005,

284—CTA Legislative Relations Department, "Race to the Top: One-Size-Fits All Hurts Students," Position Paper, No date.

285—Chris Reed, "Public employee unions: Please, someone, anyone, explain how their clout has helped liberal causes?", America's Finest Blog, May 14, 2009.

286—Dana Goldstein, "The Democratic Education Divide," *American Prospect*, August 25, 2008.

287—Lisa Snell, "Teacher Unions Crush Philanthropy and Volunteerism," *School Reform News*,

288—Stefan Gleason, "Friedrich Naumann Foundation Conference on Choice in Education," National Press Club, Washington, D.C., October 11, 2002, http://www.nrtw.org/b/shgfnfccg.htm (accessed September 20, 2009).

289—Art Pedroza, "Pandering to Unions Doesn't Pay," Candidate Statement for Republican Party Central Committee, June 6, 2006 election.

290—Erica Perez, "Anaheim school plans derailed," *Orange County Register*, January 20, 2006.

291—Susan Anderson, "The School That Wasn't," *Nation*, May 18, 2000.

—CHAPTER SEVEN—

292—Ludwig von Mises, *Bureaucracy*, (New Haven, Conn.: Yale University Press, 1946), 44.

293—Roger Congleton, "The Politics of Government Growth," Center for the Study of Public Choice, George Mason University, January 20, 1999.

294—Josh Barro, "April 13 is Tax Freedom Day," Tax Foundation Special Report, April 2009.

295—U.S Debt Clock Web site , http://www.usdebtclock.org/, (accessed September 20, 2009).

296—Richard W. Fisher, "Storms on the Horizon," Remarks before the Commonwealth Club of California, San Francisco, May 28, 2008, Federal Reserve Bank of Dallas Web site, http://www.dallasfed.org/news/speeches/fisher/2008/fs080528.cfm, (accessed September 20, 2009).

297—Michael Hodges, "Rapid Expansion of State & Local Governments," *Grandfather Economic Report* series, http://mwhodges.home.att.net/state_local.htm, (accessed September 20, 2009).

298—Alex Newman, "Cancerous Growth of Government," *New American*, April 27, 2009.

299—Brian Balfour and Michael LaFaive, "What Price Government?", Mackinac Center for Public Policy, February 6, 2007.

300—Thomas A. Garrett and Russell M. Rhine, "On the Size and Growth of Government," *Federal Reserve Bank of St. Louis Review*, January/February 2006.

301—Paul C. Light, "Fact Sheet on the New True Size of Government," Brookings Institution, No date.

302—Michael Hodges, "Government Regulatory Compliance Cost Report," *Grandfather Economic Report* series, http://mwhodges.home.att.net/regulation_a.htm, (accessed September 20, 2009).

303—*Biography of an Ideal: A History of the Federal Civil Service* (Washington, D.C.: U.S. Office of Personnel Management), http://www.opm.gov/BiographyofAnIdeal/, (accessed September 20, 2009).

304—Brian Friel, "Unshackled," *Government Executive*, November 15, 2002.

305—Ibid.

306—No byline, "Civil Service Protection Needs the Axe," Atlantic City Scoop, June 26, 2008.

307—"Civil Service Overview Sheet," City of Seattle, January 2008.

308—Morgan Reynolds, "A History of Labor Unions from Colonial Times to 2009," *Mises Daily*, July 17, 2009.

309—Terry Moe, "A Union by Any Other Name," *Education Next*, Fall 2001.

310—Charles Baird, "Labor Day is not Union Day," Acton Institute, No date.

311—Bruce Barsook and Danielle Eanet, "Would the Public Safety Employer-Employee Cooperation Act of 2009 Impact California Cities?", *Western City*, August 2009.

312—Michael Rozeff, "Public-Sector Unions and Their Government Bosses: Partners in Crime," LewRockwell.com, December 26, 2005.

313—Cyril Northcote Parkinson, "Parkinson's Law," *Economist*, November 19, 1955, http://www.economist.com/businessfinance/management/displayStory.cfm?story_id=14116121, (accessed September 20, 2009).

314—Craig Steiner, "The Truth about Taxes, the Rich, and the Poor," Craig Steiner, U.S., Common Sense American Conservatism, October 31, 2006.

315—George Will, "While government diminishes America's comparative advantage over rest of world, liberals clamor for higher taxes," *Fort Worth Star-Telegram,* July 11, 2009.

316—Matthew Falconer, "Government spending lowers the quality of life," Orlando Opinionators, May 22, 2009.

## —CHAPTER EIGHT—

317—Marcia Fritz, "Some Solutions to California's Fiscal Crisis," *California Foundation for Fiscal Responsibility Special Report,* November 14, 2008.

318—Ibid.

319—Ibid.

320—Editorial, "California's pension powder keg," *Los Angeles Times,* August 24, 2009.

321—Editorial, "The coming 'civil' war/Reforming state government won't be easy," *Gazette* (Colorado Springs, Colo.), October 10, 2003.

322—Kelly Heyboer, "Teacher tenure: It's time to end Newark's antiquated tenure system," Newark *Star-Ledger,* April 10, 2009.

323—Lance Izumi, "Why We Need Choice," *New York Times,* October 22, 2008.

324—Dick Armey, *The Red Light Running Crisis—Is It Intentional?,* Office of the Majority Leader, U.S. House of Representatives, Position Paper, May 2001.

325—Steve Stanek and Leonard Gilroy, "Sandy Springs Incorporates, Inspires New Wave of 'Private' Cities in Georgia," Reason Foundation, November 1, 2006.

326—James Sherk, "What Do Union Members Want? What Paycheck Protection Laws Show About How Well Unions Reflect Their Members' Priorities," *Heritage Foundation Center for Data Analysis Report #06-08,* August 30, 2006.

327—Virginia Postrel, "Unions Forever? A new vision for America's workers," *Reason* magazine, May 1998.

328—Girard Miller, "A Dirty Little Secret Retro-Pension," *Governing,* August 2008.

329—Peggy Lowe, "Supervisor says deputies' pensions are illegal," *Orange County Register,* July 21, 2007.

330—Peggy Lowe, "County's retiree medical debt reduced," *Orange County Register,* March 21, 2007.

# INDEX

Localities, facing bankruptcy, 26, 89

Lockyer, Bill, 149–150

Long, Robert, 116

Lopez, Nativo, 194

Lopez, Steve, 191

*Los Angeles Daily News,* 35, 59, 169

*Los Angeles Times,* 20, 54, 74, 78, 91, 105–109, 131, 134, 139, 141, 150, 153–154, 164,
    183, 189, 191, 226

Los Angeles Unified School District (LAUSD), 105–108, 168, 181, 195–196

Ludwig von Mises Institute, 198, 211

Lungren, Dan, 144


**M**

MacDonald, Ashley, 130

MacDonald, John, 78

Malanga, Steve, 22, 140

Malkenhorst, Bruce, 10

Manger, J. Thomas, 121

Manhattan Institute, 22, 86, 178

Manufacturing, shipped overseas, 174

Marin, Carol, 112–113

*Marin Independent Journal* (CA), 67

*Marin Republican Examiner* (CA), 86, 160

Marquette Warrior (blog), 179

Maryland Law Officers Bill of Rights, 121

Massachusetts Turnpike Authority, 73

Mauk, Tom, 42

McCarthy, Eugene, 209

McClintock, Tom, 99, 136, 148–149, 153, 157

McCraw, Sharon, 63

McGrath, Mary Jo, 176

McGrory, Jack, 92

McIntosh, Andrew, 16

McMahon, E.J., 86

McNamara, Joseph, 111

Mencken, H.L., 218, 222, 241

Mendell, Ed, 76, 88

Mendoza, Tony, 137